F. Zinke effig. p. 1744

G. Vertue del. & sculp. 1748.

HOUGHTON HALL

The Prime Minister, The Empress and The Heritage

Frontispiece The Enfilade, viewed from the Green Velvet Bedchamber

HOUGHTON HALL

The Prime Minister, The Empress and The Heritage

Edited by Andrew Moore

PHILIP WILSON

ENGLISH HERITAGE

First published in 1996 by Philip Wilson Publishers Limited
143–149 Great Portland Street, London W1N 5FB

Distributed in the USA and Canada by
Antique Collectors' Club Ltd, Market Street Industrial Park
Wappingers' Falls, NY 12590, USA

ISBN 0 85667 438 9

Designed by Christopher Matthews and Ian Muggeridge
Edited by Celia Jones
Printed and bound in Italy by Società Editoriale Libraria per azioni, Trieste

The present locations of paintings formerly at Houghton are given where known.

The dimensions of all paintings and works of art are given in centimetres, unless stated otherwise, and presented as height x width x depth.

Contents

Foreword 6
The Marquess of Cholmondeley

Preface and Acknowledgements 7
Andrew Moore

Introduction 9
The Marquess of Cholmondeley

Inventories 10
Abbreviations 10

THE MAKING OF HOUGHTON

1 **Britain's First Prime Minister** 12
William Speck

2 **The Architecture of the House** 20
John Harris

3 **Craftsmen at Houghton** 25
Geoffrey Beard

4 **The Genesis and Creation of a Great Interior** 29
John Cornforth

5 **The Planting of the Park** 41
Tom Williamson

6 **Sir Robert Walpole: The Prime Minister as Collector** 48
Andrew Moore

7 **The Sale to Catherine the Great** 56
Andrew Moore

8 **The Genesis of John Boydell's *Houghton Gallery*** 65
Gregory Rubinstein

9 **The Cholmondeleys at Houghton** 74
Chloë Archer

THE CATALOGUE

Sebastian Edwards · Andrew Moore · Chloë Archer

Introduction 82

Portraits of Sir Robert Walpole 83

A Tour of the House 86

THE GROUND FLOOR
The Breakfast Room 87
The Hunting Hall 90

THE FIRST FLOOR · THE FAMILY ROOMS
The Common Parlour 94
The Study 97
The Little Bed Chamber
and Little Dressing Room 102
The Drawing Room 105
The Great Staircase 110
The Stone Hall 113
The Saloon 119

THE FIRST FLOOR · THE STATE ROOMS
The Carlo Maratti Room 124
The Dressing Room 129
The Embroidered Bed Chamber 131
The Cabinet 135
The Marble Parlour 139
The Gallery 145

The 1779 Sale to Catherine the Great 151

Houghton Today 156

Sir Robert Walpole: A Chronology of his Life 162
The Walpole and Cholmondeley Families 163
Walpole Family Houses and Residences 164
Select Manuscript Sources 166
Select Bibliography 167
Exhibitions 170
List of Lenders 171
Contributors 171
Index 172
Photographic Credits 176

Foreword

THE FOCUS OF THIS VOLUME is the exceptional collection of paintings and sculpture assembled by Sir Robert Walpole, Great Britain's first Prime Minister, and the subsequent dispersal of the most important paintings by Sir Robert's grandson to Catherine the Great of Russia. Yet the history of the collection is linked inextricably with the eighteenth-century rebuilding of Houghton Hall, Sir Robert's family seat in North Norfolk, and the work of William Kent, who designed the sumptuous interiors and furniture of the State Rooms. Thus the story becomes as much that of a house and its owner as of the great works of art which were destined to fill it. Houghton was, as Sir Robert's youngest son, Horace, remarked, 'the lasting monument to his father's greatness', and I hope that those readers whose interest in Sir Robert and his world has now been kindled will come to see his magnificent creation: the house once more opened to public view after two years of restoration in the spring of 1996.

At his death, Sir Robert's estate was encumbered with debt, and the house and its contents were threatened with catastrophe. Yet, despite the loss of the finest pictures to Russia, and a fire that destroyed much of the North Wing, the structure and the original furnishings of the rooms have survived in remarkably good condition. Saved once by the 1st Marquess of Cholmondeley, who inherited the house from his great-uncle and mentor, Horace Walpole, Houghton later passed through over a century of neglect while successive Marquesses, who lived mainly in Cheshire, tried vainly to sell the whole estate. It was left to my grandparents who moved in after the Great War, to breathe new life into the musty rooms. Houghton underwent an extraordinary Renaissance, and it can be seen from the records of the Clerk of Works how much was accomplished in a few years, both in and outside the house.

When she died in 1989, my grandmother had been chatelaine of Houghton for just over seventy years and every room in the house bore her unmistakable imprint. As a child, during summer holidays at Houghton, I remember the feeling of awe and wonder when she took us round the state floor as a special treat, pointing out the details and explaining the mythological scenes in the tapestries and on the ceilings. Our life as children was centred on the nurseries in the Cupolas and there were strict limits on where we could go in the house and when. Occasionally we escaped and set off, armed with torches, on secret explorations of attics and cellars. To this day the house and its mysteries have an endless fascination for me.

The large-scale restoration work carried out over the last few years has given the opportunity to rethink the displays of works of art, both in the public and private parts of the house. While sales have been necessary to provide a capital fund, a number of acquisitions have been made, thereby keeping the collections very much alive. Wherever possible we have attempted to restore rooms to how they would have originally looked, and I hope that visitors will find a house that feels welcoming and lived-in yet retains much of its eighteenth-century atmosphere. There are plans also to replace the various features of the original garden front and West Park, including ha has, and the old walled gardens have already been re-planted and are now open to the public for the first time.

In short, there could not be a happier moment for the publication of this excellent volume, which also contains the catalogue to the accompanying exhibition. I hope that our readers and visitors to Houghton itself will agree that the story of Sir Robert's great Palladian masterpiece and its collections is far from over. I should like to express my appreciation to all the contributors, both to the exhibition and to this book, in particular Andrew Moore for bringing this project into existence.

The Marquess of Cholmondeley

Preface and Acknowledgements

THIS BOOK, published to coincide with the exhibition *Houghton Hall: The Prime Minister, The Empress and The Heritage* (Norwich Castle Museum, 12 October 1996 – 5 January 1997; The Iveagh Bequest, Kenwood, 23 January – 20 April 1997) includes essays by a number of invited contributors, as well as the catalogue to the exhibition. The body of the catalogue is presented as a tour of the private and parade rooms of Houghton Hall as originally conceived by Britain's first Prime Minister, Sir Robert Walpole.

Effectively, this volume has four stories to tell: that of Sir Robert Walpole and his collecting; of his country seat built in Norfolk; the extraordinary story of the sale of his pictures by his grandson to Empress Catherine 'the Great' of Russia; and finally the continuing process by which Houghton Hall, under the ownership of the Cholmondeley family, remains one of the finest country houses in Britain today. This is the place to acknowledge the many contributors to both the exhibition and this publication.

My first debt is to those lenders without whose generous support the exhibition would not have taken place. Listed separately at the end of the book, they have all been consistently helpful in providing as much information as possible concerning the items loaned for the exhibition and in answering numerous requests for help. While some prefer to remain anonymous it is a pleasure to record those sources who have ensured as full a story as possible may be told. I particularly wish to express my gratitude to Lord Cholmondeley, without whose personal enthusiasm and support the project could not have hoped to develop. In addition, the exhibits provided from Houghton Hall have greatly increased the depth of interest offered by the exhibition. On behalf of all the contributors to this project I extend the warmest gratitude to Lord Cholmondeley for his ready and consistent help. I would also like to express my appreciation of the support I received from Professor Mikhail Piotrovsky, Director of the State Hermitage Museum, St Petersburg, who agreed at an early stage to three major loans from his museum; this assurance also ensured the viability of the exhibition. The items on loan for the exhibition have been indemnified by Her Majesty's Government under the National Heritage Act 1980, and thanks go to the Museums and Galleries Commission and Department of National Heritage for its help in arranging this indemnity.

On behalf of Norfolk Museums Service, principal partner in the project, and also English Heritage (through the Iveagh Bequest, Kenwood), I wish to pay tribute to the major sponsors who have made generous contributions. Thanks go in particular to the principal sponsors of the project, Christie's, who have retained an association with Houghton Hall since their founder James Christie was first commissioned to value the Houghton pictures by George Walpole, 3rd Earl of Orford, in 1778. I am particularly grateful to Lord Hindlip, Chairman of Christie's, for his personal enthusiasm for the project. Three further sponsors associated with the upkeep of Houghton today also stepped in to support the project: Alsop Wilkinson, Solicitors; Strutt & Parker, Estate Agents and J.S. Hay Ltd, Building Contractors. The first two companies are currently charged with the task of helping to maintain the Houghton estate while J.S. Hay was responsible for carrying out the most recent refurbishment at Houghton Hall. All three companies responded to the opportunity to contribute towards the project to enable the story of Houghton to be brought fully up to date.

On behalf of Norfolk Museums Service I also wish to pay tribute to the generosity of our major supporters, the Norwich Town Close Estate Charity. It was their grant-in-aid that enabled Norfolk Museums Service to undertake the role of preparing the exhibition and present it first in Norwich to coincide with the 1996 Norfolk and Norwich Festival. Further grant-in-aid was generously provided by the Idlewild Trust, the Marc Fitch Fund and the South Eastern Museums Service.

I also acknowledge with gratitude those who have so generously provided written contributions to this book. I am particularly grateful to John Cornforth, not only for his essay but also for his unstinting help with many research enquiries and his enlightening tours of Houghton in the company of Lord Cholmondeley. Thanks also go to Chloë Archer, Dr Geoffrey Beard, John Harris, Gregory Rubinstein, Professor William Speck and Dr Tom Williamson for their essays, which so eloquently enhance the history of Houghton as the archetypal country house. In addition, Chloë Archer and Sebastian Edwards have joined with me in writing the catalogue section of this book. It is Sebastian Edwards who has expertly transformed this section into a tour of Houghton as it was in the time of Sir Robert Walpole. I would also like to thank Dr Wendy Evans for undertaking to contribute a catalogue entry (cat. 64).

I am indebted to a number of people who have helped in connection with previously unpublished material. Special thanks are due to David Yaxley for much help and for sharing his invaluable knowledge of the Houghton archives. I owe a personal debt of gratitude to Edward Bottoms, who undertook the role of research assistant in working on my behalf in the National Art Library, the Bodleian, Oxford, the University Libraries of Cambridge and East Anglia, and the Witt Library at the Courtauld Institute. I would also like to record my gratitude to colleagues in St Petersburg who welcomed me in my research into the Walpole pictures sold to Catherine the Great, notably Dr Elizabeth Renne and Dr Irina Sokolova.

Among those who freely gave advice, information and expertise I would like to thank David Adshead, Brian Allen, Charles Avery, David Beazley, Nigel Bumphrey, Lady Aline Cholmondeley, The Hon. Charles Cholmondeley, Charlotte Crawley, Ian Dunn, James Edgar, Richard Edgcumbe, Amelia Fearn, George Fletcher, John Guinness, Susan Hare, Tim Heathcote, Ronald Homer, Gareth Hughes, Titus Kendall, Elaine Kilmurray, Jessie McNabb, Sir Oliver Millar, Richard Ormond, François Rothlisberger, John Saumarez Smith, Martin Stiles, Philip Ward-Jackson, Robert Wenley and James Yorke. I would like to acknowledge in particular the support of the staff at Houghton, who have assisted in many ways, most notably Susan Cleaver for all her help with the administration of loans, photography and access to the archives at Houghton and also Percy Baldwin, Herbert Palmer and Olga Slegg.

I should also record my gratitude to all those who helped with the administration of loans and the provision of photographs, most notably François Rothlisberger who, through Christie's, provided considerable assistance in obtaining photographs for research and publication. In addition I thank *Country Life*, Derek Edwards, Angelo Hornak, Jarrolds, Neil Jinkerson, Martin Smith and Christopher Sykes for providing photographs of Houghton. Full photographic credits are listed separately.

Finally, thanks go to Philip Wilson Publishers for undertaking to publish this book in association with Norfolk Museums Service and English Heritage, thus ensuring that the full story of this remarkable subject may be widely available. I am particularly grateful to Anne Jackson, Susan Dixon, Celia Jones and Christopher Matthews for their support during the process of publication. I also wish to thank the Director of Norfolk Museums Service, Catherine Wilson, for her support of the project from the beginning. Colleagues in the project team at Norwich Castle Museum provided full support and advice throughout, notably Chloë Archer as Exhibition Curator and Caroline Ellis. I am also grateful to Joan Allman, Bridget Baldwin and especially Gudrun Reinke for their work on the Norwich research archive on the Houghton pictures. Among colleagues at English Heritage I especially thank Julius Bryant for his early support, his successor Judith Rutherford, Ian Dejardin, Cathy Power, Juliet West and members of the London and South East Region, and Sebastian Edwards, who acted as Exhibition Representative for the Iveagh Bequest, Kenwood. As ever, my thanks go to Judith Moore for her support and understanding.

Andrew Moore

Introduction

THIS IS THE FIRST major study to be devoted to Sir Robert Walpole as a collector and patron of the arts. It not only acts as an essential guide and catalogue to the related exhibition organised by Norfolk Museums Service in association with English Heritage, but adds considerably to the understanding of the larger-than-life figure of Sir Robert Walpole, who bestrode the European scene for over twenty years, and who was the first to take the title of Prime Minister, under both George I and George II.

As with his Whig neighbours, the Townshends of Raynham, Norfolk was Walpole's power base; his family had been landowners for hundreds of years and it was important to establish Houghton as a symbol of that power. Although as Prime Minister he would eventually only be able to escape to the country for two short breaks a year, the house soon became a centre for scheming and planning the next session's parliamentary business.

The majority of contemporary visitors were dazzled and awestruck by Houghton: the bronze gladiator in the stairwell and the vast lantern hanging in the Stone Hall; the profusion of fine materials – gold leaf and mahogany, rare marble and silk velvet; and of course the pictures. The decoration of the house is indeed a virtual ode to Sir Robert's achievements and aspirations, with Classical references to Mars and Apollo on Kent's ceilings, and the Garter Star, of which he was so proud, vying with the Saracen's Head (the Walpole crest) on almost every pediment, side table and lead drain-pipe. Sir Robert had proved beyond a doubt that a Norfolk squire could more than equal the old noble families in splendour and magnificence.

Even at a time when vast sums could be amassed by those in high office, Sir Robert's spending-power was extraordinary. His extravagance and lavish entertaining, both in Norfolk and his various London residences, was the source of frequent scandal and satire, while his enormous bulk (he was said to weigh over twenty stone) was an easy target for cartoonists. Yet whatever he was able to make from his political and financial activities does not seem to have been sufficient, and his unfortunate heirs discovered debts amounting to over £20,000 at his death in 1745. It is perhaps small wonder that the picture collection had to be sold. These debts were further compounded by his eldest son who died in 1750 and his daughter-in-law who lived to a great age with various lovers in Italy.

A remarkable side of Sir Robert's character was his attention to detail. Just as in the political field he would take a personal interest in even junior appointments and commissions, so at Houghton he was in close touch with his agent and issued constant directives about work to be carried out during his absence. How much artistic freedom he allowed Kent and his architects is unclear, but he was certainly familiar with current architectural ideas and was seemingly involved in planning every stage of Houghton's development. The same sort of approach is evident in his acquisitions of paintings and sculpture, although he relied heavily on the expertise of his agents abroad. The great number of commissioned portraits of Sir Robert and his family by Wootton, Jervas and other English artists also marks him as a considerable patron.

Sir Robert was very much a countryman at heart: he had been brought up in the old manor house at Houghton by his grandfather, and probably felt more at home with local farmers and landowners than with courtiers and London society. At Houghton he often negotiated rents with the tenants himself, and took a keen interest in farming, forestry and the development of the Park. Detailed records were kept of fruit trees in the gardens, fish taken from the various ponds and deer culled in the grounds. Sir Robert also kept two packs of hounds and the fox or hare was hunted six days a week.

However, the bluff exterior and a well-known penchant for bawdy jokes hid a civilised and cultured man. Like his father, who was highly educated and an MP until his death in 1700, Sir Robert had been a Classics scholar in his youth, and his library at Houghton encompasses French and English literature, history and natural sciences, as well as the Classics. As his mahogany-panelled bedroom was next to the library, it is reasonable to assume that he used it as his personal sitting-room, and did much of his work here.

In his family life, Sir Robert seems to have taken on the responsibility for his younger brothers and sisters at an early age, and later presided over his own growing family, siring three sons and a daughter by his first wife, Catherine Shorter, and a daughter by his mistress Maria Skerrett, whom he later married. The one surviving letter to Catherine shows a sensitive warm spirit, and certainly his youngest son, Horace, whose correspondence tells us so much about the period, had great affection for him as a father and respect for his extraordinary accomplishments.

Yet Horace later bemoans his father's extravagance, and we are left with the portrait of a man of many paradoxes; a statesman of great integrity, who nevertheless lined his own pockets in a fairly shameless manner; a financial wizard who, as Chancellor of the Exchequer, could unravel the greatest complexities, yet left his own affairs in chaos for his heirs to cope with as best they might. Perhaps the most telling image (again from Horace's correspondence) is of Sir Robert, now in forced retirement and in failing health, weeping alone in his library at Houghton because he could not find a single volume to distract his anguished mind.

The Marquess of Cholmondeley

Inventories

The following are the most frequently referred to inventories of the Houghton Collection in the text. (see also the list of manuscripts on p. 166)

1736 The earliest record of Sir Robert Walpole's collection of paintings at Houghton, Grosvenor Street and Chelsea. [see cat. 17]

1744 Inventory of paintings and the earliest plan of the picture hang in the Gallery at Houghton [see cat. 18]

1745 Inventory of the contents of Houghton Hall, taken on Sir Robert Walpole's death [see cat. 21]

1792 Inventory of the contents of Houghton Hall, taken at the death of George Walpole, 3rd Earl of Orford, 17 June 1792 and following days

1797 Horace Walpole's will included 'a list of pictures in London to be sent to Houghton'

Abbreviations

bt — bought

c. — *circa*

cat. — catalogue number

CUL — Cambridge University Library

Eng: — engraving, engraved

Exh. — Exhibited

Fig. — Figure

fl. — *floruit:* indicates the time an artist was working

ht — height

HW — Horace Walpole

illus — illustration, illustrated

Insc: — inscription

Lit: — literature

MS(S) — manuscript(s)

n. — note

NAL — National Art Library, Victoria and Albert Museum, London

Prov. — Provenance

RIBA — Royal Institute of British Architects

SHM — State Hermitage Museum, St Petersburg

THE MAKING OF HOUGHTON

Edmund Prideaux, *Houghton Hall from the west*, *c*.1725; pen and wash (see cat. 15)

I

Britain's First Prime Minister

William Speck

The Great Man

Sir Robert Walpole (1676–1745) was a great man in more ways than one. He was physically great; even an admirer such as Queen Caroline could shudder at 'that gross body, those swollen legs, and that ugly belly.' A critic such as Lady Mary Wortley Montagu claimed that his stomach protruded 'at least a yard before his nose'. Satirists depicted him as corpulent to the point of grotesque obesity.

He was also larger than life (Fig. 1). He projected the image of a gross Norfolk squire, boasting that he read letters from his gamekeeper before those of Cabinet ministers, and rarely read books. He was renowned for the coarseness of his humour, cracking crude jokes accompanied by hearty belly laughs. Yet this unsophisticated man had the best head for figures of his generation, and was able to understand the complexities of a new financial system that baffled most contemporaries. He had mastered the machinery of public credit created by the financial revolution of the 1690s. This had given rise to the national debt which was based on confidence in the ability of Britain to honour it. These attributes of the common touch and aptitude for finance contributed not a little to giving him the longest period in power ever enjoyed by anybody other than a king or queen, in British history.

It also led him to be referred to satirically as 'the Great Man'. This appellation alluded not only to his bulk but to his dominance on the political scene; he was called 'prime' minister or 'sole' minister at a time when such terms were not complimentary but pejorative. The office of Prime Minister, although Walpole is often acknowledged to have been the first incumbent, was not officially recognised during his administration. The King was still the fount of all honours and, in theory at least, picked his own ministers. In practice too the first two Georges ruled as well as reigned. When he succeeded to the throne in 1727, George II taught Walpole the hard way that his position depended upon the King. He indicated his intention of replacing Walpole with a political rival, Sir Spencer Compton, and

Fig. 1 John Wootton, *Sir Robert Walpole c.*1725; oil on canvas, 86.3 x 76.2 cm; The Marquess of Cholmondeley

Walpole had his work cut out to survive this apparent dismissal. Fortunately his friendship with the Queen gave him a powerful advocate at court, while Compton demonstrated his financial incompetence by relying on Walpole to secure a favourable settlement from Parliament for the new monarch. It could even have been the case that George intended no more than to remind the 'prime' minister where power ultimately lay. If that were so, it was a lesson Sir Robert never forgot.

Yet the notion that he had inordinate power as a minister was not without foundation. During the 1720s he gradually eliminated rivals within the ministry, a process that culminated in the resignation of his powerful brother-in-law Lord Townshend in 1730. Insofar as he could be said to have been premier, his premiership dates from that year.

Walpole's elimination of competitors was only partly due to the backing of the Crown, for he had another power-base in Parliament. In February 1739 he declared to the House of Commons that its approbation was 'preferable to all that power, or even Majesty itself, can bestow'. Walpole's decision to remain in the lower house was crucial to his successful career of twenty years as the leading minister. All his predecessors had either been peers or had been promoted to the peerage; he himself was not averse to a noble title, obtaining one for his eldest son in 1723 and becoming Earl of Orford on his fall in 1742. The House of Lords was still immensely powerful under the early Hanoverians, and nearly all of Walpole's Cabinet colleagues sat in it. However, as First Lord of the Treasury and Chancellor of the Exchequer, he felt that his presence was needed in the lower chamber, which alone could initiate financial bills; by convention the peers could not alter or amend them but only pass or reject them.

Foreign Affairs

Money supply was vital to give the Georges the free rein in foreign affairs that they sought as kings of Great Britain. The conduct of foreign policy was the most important function of government in the eighteenth century; indeed, if one includes national security as part of foreign policy, then it was almost the only function, since the State did not then assume responsibility for even such routine activities of modern governments as road construction, let alone the health and welfare of private citizens. Naturally, one of the chief concerns of the Hanoverians was the interests of their electorate – they wished to use British resources to enhance their role in Europe as electors of Hanover. And, just as naturally, their parliamentary critics paid prime attention to their exploitation of Britain's strategic influence to further Hanoverian interests. Most of the set-piece debates in the Commons concerned the implications of the ministry's foreign and defence commitments.

Walpole as the chief minister in the lower house, with a responsibility for finance, found himself in the firing line between the ambitions of the kings he served and the criticisms of the Commons against German entanglements. Usually his role was to defend the monarchs against such criticisms, but when he felt that their foreign ambitions were contrary to British interests he was prepared to dig his heels in and resist them. His rift with Townshend arose chiefly from his conviction that the Secretary of State was jeopardising Britain's traditional alliance with the Austrian Habsburgs. After Townshend's fall Walpole virtually took over the running of foreign policy. He not only mended

Fig. 2 *The Stature of The Great Man or The English Colossus*, 1740; anonymous engraving, 29.2 x 18.4 cm; British Museum

fences with the Habsburg emperor but even persuaded George II, against the King's better judgement, not to become involved in the War of the Polish Succession when it broke out in 1733. It was this kind of influence that led to charges that he was not only 'prime' but even 'sole' minister.

Walpole justified his policy of non-intervention on the grounds that it spared British lives. As he said to the Queen, 'Madam there are fifty thousand men slain in Europe this year, and not one Englishman'. Such sentiments were not primarily pacifist, but based on his experience that involvement in European war required expenditure on a scale that placed great strains on British society, and consequently seriously threatened political stability. Unprecedentedly high levels of taxation had been necessary to sustain the 'sinews of power' on which what has been called the 'fiscal-military State' depended. That state had really come into being with the Revolution of 1688, or rather in the settlement that succeeded it. Defence of the Revolution settlement against counter-revolution demanded a military establishment sustained by a system of public credit ultimately underwritten by taxation. This was due to the fact that the exiled Stuarts, James II until his death in 1701 and thereafter his son James Edward, threatened to invade Britain with foreign help to retrieve their kingdoms. William III and Queen Anne had had to fight enormously expensive wars against Louis XIV to defend their revolutionary claims to the throne. The money to sustain a greatly increased army and navy had been raised partly by borrowing and partly by taxation. Those who lent money to the government tended to do well out of the war, while those who paid the taxes tended to do badly. Direct taxation fell mainly on landowners who paid the land tax, really a rate on rental values, which in wartime could rise as high as four shillings in the pound, or twenty per cent. Indirect taxation, in the form of excises on a range of consumer goods, hit the poorer sections of society hardest. Both groups complained bitterly about the unfair burden they felt they were carrying and called for an end to hostilities. The tension between the public creditors and the taxpayers had threatened serious political disruption under William and Anne.

Walpole had served his political apprenticeship at the heart of this new fiscal-military State. His political mentor had been Lord Godolphin, who served as Lord Treasurer from 1701, the year Walpole entered Parliament, until 1710. The future Prime Minister's ministerial experience had been in departments servicing the war effort. He spent the years 1705–8 on the admiralty council that advised the Lord Admiral, Prince George, Queen Anne's husband. In 1708 he replaced Henry St John, who as Viscount Bolingbroke was to become his arch rival, as Secretary at War. The following year he became Treasurer of the Navy.

Walpole's Whiggism

The expansion of the power of the State after the Revolution also expanded the opportunities for patronage at the disposal of the government, and critics alleged that this increased opportunities for corruption. The notion that the State's servants were actually profiting from the wars fuelled the bitter complaints of the taxpayers. Walpole himself seemed to provide proof of this contention when he was expelled from the Commons in 1712 and spent six months in the Tower of London for alleged peculation as Secretary at War. In fact, Walpole was almost certainly innocent of the charge, and the victim of party-political vindictiveness. At the time of his consignment to the Tower the Tories were in the majority in Parliament, and were waging a vendetta against the Whigs, of whom Walpole was the leader in the Commons. One of the Tories' main charges against the Whigs was that while in power they had deliberately prolonged the War of the Spanish Succession in order to feather their own nests. The row between the State's creditors and the taxpayers had polarised along party-political lines, with the Whigs identified with the creditors and the Tories with the taxpayers.

Although the debate over war and war finance loomed large in party propaganda in the last four years of Queen Anne's reign, the underlying issues went deeper than that. Walpole's commitment to the Whig cause was sincere, and his whiggism is crucial in any explanation of the trajectory of his political career. At its heart was a commitment to the Protestant Succession in the house of Hanover against its enemies at home and abroad. He defended the Revolution of 1688, which had sent the Catholic James II into exile in France, and the subsequent settlement, which gave the succession to the Crown to the Lutheran Electors of Hanover against the hereditary claims of James and, after his death, that of his son James Edward Stuart. Stuart supporters, known as Jacobites, were the main domestic opponents of the Protestant succession.

Among them Walpole included the Tories, and this view lay at the heart of the trial of Dr Sacheverell in 1710, in which he had played a leading role. Sacheverell was a High-Church clergyman who preached a sermon in St Paul's Cathedral upholding the principles of passive obedience and non-resistance, and condemning the notion that resistance could be justified. He denied that it had been employed in the Revolution. For this assertion and his criticism of the toleration of Protestant dissenters he was impeached. Walpole was one of the managers of the impeachment for the House of Commons, and upheld the right of resistance, claiming that to prove it had been used in 1688 was tantamount to proving for form's sake that the sun shone at noon. Tory lukewarmness for the Revolution settlement convinced Walpole that they were insincere supporters of the Protestant succession and were in reality Jacobites. The only staunch champions of the settlement and the succession it had entailed were the Whigs and their adherents, the Protestant dissenters.

Walpole retained these convictions throughout his life. They seemed to be confirmed when Bolingbroke, a leading minister in the Tory government of 1710 to 1714, went to join James Edward Stuart in exile in 1715. Shortly afterwards a Jacobite rebellion with the aim of restoring James

III, as his adherents called James Edward, or the Pretender, as his opponents preferred to call him, broke out in Scotland and even penetrated England before it was suppressed. In 1723 Walpole's spies exposed another plot to restore James to the throne. Suspicions came to centre on Francis Atterbury, Bishop of Rochester, as the ringleader of the conspirators, and Walpole pursued him relentlessly to obtain a conviction. Atterbury's friends insisted that the bishop had been framed. Walpole was convinced of his guilt and was ruthless in getting his victim expelled from the kingdom.

Later Walpole looked back to 1723 as the last year in which the Whigs had been a united party. Not a single Whig, he observed, had voted for the Bishop of Rochester. After that those Whigs who were led by William Pulteney, formerly a close political ally, had gone over to the Opposition and persistently opposed Walpole's ministry. Pulteney was, in fact, taking a leaf from Walpole's own book. After the accession of George I in 1714 almost all Tories had been removed from office and replaced with Whigs. Walpole profited from the Whig triumph immediately, by becoming first Paymaster of the Forces (Paymaster General), and then First Lord of the Treasury and Chancellor of the Exchequer. But in 1717 the triumphant Whigs had quarrelled among themselves. In the ensuing power struggle the Earls of Stanhope and Sunderland emerged as victors, outmanoeuvring Townshend and Walpole, who had gone into opposition and even allied with the Tories against a Whig ministry.

The 1717 Whig schism set the pattern for other dissident Whigs to leave office and oppose their former colleagues. A major difference was, however, that while Walpole and Townshend had exploited their nuisance value to return to power, none of those who went into opposition under Walpole managed to get back into office. This difference was partly due to Walpole's success in branding the Tories as Jacobites with whom no staunch Whig, even when opposed to the government, could ally. Religious distinctions between Tories and Whigs were another obstacle to the formation of a Country party from the two elements in opposition to the Court. The Tories long remained identified with High Church Anglicanism, while the Whigs continued to befriend dissenters. Curiously, opposition Whigs tended to be more closely associated with nonconformity than were ministerial Whigs. When dissenters mounted a campaign in 1736 to have the Test and Corporation Acts repealed, dissident Whigs took up their cause while Walpole declined to do so. These acts confined offices in national and local government to communicating Anglicans. Dissenters resented these restrictions on their full participation in the State, but although Walpole sympathised he had no wish to alienate the Anglicans. His solution to the dissenters' predicament was to pass legislation granting immunity from prosecution to those who took office. Most nonconformists seem to have accepted this compromise; only the more militant sought full repeal of the acts, a move that divided the Tories from dissident Whigs who supported the campaign.

Walpole and his brother-in-law succeeded in 1717 because they organised a defeat of the government in the House of Commons over the issue of the peerage bill. No future combination of Tories and dissident Whigs was able to do this. The peerage bill was an attempt by Stanhope and Sunderland to freeze the number of peers in order to retain control of the House of Lords. Walpole persuaded country gentlemen of both parties that this would thwart their ambitions to ennoble their families, and the bill was defeated. He and Townshend were taken back into the government at an opportune time, just before the bursting of the South Sea Bubble.

The South Sea Bubble

The South Sea Company had been created in 1711 to exploit the opportunities of trading with Spain and its overseas possessions which were expected to be granted in the peace treaty ending the War of the Spanish Succession. Although the Treaty of Utrecht of 1713 did not give all the concessions anticipated, the company nevertheless did profit from trade with South America. It also gave money to the government in return for its commercial privileges. It was a reasonable extension of this practice to get the company to take over that part of the national debt which was not secured against revenues. State creditors in this category were to have their loans transferred into company stock. Had the scheme simply converted the unfunded debt there is no reason to believe that it would not have worked. Unfortunately, it offered creditors stock at par, so that any increase in the market price raised additional capital for the company over and above the sum owed to the State. All means were therefore employed to raise the value of the company's stock on the exchange. Some of the methods employed were to say the least dubious, involving gifts of stock to influential parties in Parliament and even at court. At first the results were positive, and in the summer of 1720 South Sea stock sold at ten times its face value. Then prudent investors withdrew, and the slide started. Once it had set in, panic ensued, and as the market value of stock fell many were ruined. There was a call for scapegoats; some directors fled the country, and one junior minister,

James Craggs the younger, committed suicide.

Walpole was lucky to have re-entered the ministry after the scheme was started. He had a reputation for sound finance. He had started the Sinking Fund to redeem the national debt, and had consolidated and reduced the interest on it, before he left office in 1717. As Sir Richard Steele observed of this financial management at the time, 'Walpole must be a very great man.' Although he was no wiser than the next man about the fragility of the South Sea scheme, and burned his fingers investing in the stock in 1720, this reputation stood him in good stead when he took over responsibility for the nation's finances. While his own solution to the crisis, which involved the Bank of England assuming liability for the unfunded debt, proved abortive, he nevertheless restored confidence, and with it the City weathered the storm.

He also limited the political damage from the crash. Cries for scapegoats threatened leading politicians and even the King's confidantes. But Walpole contrived to cover their tracks, and only threw one sop to the wolves, John Aislabie, the former Chancellor of the Exchequer, being obliged to abandon his political career. The fact that more powerful men escaped led to Walpole being described as the 'screen master general' and being depicted as a screen in satirical prints. It was a small price to pay for gaining the complete confidence of the King and the backing of Parliament. The Bubble ruined the reputations of his rivals but secured his position as Prime Minister, an office, albeit unofficial, which he was to hold for an unrivalled twenty-two years. So long was he at the helm that his period in power became known as the 'Robinocracy'.

Corruption and the Robinocracy

Critics alleged he obtained the premiership by exploiting the scandal of the Bubble for his own advantage and sustained it by systematic corruption. Clearly politicians in power were corrupt at the time, and Walpole was saved by the good luck of being out of office when the key decisions were taken. His own rise to fame and fortune invited suspicions. Where today myths of advancing from log cabin to White House merit applause, then men who rose from humble origins to public prominence were suspect. Charles Davenant, a Tory writer, had characterised the archetypal careerist Whig in the fictitious character Tom Double. Double rose from being a penniless proof-corrector in a garret to becoming a wealthy country gentleman by thoroughly unscrupulous exploitation of the machinery of public credit and finance created after the Revolution. In the eyes of his opponents Walpole embodied the stereotype. Although his origins were scarcely humble they were relatively obscure. How a middle-income Norfolk squire acquired the means to demolish and rebuild his house on a grand scale, moving a village in the process, does indeed invite speculation. Houghton, although not a palace on the scale of Blenheim, is nevertheless a most imposing edifice, and, filled as it was with paintings and artefacts from all over Europe, clearly required expense on a scale far above that of Walpole's neighbours. In 1730 the *Craftsman*, the main opposition paper, claimed that the weekly housekeeping costs at Houghton amounted to £1,500. Few of the Norfolk gentry could have afforded to maintain a London town house on the scale of Walpole's establishments at Chelsea and Downing Street. He even had a mistress, Maria Skerrett, set up in a government residence in Richmond Park, along with their illegitimate daughter, while his first wife, Catherine Shorter, was alive. This extravagant way of life must have incurred far more expense than his income of about £9,000 a year as a minister could cover. Where the difference between them came from cannot now be ascertained. But that Walpole was not exactly scrupulous about the means whereby he sustained his standard of living is suggested by the fact that he had no compunction about acquiring Holland lace or French brandy from smugglers.

The Opposition not only charged him with personal corruption but also endlessly accused him of maintaining a majority in Parliament by corrupting members of both Houses. There was undoubtedly a sleaze factor under the Robinocracy. Some of Walpole's cronies were regarded even by his supporters as 'dunghill worms'. One such was Sir William Yonge, who had been one of the members bribed by the South Sea Company with a present of its stock in 1720. Although he became a Commissioner of the Treasury under Walpole, George II referred to him as 'stinking Yonge'. In the 1730s there was a succession of scandals involving MPs associated with Walpole, of which the Charitable Corporation and the Derwentwater Trust were the most sensational. The Charitable Corporation lent small sums to poor persons at legal rates of interest to prevent them falling into the clutches of loan sharks. One of its managers was Sir Robert Sutton, who persuaded the government to increase the corporation's capital in 1728 and again in 1730. On each occasion Sutton profited from what would now be termed insider dealing. In 1732 an inquiry into the ways in which the managers had benefited from the manipulation of the corporation's shares led to charges of defalcation against Sutton. The Opposition moved in for the kill, and Walpole, suspecting that the defence of a supporter would also implicate his ministry in

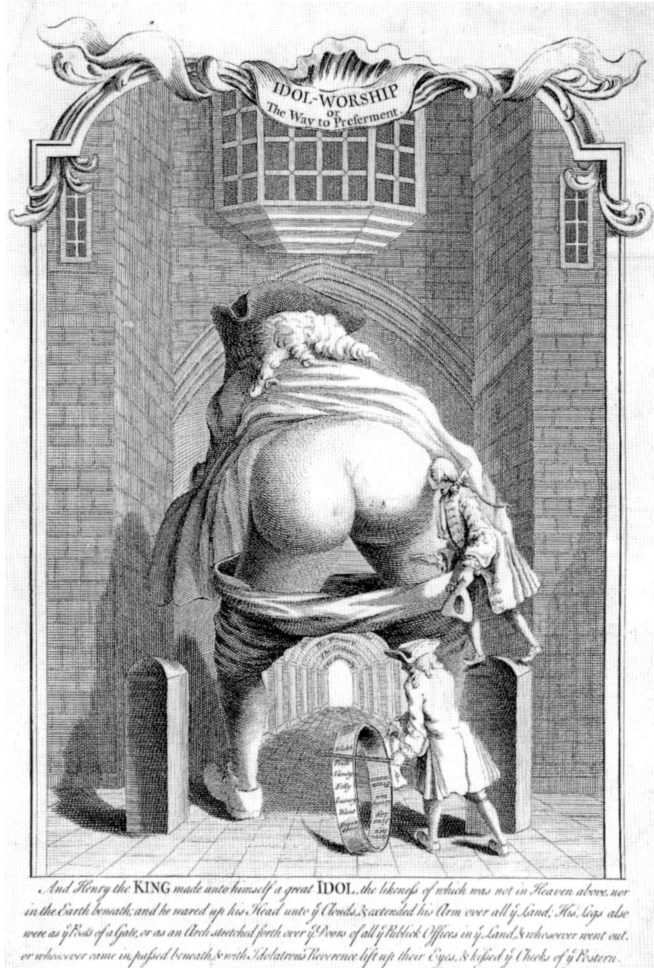

Fig. 3 *Idol Worship, or The Way to Preferment*, 1740; anonymous engraving, 35 x 25 cm; British Museum

corruption, left Sutton to twist in the wind. The Derwentwater Trust had been set up to administer estates confiscated from Jacobites after the 1715 rebellion, but it emerged that its managers had plundered its assets. Walpole intervened to shield one of them, Sir John Eyles, from investigation, reviving memories of how he had screened people involved in the South Sea scandal. The notion that Walpole bribed MPs to support him has been passed down with the legend that he said of them 'every man has his price'. In fact he said that of his Whig opponents. An exhaustive enquiry into his administration could find direct evidence of him paying MPs for votes on only two occasions.

There were, of course, more subtle ways of buying support than direct bribery. One was to reward members with posts in the administration (Fig. 3). The number of 'placemen', as MPs with jobs under the Crown were called, undoubtedly increased during the Robinocracy, reaching a peak of perhaps one hundred and fifty. Although the Opposition never wearied of denouncing them all as so much lobby fodder for the ministry, and sought means to reduce their numbers, they were by no means all automata, ready to do Walpole's bidding whenever he required their votes. And even if they had been, they never came near to forming a majority.

Another method of influencing the behaviour of MPs was to influence their returns. Electoral bribery was held responsible by the Opposition for the built-in majority that the ministry commanded after every general election. Yet, again, the resources available to the government could not have bribed a majority of voters even in the days of the unreformed Parliament and its rotten boroughs.

The Excise Scheme

The greatest test of his appeal to the electorate at large that Walpole faced was the general election of 1734. This was because his opponents made their greatest effort to exploit a national issue at the polls, the Excise Scheme. Introduced in 1733, it represented the culmination of the Prime Minister's long-term aim to shift the burden of taxation from direct taxes on land to indirect taxes on goods. He had already applied the excise to cocoa, coffee and tea in 1724, and this had helped him to reduce the land tax from three shillings in the pound in 1729 to one shilling in 1732. He now sought to improve the yield from tobacco and wine by removing them from the customs, where they were subject to massive evasion by smugglers, and imposing excise duties on them instead. He assumed that this would be popular with the country gentlemen who paid the land tax and who made up the bulk of the membership of the Commons.

To his astonishment the scheme blew up in his face. So far from being popular it was presented by the Opposition as the prelude to a general excise. The tax was widely disliked because its collection depended on officials who were given wide powers to search for goods subject to the duty. Addresses and petitions for it to be abandoned poured in. Public meetings were held, some of which occasioned violence. Walpole witnessed his majority fall steadily as the campaign against the bill increased the pressure. In the event, he decided to abandon the measure before he lost it in the House. Although his opponents never defeated it on the floor of the Commons, they came closer to achieving a combination of Tories and dissident Whigs than at any time during his long administration. They were jubilant in obtaining the goal to which the *Craftsman* had long aspired, the uniting of the Opposition into a Country party against the Court.

Fig. 4 Joseph Goupy, *Sir Robert Walpole addressing the Cabinet*, *c.*1735; gouache; British Museum

This coalition held together until the following year largely because a general election was then due. Opponents of excise made their maximum efforts in large open constituencies, such as counties and cities where the electors could vote relatively freely. Those who did so voted overwhelmingly against supporters of the scheme. In Walpole's own county of Norfolk, which normally returned two ministerial Whigs, the Tories were triumphant. Yet the ministry emerged from its ordeal at the polls with an overall majority. This result stemmed not from its use of bribery and corruption, as its opponents claimed. Although the Treasury spent more money on the secret service than in any year since the Glorious Revolution they did not do so in the majority of constituencies; many did not even witness a contest. These were for the most part small boroughs which had long before succumbed to the growth of oligarchy, entrenching the electoral interests of their Whig patrons so firmly that a challenge was hopeless. By 1734 the oligarchic element in the electoral system, which tended to support the Robinocracy, had more impact on the outcome of elections than the popular element, which demonstrated wherever it could manifest itself that the Robinocracy was deeply unpopular.

Walpole and the People of the Robinocracy

The unpopularity of the Robinocracy is a paradox in view of the widely held assumption that Walpole prevailed over political stability which rested on a consensus. Certainly he did little to endear himself to the Tories, whom he accused of Jacobitism, or the dissident Whigs, whom he traduced as opportunists. Nor did his dislike of combinations, or early trade unions, betray a concern for the mass of the population below the elite. On the contrary, his support for such measures as the Waltham Black Act apparently showed a determination to keep the lower orders in their place. This statute, originally passed in 1723 as a temporary measure but later made permanent, was primarily aimed at gangs of deer stealers who were allegedly attacking deer parks in the vicinity of Waltham in Berkshire. It made a capital offence of blacking faces to avoid detection, which the gangs were alleged to do. It also made capital an estimated fifty other offences, from breaking fish-ponds to mutilating bushes. In so doing, claim Marxist historians, Walpole was riding roughshod over traditional rights in the forests in order to assert the propertied rights of those Whigs who, like him, had risen with the fiscal-military State.

Sir John Plumb, by contrast, argues that Walpole presided over political stability based on a consensus. In his view, the majority of Britons accepted the country's political institutions, and the classes of men who controlled them. Plumb's definition of political stability still seems to be acceptable. Those historians who have claimed that the alternative of Jacobitism appealed to over half the nation have not substantiated their case. Most Britons seem to have accepted the Protestant succession in the house of Hanover and the Revolution settlement on which it was based. Indeed even Walpole's main rivals accepted that the Revolution restored the traditional balanced constitution of king, lords and commons, and that in theory at least this was the most perfect policy that human ingenuity could devise. They merely argued that in practice certain corruptions had been introduced which had tipped the balance ominously towards the Crown and its ministers and against the two Houses of Parliament.

Walpole himself accepted many of these propositions, though with modifications. He argued that the Revolution had established rather than restored the balanced constitution. He also denied the implication in some of the Opposition's assertions that sovereignty lay with the people. To him and like-minded Whigs it lay with the King in Parliament. Partly this was a cynical acceptance that the body of the people did not support them. As a ministerial paper put it after the 1734 election, 'supposing it is true that the majority of the people are against the ministry what does that prove? The people are sometimes right and sometimes wrong.' This reflected an important shift in the prevailing ideology. Whig philosophy before Walpole could accommodate ideas of both parliamentary and popular sovereignty. During the Robinocracy the Court Whigs upheld the former while the Country Whigs maintained the latter.

Walpole's Fall from Power

In the late 1730s dissident Whigs dominated the Opposition. Bolingbroke, who had been allowed to return to England in 1723, and who became the leading Tory advocate of Country ideology, returned to France disillusioned by the outcome of the 1734 elections. The chief challenge to the Robinocracy was then mounted by men such as the Earl of Chesterfield and Viscount Cobham, who had been dismissed from office for their opposition to the Excise Scheme. These led a group of self-styled patriots who attacked Walpole for allegedly undermining the country's interests. They found a cause in the harassment by Spain of British merchants trading with South America. Walpole tried to negotiate a peaceful solution of the problem while they clamoured for war. Invidious comparisons were made between the alleged appeasement of Spain by George II's ministers and the stout defiance of the Spaniards by Queen Elizabeth. This clamour played a role both in the breakdown of diplomatic efforts to reach an agreement and the outbreak of the War of Jenkins' Ear in 1739 followed by the rapid decline into a general European war – the War of the Austrian Succession.

The issue of war with Spain also played a part in the general election of 1741, when Admiral Vernon, a popular 'patriot' hero, stood in several constituencies to great acclaim. As in the previous contest, Walpole could ignore public opinion in the open constituencies, but he was vulnerable to defection in the smaller boroughs by supporters of Frederick, Prince of Wales. Frederick had quarrelled with his parents and gone into opposition in 1737. His electoral interest in the small boroughs of Cornwall was extensive and was used against the ministry. Walpole had also alienated the Duke of Argyll, whose influence was great in some of the tiny Scottish constituencies. The result was much closer than in 1734; everything depended upon control of the Committee of Privileges and Elections, which then decided the fate of petitions from defeated candidates. In the event, the ministry lost control of this crucial committee, which normally used its powers blatantly to 'weed' the House of opposition members and thus increase the government's majority. On this occasion it employed them

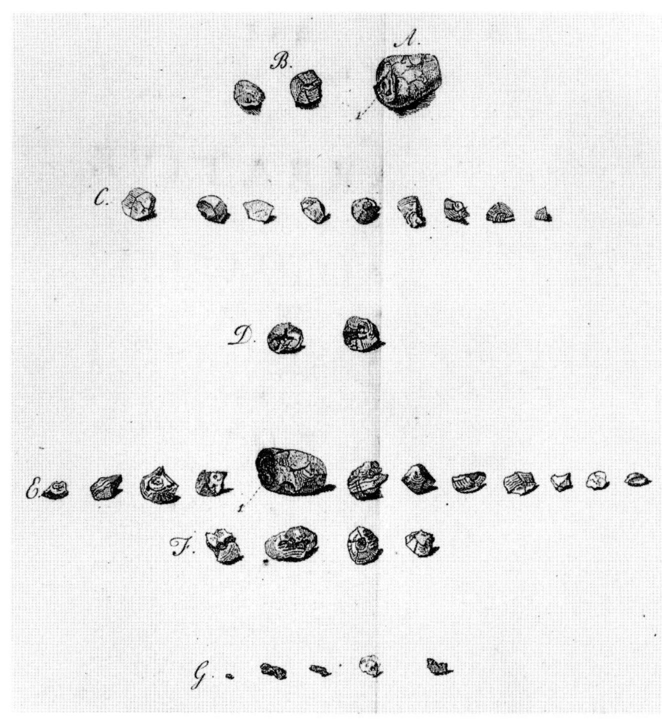

Fig. 5 *The Stones passed by Sir Robert Walpole on 4 February 1745* (no scale is given); engraving, 16.5 x 15.2 cm; Wellcome Institute Library, London

to oust ministerial supporters. Walpole saw power slipping from him and resigned.

He survived another three years, dying in 1745 at the age of sixty-seven. As Earl of Orford he could find some consolation for the loss of power in the role of elder statesman. But he also suffered a sad decline. The loss of his second wife, his former mistress, Maria Skerrett, in 1738 had been a bitter blow from which he had never quite recovered. Now advancing years and incapacity also took their toll. He had never enjoyed excellent health despite his apparently robust constitution. Fevers, gout and other illnesses had plagued him at intervals throughout his life. Now kidney stones afflicted him with chronic pain (Fig. 5). The attentions of his doctors seem rather to have aggravated than relieved his distress, yet he bore their attentions stoically. As he said to one of them, ''Tis impossible not to be a little disturbed going out of the world, but you see I am not afraid.' Those were the dying words of a brave if not of a great man.

Yet he was a great man in every sense of the word. He bestrode his world like a colossus. And if he sometimes abused his power he also used it to achieve goals which he considered honourable. As Sir Winston Churchill put it, 'the pursuit of power with the capacity and in the desire to exercise it worthily is among the noblest of human occupations.'

2

The Architecture of the House

John Harris

AMONG THE GREAT Palladian houses of England, primacy must be given to Houghton, although it would be a close run thing if Wanstead in Essex was still with us. Houghton is considered to have reached its perfection by the relentless obsession of a great and rich magnate to achieve his goal in one considered and faultless building operation. But was it? Even in *Country Life* in 1907 it was observed that in Isaac Ware's folio, *The Plans, Elevations and Sections of Houghton in Norfolk*, of 1735, no mention is made of Colen Campbell, and Thomas Ripley was given as the architect of the exteriors. This is quite extraordinary, because Ware was working with Ripley at the time, and knew exactly what the situation must have been. In fact, in the space of less than ten years there is a real compote of architects on the job: Ripley, James Gibbs, William Kent, Campbell and Ware. If we see perfection today, it was accomplished by a collage of architects, and one suspects through a draconian surveillance by its owner.

A few dates can be tabulated: Sir Robert, whose family was of ancient lineage traceable to the early thirteenth century, inherited the estate and its brick Restoration house in 1700. He soon began to modernise the old house, ordering new sash windows, fireplaces, doors and panelling, and a new barn was also programmed. Further alterations and improvements were carried out in 1716 and 1719. The decision to demolish the old house and build a new mansion is not likely to have been made any sooner than the late summer of 1720. According to Sir Matthew Decker in 1728, the plantations were begun around 1707, perhaps coinciding with orders for the reconstruction of the house. The most likely recipient of these orders is Henry Bell of King's Lynn (1647–1711), a prosperous merchant who was also skilled gentleman-architect. In 1702 Bell had withdrawn his papers to stand for Parliament in favour of Walpole. This generosity was much appreciated. Exactly what was done to the old house in 1707, and apparently again in 1716, but by another architect, is unknown. It is uncertain if the 'New Design of my Invention', dedicated to Walpole and published by Campbell in *Vitruvius Britannicus* in 1717, was inspired by rumours of Walpole's need

Fig. 6 James Gibbs, side front for Houghton, *c.*1720; Pen and wash, 32 x 46 cm; British Architectural Library Drawings Collection

for a new house. However, as a preliminary to the great rebuilding of the 1720s, Thomas Badeslade (d.? 1742), the land surveyor, prepared a survey. This shows a large house of conventional oblong plan with recesses to the end fronts (possibly indicating two long fronts of different dates) and straight office ranges flanking a forecourt. The garden was one of serpentine paths, inspired by the work of Stephen Switzer (1682–1745), that survived until about 1730. However, what Badeslade must have witnessed was the building of the new stables due south of the old house. These are believed to have been begun in *c.*1719, although they were not covered in until November 1721, and their architect is unknown.

Thomas Ripley was appointed supervisor of the forthcoming building works on the new house in 1720, and it can be assumed that Isaac Ware, apprenticed to Ripley from 1 August 1721, was employed in the site office.

Fig. 7 Colen Campbell, 'First' design for the court front 1723; pen and wash, 31 x 50 cm; British Architectural Library Drawings Collection

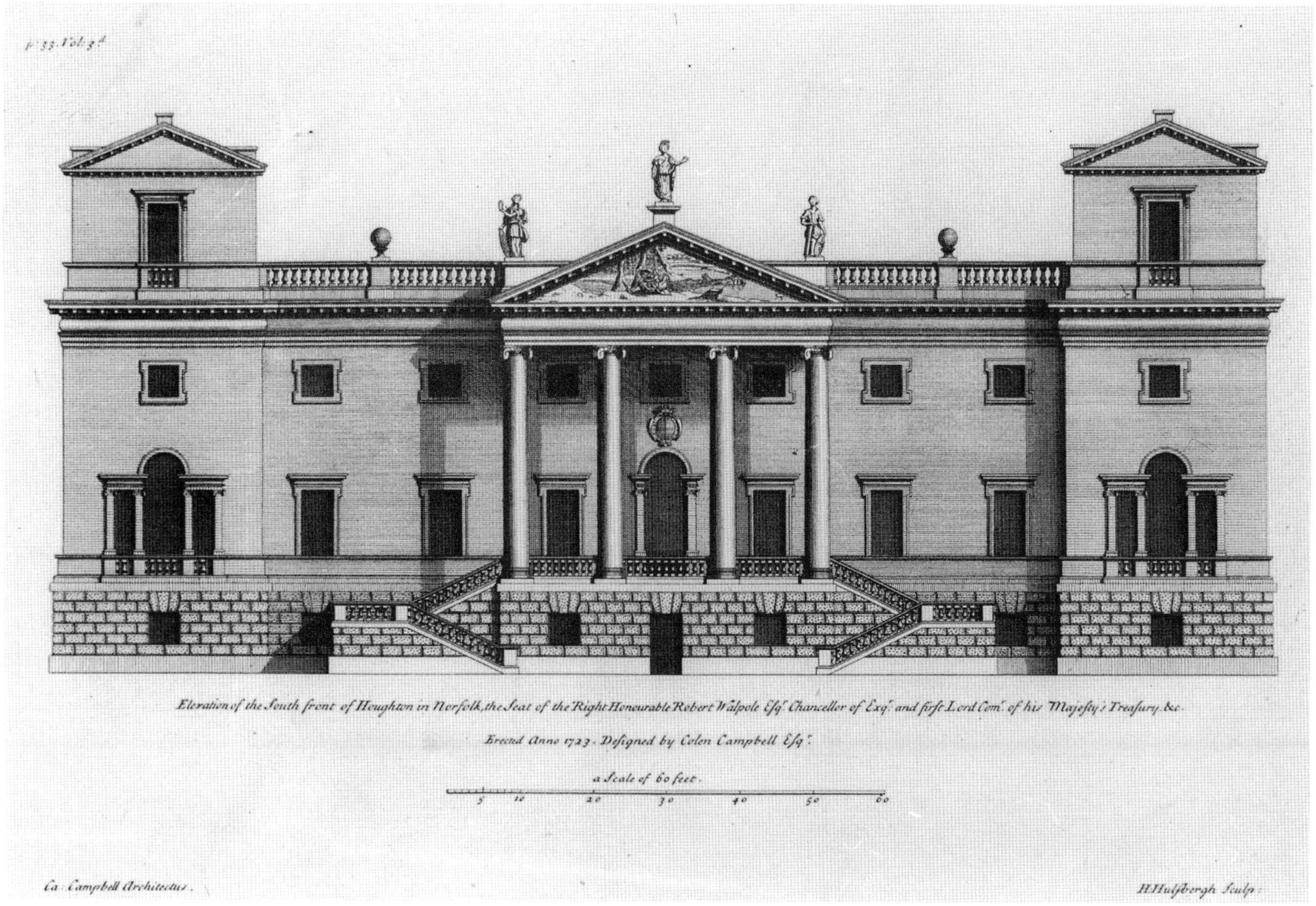

Elevation of the South front of Houghton in Norfolk, the Seat of the Right Honourable Robert Walpole Esq.r Chancellor of Exq.r and first Lord Com.r of his Majesty's Treasury &c.

Erected Anno 1723. Designed by Colen Campbell Esq.r

a Scale of 60 feet.

5 10 20 30 40 50 60

Co. Campbell Architectus. H.Hulsbergh Sculp.

Fig. 8 Colen Campbell, engraving from *Vitruvius Britannicus* III, 1725, portico front design said to have been erected 1723

Ripley was no nonentity; he became Master Carpenter in the Office of Works on 10 August 1721, and by 1726 had risen to the highest post in his profession, that of Comptroller. He would establish his reputation in the county as the architect of Wolterton Hall for Horatio Walpole, Sir Robert's brother, in 1727 and would be in charge of the substantial alterations to the interior of nearby Raynham Hall, said to have been designed by Kent. In June 1721 he had been viewing timber for Houghton, and also investigating stone quarries in Yorkshire. In August, too, Robert Hardy was appointed Clerk of Works. Celebrations were afoot on 24 May 1722, when the first stone was laid. By December the brick cellars had been completed and the first stone course laid. In 1723 (and presumably after March of that year) Campbell dates his 'First Design' for the 'Court' and 'Garden' fronts, but significantly does not date any designs for the plan (Fig. 7). In his *Vitruvius Britannicus* III (1725), he gives a date of 1722 in his textual introduction and 1723 on his plates. There is fudging here. In 1725 William Kent began to provide designs for the interiors, and Campbell was still at Houghton in that year with 'A Design for the Garden front of the offices'. Then, also in 1725, James Gibbs surprisingly intervened with the provision of the first of four domed cupolas. In 1726 Campbell was still around with 'One wing of the offices', and Kent was now in complete control inside the house. In 1727 Gibbs's second cupola was completed, and in 1729 his fourth one. As far as the exterior of the house is concerned, all is complete except for Kent's last major intervention in 1733 with the characteristic new stables built to the west of the old.

It has always been assumed that Campbell made the first plan for which the foundation stone was laid, but annoyingly his Palladian pavilion towers proved inadequate and were replaced by Baroque domed cupolas by his avowed enemy Gibbs! But as the tabulation of known dates shows, one must have serious misgivings about this interpretation; there are many flaws. Firstly there is the obvious one that a foundation laid in 1722 with the first course up by the end of the year, confounds Campbell's dating of his 'First' designs. Then there is a stylistic flaw. The upper windows on the side of Houghton today might be described as auricular – the keystone presses out of a pair of broken inturned scrolls, and below, the scroll turns inwards against the frame. This is not Campbellian. The style is of the 1680s, and it may not be a coincidence that windows of this sort appear by Henry Bell at the Sessions House, Northampton (1676) and at Kimbolton Castle, Huntingdon (1685). But they also appear on a side elevation of one of two designs by Gibbs that have always been assumed to have been drawn up in order that Walpole would be best able to judge the look and proportioning of the domes. However, once we examine these in detail there are so many discrepancies to the house as built as to confirm that they are, in fact, designs for the first house. As they came to the Royal Institute of British Architects (RIBA) with Campbell's own collection of designs, Campbell must have acquired them at Houghton. Once a comparison is made between Gibbs's drawings and the house as built, or to Campbell' s own plans and elevations, the discrepancies are glaring: window details, sizes, variations in the details of the rustic or basement storey, a different portico door, different approach stairs, varying proportions and ratios of wall to void, and the actual measurements of the block plan.

This is all puzzling. We are confronted by the distinct possibility that Gibbs was the architect at Houghton between 1720 and Campbell's 'First Design' of 1723. Obviously Campbell took over the designs, and not liking Gibbs's French Baroque style cupolas, worked out his own solution with pavilion towers similar to those at Wilton House in Wiltshire. Gibbs may of course have been the architect of the stables, if not the architect of the second reconstruction in 1716. His role can be buttressed by another document in the RIBA: a plan inscribed 'Sr Robt Wallpole's at Houghton' that is, suspiciously, in Gibbs's hand (Fig. 9). It does not come from the Campbell collection. Not only does it fit Gibbs's elevations, but it has an identical arrangement of stairs to the Saloon front. Its extended double-pile plan, derived from that of Roger Pratt for Clarendon House in London (1664–7), is Gibbsian not Campbellian. Even more significant are the parallels between Gibbs's plan, the plan of Gibbs's Ditchley Park, Oxfordshire, begun in 1720, and Houghton as built. In fact, the plan of Houghton is old-fashioned. On the west side a group of rooms was made as a self-contained unit for the family with a separate garden entrance, and all derive from Pratt's Clarendon House. Gibbs is further implicated by John Cornforth's discovery among miscellaneous architectural drawings at Houghton of a section through a two-storey hall of five bays width – a design in the style of both Gibbs's drafting and his interior architecture.

It is possible that Cambridge was the meeting place for Walpole and Gibbs; Edward Harley, later 2nd Earl of Oxford, was Gibbs's constant promoter. Walpole was a generous contributor to the building of the Senate House in 1721 and King's College in 1723, and must have known their designer Gibbs. In any case Harley had sent Walpole Gibbs's designs for the Senate House in 1721. In 1732 Harley criticised Houghton in words that have proved con-

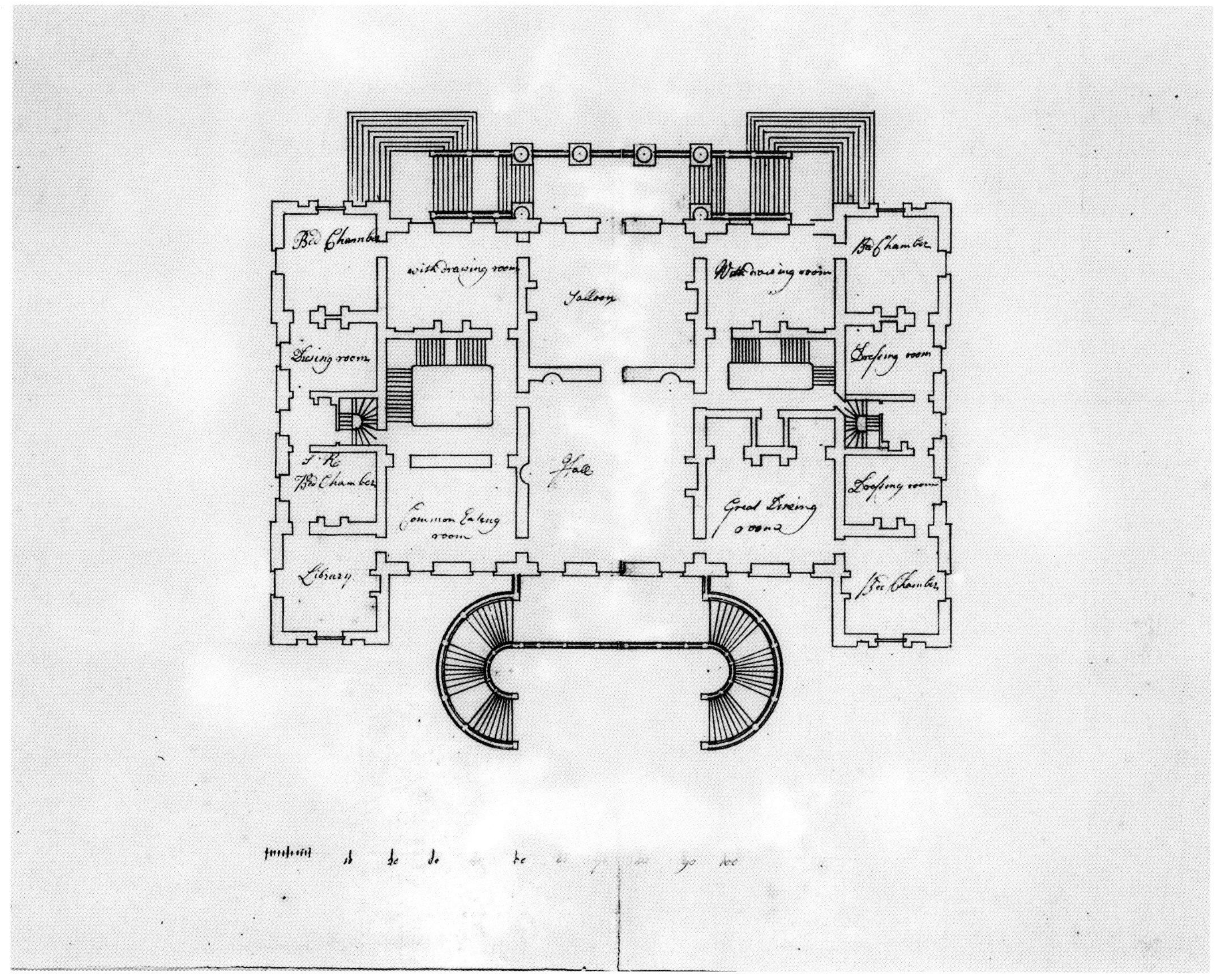

Fig. 9 James Gibbs, preliminary plan for Houghton, *c.*1720; pen, 55.5 x 53.5 cm; British Architectural Library Drawings Collection

fusing to scholars: that the domes were 'altered by Mr Gibbs from the *first design* [my italics]. The house as it now is [is] a composition of the greatest blockheads and the most ignorant fellows in architecture that now are. I think Gibbs was to blame to alter any of their designs or mend their blunders.' By 'first design' Harley must surely mean the RIBA drawings: that Gibbs made the first design for Houghton, and was superseded by the 'greatest blockheads', meaning Campbell and Kent. He is here critical of Gibbs for bothering to 'mend their blunders' by adding domes to a house that, as Edmund Prideaux shows in his wash view (cat. 15), had been finished off with a conventional hipped roof, not the pavilion towers of Campbell's many elevational designs.

It may all have been a matter of taste. At Ditchley Gibbs was superseded by Kent by 1725. By 1717 he had been replaced at Lord Burlington's Chiswick and Burlington Houses by Campbell, who very soon would be replaced by Kent. However, Kent's intervention at Houghton is astonishing considering he had nothing substantial to his credit in 1724 apart from some decorative painting. His work at nearby Raynham Hall (where Ripley was in charge) is later, as is that at Holkham. As far as we know he had not graduated to architecture, yet by 1727 at the latest he had provided the executed design for the great rusticated entrance to the piano-nobile on the east front. This must have infuriated Campbell who had proposed something like the central window in the style of Inigo Jones at Wilton. Kent must have been regarded as the 'New Wave', and we can understand Harley's annoyance if we recollect that Kent had trounced Sir James Thornhill, one of Harley's creatures, in securing the commission to paint the Cupola Room at Kensington Palace in 1721, a job in the gift of Sir Robert's brother, Horatio.

A putative scenario may be constructed: that Henry Bell is Walpole's first architect, and in Walpole's hands are his designs for a new house that may incorporate the auricular window. If Gibbs designed the first stables, then he was known to Walpole in 1720. He makes designs. Much must have been executed, not least some of the interiors on the ground floor, where the chimneypiece in the Hunting Room is Gibbsian. These designs likewise pass to Walpole. Then along comes Campbell, whose Burlington House and Great Gate on Piccadilly (around the corner from Walpole's house) was an advertisement for the new taste. He modifies Houghton, but before he can obtain a grip on the interiors, is superseded by Kent, whose merits could have been conveyed to Sir Robert by brother Horatio, if not by Kent's old travelling companion, Thomas Coke of nearby Holkham Hall. And finally, and not to be forgotten, there is the mysterious Ripley whose contribution to Houghton is perhaps underestimated and undervalued. There is obviously overlap all the way. This is demonstrated by Campbell's designs for offices in 1725 and 1726. A farcical situation could be imagined when in 1725 Ripley, Gibbs, Campbell and Kent might all have been avoiding each other's gaze!

Today it is difficult to understand this overlap of architects. We are used to the notion of one following another in distinct succession. Perhaps we cannot appreciate how such architects were in servitude to Sir Robert, the powerful Maecenas of his day, and must do his will. Perhaps we also belittle his own creative contribution, because his character as a hunting man has been limned to his disadvantage by Horace Walpole. I can envisage an office or library full of architect's designs, and Sir Robert sifting and commanding alterations, 'put that window here', 'replace that door there'. He required a house of sufficient splendour to celebrate a great county gentleman, a great statesman, and the recipient of the Order of the Garter. It is surely the Garter that determined so much after 1726.

Isaac Ware's folio of 1735 is not only a trophy of the completion of a great house, but is also the first monograph on a British country house. It must be seen as a statement of the supremacy of the Palladian style over the Baroque of the Harley–Gibbs faction. So complete was Houghton then, and so few have been the changes to its external fabric over the years, that Ware's folio could also serve today as a modern monograph. Had Sir Robert, then Earl of Orford, not died in 1745 with immense debts (accrued through his profligate expense) upon the house and its contents, Houghton might have suffered from the alterations made in accordance with subsequent fashion and taste. It did not because, after the pictures were sold to Russia in 1779, the place was often empty and subject to gradual decay.

Fig. 10 William Kent, design for the Great Door of Houghton on the east front, *c.*1727; pen and wash, 23 x 18 cm; Ashmolean Museum, Oxford

When James Grigor visited Houghton in 1841 for Loudon's *Gardener's Magazine*, he could bemoan that 'Everything, except the trees, seems to have suffered by the long lapse of years: on their heads it has put fresh honours; and if in some instances they are sinking into dilapitude, their decay is unattended by any of that regret which we experience in beholding the untimely abandonment of the buildings.' This 'abandonment' was total, for although the house ticked over, the Cholmondeleys preferred the informal comfort of their family seat at Cholmondeley Castle, Cheshire. After Waterloo Houghton was offered to Wellington, and refused because of its formality, and in 1886, through Court of Chancery, Lord Cholmondeley offered it for sale with 4,050 hectares. So unattractive and unfashionable was it then regarded that it only received a bid of £30,000. What a relief! What might have happened to it if sold?

3
Craftsmen at Houghton

Geoffrey Beard

On 24 May 1722 the foundation stone of Sir Robert Walpole's imposing Norfolk mansion, Houghton Hall, was laid. Twenty-five years later, in 1747, when Horace Walpole dedicated to his father the imposing *catalogue raisonné* of its splendid collections, he concluded the dedication thus: 'Could those virtuous men your father and grandfather, arise from yonder church, how would they be amazed to see this noble edifice and spacious plantations where once stood their plain, homely dwelling.' In the creation and decoration of 'this noble edifice' various craftsmen played an important part. Many details of who did what are, alas, lacking, through a conscious decision by its original owner to suppress documentation. It is nevertheless possible to advance some details from somewhat unlikely sources among the archive, variously at Cambridge University Library (CUL) and at Houghton itself.

The long, involved process of building began in 1721, when John Glover supplied 100 trees, delivered sawn, in 227 loads. Other timber came from King's Lynn, from the merchant Samuel Browne – eighty Frederickstadt deals, a barrel of tar, six bunches of fir laths, deals and sawn deals. The ship *Benjamin Susan* held '100 Large Spars, short and half deals', which Thomas Ripley had paid for on 4 November 1721. Ripley, a senior officer of the Board of Works, supervised the building's erection and made all payments for the work done. While the record is far from complete, in the main years of activity between 1726 and 1733 he disbursed some £22,000. Ripley had been born in *c.* 1683 in Yorkshire; he owed his preferment to Walpole and, indeed, had married one of the Houghton servants. His knowledge of Yorkshire may have accounted for the connections that led him to use stone from Aislaby, near Whitby, for the carcase of the house rather than that from quarries nearer to the site. The Yorkshire stone was delivered by sea to King's Lynn and Heacham and 130 tons were carted to Houghton (CUL, 1722–4 vouchers), but this may only represent a proportion of the whole; there was much work for local men, apart from leading London artificers, and a list of twenty masons and ten carpenters – all freemen of King's Lynn – is among the 1722 vouchers.

The vast quantities of nails, bricks, timber, hinges, poles, sand and lime – all the impedimenta of building – came to the site from many places. Samuel Thurlow supplied Dutch and other pantiles and, as time advanced, more exotic suppliers were obtained. In 1725 'Lateward, Butlin and Partners' supplied 305 mahogany planks from Jamaica, and Captain Hannar's *Dolphin* and *The Rose* brought in a further 26 and 88 planks respectively. John Griffiths was busy sawing it (CUL, 1725 vouchers), whilst the London plumber George Devall was given £300 on account. His estimate for work in lead and plumbing for 1730–6 also survives.

The humdrum catholicity of the duties of one member of the Houghton household staff included recording the consumption of wine, and by whom, and in the absence of more relevant documents, the listing is useful in noting the presence of several craftsmen. Of course there are gifts of wine to 'Mr Ripley' and to 'Mr Cass' (Christopher Cass, the London mason in partnership with Andrews Jelfe), and to Italian stuccoists. There are occasional and incomplete records too of whose horses were stabled – clues that indicate at least the presence of certain craftsmen. This helps to build a fuller picture of activity, including the sombre record of the price paid in suffering: of William Morris scalded by lead (1725), of workmen falling from scaffolding and of the expenses of doctors attending them.

One of the most important contributions to Houghton's decoration was made by Italian stuccoists. Stucco in England, as distinct from plasterwork, enjoyed only brief popularity on two occasions: it was used for a short time in the reign of Henry VIII, when Italians worked at Nonsuch Palace, and again in the first half of the eighteenth century, from about 1709 to the last recorded use at Shugborough, Staffordshire, in 1763. Throughout both periods and in the intervening years, British plasterers, working to long-established methods – that is, adding animal hair for strength, rather than stucco's (ideal) requirement of marble-dust and supporting armatures – were active alongside their foreign competitors, and some learned new tricks to add to their cherished apprentice-learned repertoire.

Fig. 11 The ceiling of the Stone Hall

The *stuccatori* who worked in England in the eighteenth century came, almost without exception, from the canton of Ticino in Italian Switzerland. Two of the best known were Giovanni Bagutti of Rovio, near Lugano, and Giuseppe Artari of nearby Arogno. They worked together in England as partners until a little after 1730, with the older man, Bagutti, usually taking the main responsibility. They did their most important work for the architects John Vanbrugh, James Gibbs, Colen Campbell, Giacomo Leoni and Francis Smith, with Bagutti, at Vanbrugh's Castle Howard, Yorkshire, as early as 1709, thereby accepting the first recorded eighteenth-century stucco commission in England.

It is always interesting to speculate (even when, as at Houghton, no satisfactory answer is forthcoming) on the sources, engraved and otherwise, on which stuccoists relied. Another Ticino stuccoist, Francesco Vassalli, working in England and known to Artari, informed one of his patrons, Richard Towneley, in 1729 that, 'since I have been in Italy, it is in my power to satisfy you more than I could have done before I returned into Italy'. This was presumably a reference to work seen there and engravings obtained of it. For example, Bagutti and Artari's hall ceiling at Clandon Park, Surrey (*c.*1732), is based on that by the Carracci brothers in the Farnese Gallery in Rome. The representation of Hercules and Iole painted there was engraved many times (in 1657 and 1674, and by French artists such as Nicolas Mignard). The Farnese ceilings, together with those by Pietro da Cortona in the Palazzo Pitti in Florence, were but two of a wide repertory of sources adapted from engravings by stuccoists for later use in England and elsewhere.

Among the 1727–8 vouchers in the Houghton archive, a most significant entry occurs on a mere scrap of paper, 'To Mr Altery for Saloon ceiling, £131 14*s.* 5*d*', part of three payments to the stuccoist (totalling £560 10*s.*) made between February and May 1728. The 'Saloon' ceiling, in this case, was the one in the Stone Hall, as only a painted ceiling by William Kent is in the adjoining Saloon itself. On 16 June 1726 Sir Robert had been elected a Knight of the Garter – the expenditure on the celebrations (CUL, 1726 vouchers) was extraordinary, even by early-eighteenth-century standards – and the Garter Star is found liberally scattered across Giuseppe Artari's Stone Hall ceiling. The record of wine consumed notes many bottles of 'Red Port' (occasionally white, Lisbon or 'Mountaine') as given 'To ye Italians', almost daily between 10 July and 10 October 1726. If one accepts the reliability of this record of drinking habits (always allowing for the tried and tested method of adding some to the stucco-mix to help its plasticity), Artari and his team were at the house for those four months at least.

The most engaging of the stucco decorations was reserved for the deep cove, with its cavorting overfed male and female *putti*, swinging between swags of leaves, flowers and shells with female sphinxes at each corner. It has been noted (Plumb, 1956, p. 84) that 'a well-concealed bawdy joke in the stucco dado of the Stone Hall could never have been made by Artari without Walpole's permission' – it has all to do with one cherubic girl *putto* among a bevy of cavorting naked boy *putti*. At the centre points of each side of the cove the swags and *putti* centre on bas-relief profile heads of Sir Robert, his first wife, Catherine Shorter, his son Robert, later 2nd Earl of Orford, and Robert's wife, the Devonshire heiress, Margaret Rolle.

The swags usually had at their centre a strong wire pinned into the ceiling joists above the ceiling. Then the individually moulded leaves and flowers, each with its own 'armature' of wire, would be twisted around the core wire. The *putti* themselves, sometimes made from neat gypsum

(Plaster of Paris) alone, were usually hollow, with a metal armature (wrapped in twine and straw to prevent iron oxide leaching its way to the surface) driven into the ceiling's wood and plaster structure. The profile heads were one of the few free-modelled features and were usually based on portraits, engravings or, in the case of Roman emperors, on images on coins. Stuccoists knew little of English plasterwork methods and usually worked their decorations after a plain three-coat plaster ceiling had been established by a craftsman such as the York plasterer Isaac Mansfield, whom we know worked at Houghton.

There is no reason to believe that Giovanni Bagutti helped Artari at Houghton. Whilst they had worked together at James Gibbs's London church of St Martin-in-the-Fields (1725), and were to be active again at Moor Park, Hertfordshire (1729–30) and elsewhere, there were other members of Artari's family in England. In particular, his brother Adalbertus could have been with him as they worked high on the Houghton ceilings and also drank their daily allocation of Sir Robert's wine.

Specific archival mention of important goods for Houghton is rare. Apart from 184 yards of fine Dutch canvas to line tapestries, charged at *9d.* a yard (CUL, 1726 vouchers), and 62 squares of crown glass 'for the chamber windows over the 2 Arcades to west front' (1729), much is not known. Two dates can be noted, however, first, February 1729, when John Cleaves, a London smith, provided '3 Brass window Barrs with Catches & Screws for the Salloon', and, second, October 1730, when marble was obtained for the Marble Parlour (or Dining Room). The record (CUL 1730 vouchers) of the cubic capacity of Plymouth, black-and-gold, purple-and-white and veined marbles was all placed to Mr Cass's account, after being obtained from Henry Bowman. There is, unfortunately, no record of payment for work by the leading sculptor, John Michael Rysbrack (1694–1770). He had supplied two marble reliefs to go over the chimneypieces in the Marble Parlour and Stone Hall and probably the chimneypieces as well. There are also stone reliefs and reclining figures by him over doors in the Stone Hall, and a group of Neptune and Britannia on the façade over the original entrance, 1730. A full-size cartoon by Rysbrack for the relief in the Marble Parlour was presented by the family to the British Museum in 1952 (cat. 57). Additionally, there is at Houghton a marble bust of Sir Robert Walpole by Rysbrack (cat. 33) and a terracotta, similar to it (National Portrait Gallery, London). The Marble Parlour chimneypiece may well have been by the London craftsman, Abraham Swan, as there is a record (1732–3) of 'Swan the carver' being paid 'for travelling to Houghton & return on Acct. of the Dining Room chimneypiece'. Swan later published (*c.*1745) an important treatise on staircases, much used by joiners in England and North America. Finally, Cass and Jelfe, who were busy in 1733 on the stable-block, cleaned the Great Stairs and Great Hall and 'painted the Cornice of Main House'. This was all included in their November–December 1733 account, along with the expenses of masons travelling from London to Houghton and back again (fifty-seven days), battering axes, shuting saws, extra charges on Portland stone, carriage of tools, freight of plaster and 'Mr. Jelfe's travelling'. Aside from the stucco decorations, Rysbrack's reliefs and Kent's paintings, an important feature of Houghton's decoration was carving in wood, in mahogany and partly or fully gilded soft wood. The fine staircase, with its 9½ inch wide handrail, deeply carved balusters (some of the finest in existence), and many superb door and window-cases (such as those in the Saloon) were the work of James Richards (d. 1759), and his 'man', Ralph Kite. The accounts for 15 August 1729–summer 1730 include, 'Ralph Kite for Mr. Richards, Carver, £3' (CUL, Account Book, 40/1).

Fig. 12 The Stone Hall, detail of stucco

Richards had succeeded to the post of Master Sculptor and Carver in Wood in the Office of Works in 1721 at the death of Grinling Gibbons. He was one of the most accomplished carvers of his age, with his finest realisation the rich gilded carvings on the State Barge, designed by William Kent in 1732 for Frederick, Prince of Wales (National Maritime Museum, Greenwich). Richards had worked from at least 1717 for the architect Colen Campbell, who seems to have taken over after Gibbs's earlier work at Houghton. Nothing is known of Richards's training but he was born about 1690 and was about thirty years old when

Fig. 13 The south wall of the Saloon

he worked under Campbell at the Rolls House in Chancery Lane. In the summer of 1720 Campbell had left Lord Burlington's service, but continued to employ Richards at Mereworth Castle, Kent and Compton Place, Eastbourne, the house completed by Campbell just before his death. His daughter Elizabeth married the architect Isaac Ware, and they had a son named Walter James Ware. Involvement with Kent, whose supervision of, and active participation in the interior decoration of Houghton was so important, was the obvious mainstay of Richards's activity. He was concerned, for example, with carving in the new Treasury in Whitehall, designed by Kent (building 1733–7), and he worked there alongside the plumber George Devall, as he had done at Houghton.

The stuccoists soon had to reckon with painters such as Kent and Francesco Sleter doing in paint what they were creating in stucco; Kent worked in seven rooms at Houghton and a considerable amount of his decoration is surrounded by foliated scrollwork (White Drawing Room; Marble Parlour), or has borders with feigned busts on grounds of gold scales (Saloon), worthy of the most accomplished stuccoist. But for the moment all was harmonious. They were working to satisfy only 'The King's Minister', and where better than at his 'great, fine House'?

4

The Genesis and Creation of a Great Interior

John Cornforth

NORFOLK IS A MARVELLOUS county for the study of early eighteenth-century interiors, the relationship of decoration, furniture and works of art, and also the connection between planning, use and daily life. In this Houghton and Holkham are the great stars, and gathered round them is a constellation that includes Narford, Raynham, Wolterton and Felbrigg.

There is, however, one missing figure, James Gibbs, although, as John Harris has explained, he was probably responsible for the concept of Houghton and its cleverly worked-out plan. Within the house there are certain features that have a Gibbsian look about them, such as the chimneypiece in the Hunting Hall, or possibly derive from Gibbs's suggestions, such as the handling of the cove of the Saloon and the order of pilasters in the Marble Parlour.

William Kent played an important part in the remodelling of Raynham for the 2nd Viscount Townshend, the brother-in-law of Sir Robert Walpole, in the same years that he was working at Houghton. He also played an active role in the genesis of Holkham and its setting, but, with the exception of the library, all the main rooms were completed after his death. At Houghton, on the other hand, all the decoration on the piano nobile is by Kent: indeed, it is the fullest expression of his genius as an architectural decorator.

Despite all the attention he has received in this century, Kent is still an underestimated figure, partly because we tend not to look at the different aspects of his work in the right order and so do not fully appreciate his originality. He went to Italy in 1709 with the younger Talman, who was interested in decoration as well as works of art and produced the first English drawings to show objects in a designed setting. There he trained as a history painter; and those who supported him in Italy had high hopes of his future success in England. He also prepared himself in other directions for he wrote, 'I am making all preparations and continually a Drawing ornaments and architecture and getting things yt I think will be necessary for use in England...', and on another occasion, 'I lay what little money I have on prints and stucco figures as heads and feet etc, which will be of great use to me when I cannot see Ye Antiques. I now am make a study about my paintings if I can introduce the Italian gusto into England.' His interest in architecture may have been stimulated by his young Norfolk patron in Italy, Thomas Coke, later Earl of Leicester and builder of Holkham.

Kent returned to England at the end of 1719 with the Earl of Burlington and soon he produced designs for the Saloon at Burlington House, presumably revising a scheme by Colen Campbell.

In 1722, through Burlington's influence, he managed to land the commission to decorate the ceiling of the Cupola Room at Kensington Palace and then to paint a series of ceilings in that palace which include figurative subjects for the new 'Jonesian Revival' ceilings of the Privy Chamber and the Drawing Room. However, it soon became clear that his talents as history and figurative painter were limited. On the other hand, he proved to have great talent as a designer and painter of ornament, and he began to turn to architectural decoration, painting the walls of the Cupola Room and drawing out schemes for the Drawing Room that included his first chimneypiece and overmantel in 1724 and a proposed picture hang. About 1725 he produced his first thoughts on architectural furniture as etched tailpieces to Alexander Pope's translation of Homer's *Odyssey* published in 1725–6. One is a table, close in spirit to that in the Hall at Ditchley Park, Oxfordshire, apparently carved by James Richards in 1726. By then he was working on the remodelling of the King's Gallery at Kensington, for which he made drawings 'with all the Pictures sketcht in proper colour'. He designed and painted its ceiling with figures in grisaille against a gold mosaic ground, which echoes the work of the Italian *stuccatori* recently arrived in England, as well as designing frames carved by John Howard for the great Venetian pictures that formed part of his unified scheme.

Round about 1728, while working for Thomas Coke at Holkham, Kent began to think about landscape design, approaching it from a pictorial point of view. Then, about 1730 he produced his first architectural designs, for a classical villa at Esher for Henry Pelham, a political colleague of Sir Robert Walpole. It should be remembered also that he is the first designer to use the gothick style for domestic work and also the first to design garden buildings in a *chinoiserie* style. He is also the first architect to whom a number of pieces of furniture, as well as silver, can be attributed. Thus, he was a designer of great individuality and range.

Kent's approach to architecture was quite different from that of Lord Burlington, who always thought in terms of precedents for all he did and liked plain surfaces with little ornament. Kent had the freedom of approach of a painter and loved pattern, texture, ornament and colour – characteristic decoration of the sixteenth and seventeenth centuries. In that painterly approach he was also the opposite of James Gibbs, who was the best trained and most experienced architect practising in Britain in the 1720s, although seemingly losing jobs because of his suspected Roman Catholicism and Jacobite sympathies. As far as interiors were concerned, Gibbs was a skilled planner, but he had a somewhat limited repertoire of ideas for the decoration of grand rooms. However, he appreciated the enlivening contribution of the Italian *stuccatori*, and from the time of their arrival, about 1720, gave them the freedom to design as well as execute their schemes. Also, he liked the combination of Italianate decorative painting and plasterwork, as can be seen on a modest scale in the room from 11 Henrietta Place, London, now in the Victoria and Albert Museum. In the early 1720s he made a few designs for furniture as part of rooms. Thus, he was working as an architectural decorator possibly even before Kent moved in that direction, although it is quite hard to unravel the facts and dates.

In considering William Kent's interiors at Houghton, therefore, it is only right to think of how he was competing both with Gibbs and Campbell. In addition, the way in which his designs related to current furnishing practices needs to be recognised. How and when Kent became involved at Houghton is not entirely clear. Sir Robert Walpole, or rather his brother, Horatio, later the 1st Lord Walpole and the builder of nearby Wolterton Hall, first had contact with him in 1721–2, when, as Secretary to the Treasury (appointed by Sir Robert who was First Lord) he gave instructions that Kent should paint the ceiling of the Cupola Room at Kensington. Kent's first designs for Houghton appear to be the two proposals for the decoration and picture hang in the Saloon, dated 1725, that are the earliest drawings of their kind in England (cat. 38–39). But whether they were commissioned by Sir Robert or done on Kent's initiative is not known: certainly Kent kept the drawings and they were only sold after his death. Round about the same time Kent began work for Lord Townshend at Raynham, where Sir Matthew Decker described the hall and Belisarius Room as finished when he went there in 1728. Almost all Kent's work at Houghton includes references to Sir Robert's Garter conferred on him in 1726, but, even if work was in hand before that and went on immediately afterwards, it may have been checked in 1727 when George I died unexpectedly and Sir Robert must have wondered whether he would remain in office.

It is tantalising that none of Kent's early drawings showing picture hangs and using colour should survive, but among his other work is a rejected design for the ceiling of the Drawing Room at Kensington that is close in style to the proposed treatment of the ceiling of the Saloon at Houghton. A carefully set out drawing showing pictures in frames on one wall of the Duke of Grafton's dining room appears not to be a design but a drawing for the engraving in Isaac Ware's *Designs of Inigo Jones* of 1731. The earliest Kent drawing using colour is the one for the Library at Holkham, which must date from the late 1730s, but the decorative painting was not carried out. His earliest executed design for Houghton is his drawing of 1731 that is very close to the pier table in the Carlo Maratti Room (cat. 47).

He was not a naturally careful draughtsman, like Henry Flitcroft, who was specially trained in that direction, but his sketchy manner was always expressive enough to provide a spark for craftsmen and, when he worked on someone else's drawing – such as John Vardy's drawing for a chimneypiece in the Treasury in 1736 – his amendments bring it to life. Part of the delight of Houghton lies in the vitality as well as the variety of all the details; and they feel like expressions of Kent's imagination captured by artists and craftsmen used to working with him and interpreting his sketches.

Evidence about contact between Sir Robert and Kent is lacking, but it is not difficult to imagine them getting on well because Kent possessed a similarly robust attitude to life and people, and, like a successful modern decorator, he must have had an enviable gift for guiding, dominating, charming, cajoling and giving way to clients without sacrificing any of his Yorkshire directness. Pope said of him that he was 'by no means a respecter of persons, but using sharp speeches to the greatest'. But the buttoned-up Lord Burlington and his much jollier wife were devoted to him:

'He is such a pure good humour'd man', wrote Lady Burlington, and their children called him 'Mr Kentino'. Surely it is not difficult to feel the warmth of his personality as well as Sir Robert's in the great rooms at Houghton today.

Much of the thinking, however, must go back to Sir Robert and his particular requirements: he wanted a house that was a monument to himself and the equal of the great houses of other grandees, as opposed to the seat of a country squire, albeit one of very ancient lineage; he required a place of parade where he could receive guests as important as the Duke of Lorraine, the son of the Holy Roman Emperor, who visited Houghton in 1731 before it was quite complete; but at the same time he needed a house for his family and also a place where he could entertain his political cronies at his twice yearly political meetings at Houghton, known as Congresses. For them he needed plenty of space where rowdy company could do no damage: as Thomas Gray, the poet, wrote to young Horace Walpole in July 1736, 'You are in a confusion of wine and bawdy and hunting and tobacco, and heaven be praised, you too can pretty well bear it'. Or, as Lord Hervey wrote to the Prince of Wales in 1731, the ground floor is 'dedicated to fox hunters, hospitality, noise, dirt and business'.

Those four aspects lie behind the remarkable sense of control in the house, which must have depended more on Sir Robert, Thomas Ripley, the executant architect appointed in 1720 and on the briefing of the upholsterers than on William Kent. That can still be sensed by walking round the house with the inventory taken on Sir Robert's death in 1745 (cat. 21) and a second one taken on the 3rd Earl of Orford's death in 1792 and checking them against the rooms and the furniture. They make it possible to visualise Houghton in Sir Robert's time in a way that is unrivalled in England. The practical good sense of the everyday family rooms on the ground floor, or rustic, as it was called, and the solid comfort of the bedrooms on the second floor make an unexpected and still little-known contrast with the often illustrated principal rooms on the piano nobile; and even on that floor there is a strong sense of build-up between the rooms of the family apartment at the south end of the house and the rooms of parade in the centre and at the north end. That is not easy for a present-day visitor to Houghton to experience.

The Hunting Hall and the Coffee Room on the ground floor are still the everyday dining room and sitting room of the house and known by their original names: in the former it is easy to imagine breakfast in the late 1730s when 'everybody calls for what he will; people do not come at a time, which is wrong' – and they still do not. Since the late eighteenth century the room has been hung with a blue ground Chinese wallpaper, but when some of the paper was taken down during recent repairs, the original panelling, painted a light stone colour, was revealed and that related to the stone of the chimneypiece. Probably most of the everyday rooms as well as the circulation spaces were painted that practical colour, which was so favoured in the first half of the eighteenth century, and it is specified on a drawing relating to the Great Staircase.

Anyone considering the piano nobile needs to be aware of how carefully the climax is orchestrated. Again, this is a unique experience in England. Before embarking on a tour of the rooms, there are a number of general points to bear in mind about Kent's overall control over their design and the way and the extent to which he followed current conventions. Not only did he work within a sequence of rooms that was more or less established, but he accepted the current Baroque idea that the rooms became richer and finer as a sequence from Saloon to Bedroom. Thus the idea of hanging the Saloon with caffoy, a fairly coarse material with a bold figure that was moderately priced, and then using a finer velvet in the Drawing Room seems to have been usual, as can be seen at Erddig in North Wales, which was refurnished during the early 1720s. Similarly, the idea of parcel-gilt mahogany furniture in the Saloon being followed by gilded furniture in the Drawing Room parallels the simple walnut chairs in the Erddig saloon, which were followed by silver gesso in the Drawing Room. At Erddig the climax was provided by the bed of gilt gesso and oriental embroidery, a change of mood that could be paralleled by the needlework bed that was originally placed in the State Bedroom at Houghton. The sequence of looking glasses at Erddig also contributed to a sense of build up there, and, while that does not happen at Houghton, it is done in other subtle ways that are easy to overlook, such as the sequence of marbles. In the Saloon the chimneypiece is black with white marble, whereas in the Drawing Room it is white with black, and then black with white in the Bedroom. Also, it should be noted that all the rooms from the Drawing Room round to the Cabinet Room were done in green velvet, with a change to green damask in the Marble Parlour. That was made, because velvet holds the smell of food and is impractical for dining chairs because it marks so easily. But green may represent a change of mind: the change from crimson in the Saloon to green in the Drawing Room appears to be a break with convention that may have come about through Kent's development of the iconography of the rooms, in particular dedicating the State Bedroom to Venus, Goddess of Love and Sleep, and green being at that time particularly associated with Venus.

The next significant element in the overall effect is how the pictures were disposed to create a sense of pace and variety, with picture rooms contrasting with tapestry rooms. Sir Robert began to buy pictures in 1717 and by 1736 owned 421, of which at least 400 were acquired by him. As originally hung in the early 1730s, the large Old Masters were concentrated in the Saloon and the Drawing Room, with small pictures in the Cabinet Room; and there were full-length Van Dyck portraits bought at the Wharton sale in 1725 in the Family (Yellow) Drawing Room. The other rooms contained few Old Masters of consequence. Family pictures were hung in logical groupings in the family rooms on the ground floor, combined with pictures of horses and dogs. There were no portraits of Sir Robert or his family in any of the seven principal rooms.

It is important to realise how novel was the style of the rooms and the extent to which they were the work of someone who was both a history and decorative painter. To a generation like ours, which is not particularly knowledgeable about iconography and symbolism, that may not be obvious, but it is striking that there is a symbolic, iconographic unity to each of the main rooms, with the subjects of the ceilings being reflected in the colours of the rooms and continued into the details of the furniture and sometimes echoed in the pictures that hang on the walls.

Since it is no longer possible to mount the east steps to the main door into the Stone Hall, everyone has to use the Painted Staircase. The advantage is that it underlines the contrast between the everyday rooms and the rooms of the parade in such a striking way. The rather dark and certainly low-key Arcade or Lower Hall runs the complete depth of the house and is still furnished with its benches, twenty-four chairs with railed backs and arms, which must have been thought safer for Sir Robert's cronies than the usual kind of hall chairs for servants, and four carved stags heads first recorded in 1792 (but the original fire engine and fire buckets have gone).

A black door without any special mark opens on to the foot of the staircase. If it is the red carpet that immediately leads one's eye up, one soon takes in the four towering columns forming a not-so-miniature temple, then the extravagant carved mahogany balustrade and finally the walls lined with canvas painted stone colour to continue the idea of the Arcade and to match the stone doorcases. They are decorated with mythological hunting scenes of *Meleager and Atalanta* in grisaille set in *tromp l'oeil* frames in white and gold in a pattern close to that of the carved and gilded frames that Kent designed for the King's Gallery at Kensington; and they are flanked by *tromp l'oeil* trophies emblematic of hunting. The canvas has a pronounced twill weave to it that gives an added sense of life to the painting, which suggests that Kent must have had some experience of work in the theatre (Fig. 20).

As one starts to climb, it becomes apparent that the staircase rises the full height of the house. At first-floor level the temple becomes the base for a huge bronze *Gladiator*, a copy made about 1645 by Le Sueur of a classical original that was given to Sir Robert by the 8th Earl of Pembroke. It is a theatrical idea unrivalled in an English house, and surely Kent's way of indicating to visitors that they pause at first-floor level, go through a side door into the Stone Hall and start on what Lord Hervey called 'the floor of taste, expense, state and parade'.

In its present form, the Stone Hall is a great room by Kent, but it is only right to see it as a revision of a proposal by Campbell that appears in *Vitruvius Britannicus* III (1725), which, in turn must be a replacement of Gibbs's original concept. Gibbs's design may not survive, but bearing in mind his Great Room at Sudbrook Park, Richmond, Surrey, of about 1718, the idea of the two-storey hall at Kelmarsh Hall, Northamptonshire, and an unpublished drawing at Houghton for the outer wall of a double-height hall with two storeys of pilasters and a gallery, it is reasonable to imagine it like that. Alternatively it could have a giant order of single or paired pilasters with a shallower attic storey and perhaps a semi-vaulted ceiling; and there would have been a screen against the west wall to provide a hidden first-floor link beneath the north and south ends of the house. It was Campbell who proposed an interior more like the hall in the Queen's House at Greenwich, with the balcony and a disposition of elements similar to that existing today. Kent, however, redrew all the elements to create a bolder, richer effect with more sculpture.

The Hall is a celebration of Walpole's triumph as a new Roman and of the pleasure of the chase and country life. Watched by Rysbrack's figures of *Peace* and *Plenty* over the east door (Fig. 18), Sir Robert in toga and Garter Star presides over the room from the chimneypiece and so is raised slightly above the classical busts of emperors on the long brackets. Behind him is the relief of the *Sacrifice to Diana*, and above the doors are smaller reliefs depicting sacrifices, also by Rysbrack. They are derived from copies of earlier engravings of the Arch of Constantine used in Bernard de Montfaucon's *Antiquity Explained and represented in Sculpture*, which appeared in the early 1720s, where they were interpreted as illustrating the Hunting of the Ancients with one of them entitled 'Trajan preparing for the hunting'.

The idea of the pairs of *putti* on the pediments to the doorcases is sometimes seen as a Campbellian and some-

Fig. 14 Entrance doorway, the Saloon, leading to the Stone Hall

times as a Gibbsian idea, but it was one first made possible by the Italian *stuccatori* who may have modelled them for the first time at Orleans House, Twickenham, about 1720. In the Saloon at Burlington House, probably their next appearance, it is often said that they are due to Campbell, but as Kent painted the ceiling and must have designed the big frames on the side walls, is it not just as likely that he did the doorcases as well? At Houghton they were modelled by Rysbrack and combine with the busts to create a dancing rhythm round the hall that answers the playing putti swinging round the cove.

The two themes continue up to the ceiling; the cove with its wonderfully lively figures of putti swinging from the oak garlands that link together the roundels of Sir Robert, his first wife, his son and his daughter-in-law. The ornamental plasterwork was carried out by Giuseppe Artari either in 1726 or 1728; and above is the ceiling with a great display of the Walpole arms, crest, supporters and Garter, all set against a pale blue ground that may be original, with symbols of hunting in the segments answering the fox's mask above the chimneypiece.

But who designed the cove? Kent takes credit for it in the headpiece of his *Designs of Inigo Jones* of 1727, but I suspect that he may have been adapting an idea seen on a painted ceiling in Italy and revived for him in an engraving or taken from a French print. But given the way he thought, he probably also saw them as a prelude to the putti playing in the borders of the 'Van Dyck' tapestries in the State Dressing Room.

Facing the chimneypiece is a bronze cast of Laocoön by Girardon that Sir Robert's brother, Horatio, whom he had appointed ambassador to Louis XV in 1724, obtained for him in Paris. It stands on a plinth designed by Kent. Flanking it are a pair of marble topped tables whose scrolling frames incorporate garlands of oak leaves echoing those on the walls and in the cove of the ceiling. On the other three walls the only furniture are pairs of benches of a type specially favoured by Kent and here designed so that they fit beneath the long brackets supporting busts, with their scrolling backs answering in reverse the scrolls of the brackets (cat. 36).

Originally the Hall was lit with a lantern containing

eighteen candles, which was regarded as an extravagance worthy of satire. When the Duke of Lorraine stayed at Houghton in 1731, before the Marble Parlour was finished, he dined here; and Sir Thomas Robinson recorded that it was lit by 130 wax lights and the Saloon with 50: 'the whole expense in that article being computed at fifteen pounds a night'. That is a reminder that light was a symbol of hospitality and show; and how little light was used most of the time. The present carved and gilt chandelier was introduced by the 2nd Earl of Orford, who bought it at the sale of his brother-in-law's London house in 1748.

It is a great thrill to open the double doors in the hall and walk into the Saloon, to go from the cool stone colour into the glow of crimson and gold, and from the demesne of Diana into that of Apollo and Venus (Fig. 14). The central panel of the ceiling depicts *Apollo driving his Chariot of the Sun* and is painted in grisaille against a mosaic ground, an idea derived from Raphael. The cove has on the north and south walls roundels of Neptune and Cybele for Water and Earth, the roundels being supported by pairs of putti and the Walpole supporters and Garter Star, with roundels representing the Four Seasons on the longer west and east walls. The frieze is ornamented with the head of Diana with bows, trophies of bows and quivers of arrows, hounds and hares that is completely un-Palladian. It suggests that Kent may have looked at friezes by the seventeenth-century Florentine etcher, Stefano della Bella. Apollo's sunflower appears in the pediments over the east door and the facing window, and a bust of Venus stands on the chimneypiece.

The richness of the imagery may distract the eye from taking in the design of the room, which conceivably went back to Gibbs, or at least to a Gibbs idea. That is suggested by the way that the upper windows on the west wall are set back behind the cove, a detail never photographed because of the light, but it is a favourite idea of Gibbs, which Kent took over, or borrowed. He then carried it round the cove in what look like arches with grisaille ornament against mosaic grounds, which were intended to create a sense of vaulting. He also enjoyed challenging the Italian *stuccatori* in *tromp l'oeil painting*, as can first be seen on the walls of the Cupola Room at Kensington: here, all the ornament in the cove is painted in grey, white, green and gold against a stone coloured ground. And surely the idea of the central octagonal panel of Apollo in grisaille recalls the contemporary plaster reliefs by the Italians and the Dane Charles Stanley, while the grisaille roundels in the coves also recall a favourite idea of *stuccatori*?

It was Kent's painterly eye and his memory of late seventeenth-century Roman furniture that enabled him to conceive of architectural furniture, pier glasses and tables, chairs and stands as relating to plasterwork and decorative painting. That can be seen in his use of shells which appear in paint on the cove, in carved wood on the pier glasses and the bases of the pier tables on the west wall, and also on the chairs; while the *putti* playing in the cove of the Hall are found supporting Neptune and Cybele in the painted cove and decorating the pier glasses and tables in carved wood.

The gilding is also brilliantly planned and, considering it is oil rather than water gilding in the English tradition, still has remarkable flash after 250 years. How far to take parcel gilding is always a problem, but here the connection between carving and gilding is handled with great skill, not only on the great doorcases but on the chairs. It is noteworthy that it is only in the Great Apartment that the mouldings of the doors are carved and gilded, whereas in the Hall and family rooms the doors are moulded and not picked out.

The walls are hung with their original caffoy. Originally there was less contrast between the figure and the ground. The 164 yards costing £118 18*s*. were supplied by Thomas Roberts in the period April 1729–January 1729/30. The room was more or less complete by May 1731, when it was seen by John Loveday of Caversham, but the final touches of gilding were added in 1732.

There is no bill for the furniture, but James Richards almost certainly made the frames for the tables and glasses and the set of twelve armchairs, pair of settees and four stools. He was the leading Office of Works carver and a great favourite of Kent since he made the tabernacle frame for his *tromp l'oeil* statue of *Mercury* in the hall at Chicheley Hall, Buckinghamshire, in 1722. He also worked a great deal at Raynham, Norfolk, from 1730. The material fits the chairs so well that it must have been to hand when Kent designed them; and, what is, as far as I know, a unique survivor in England, the chairs are backed with a woollen material stamped with a figure very close to that of the caffoy.

The pair of gilt-metal chandeliers in the French style appear to be two out of four listed in 1745. They may have been supplied by William Hubert, who repaired French metal branches and girandoles for Sir Robert in 1730 (see cat. 16). When Hubert died in 1740, he was described as 'a French Gentleman, a great Dealer in Pictures, curious Stones, etc' and, according to an auctioneer's announcement of 1735, he also had 'Great choice of very curious Bronze Lustres, Girandoles, Andirons, and Branches, gilt and repaired in the finest French taste'. His Houghton bill is the only one so far recorded and it is tempting to link his name with the three surviving chandeliers.

The eye is never allowed to rest, and yet it is never tired nor bored here: the room provides endless pleasure. In addition, it originally looked out on an equally elaborate formal garden laid out a few years before the new house was conceived but an integral part of the composition.

The Drawing Room next door has been substantially altered since Sir Robert's day, because it was the first of the green velvet rooms. Presumably his grandson, the 3rd Lord Orford, found the material badly bruised by the picture frames when he sold the pictures in 1779, and by 1792 it had been replaced by green striped material, a fashionable choice. But presumably also, he did not find a way of clothing the walls with pictures, although he too was a collector. So after the visit in 1797 of the Prince of Wales to the 4th Earl of Cholmondeley, who inherited Houghton from Horace Walpole that year, the Prince gave him the brocaded silk hangings, which seem to be an English version of a Louis XVI material. They, together with the set of related chairs, the valances of the window curtains, the overdoors and John Hoppner's portrait of Lady Cholmondeley, the wife of the fourth Earl and first Marquess, in a white dress, make the room one of the best examples of 1790s decoration in England, and they echo the white grisaille painting in the ceiling.

However, they are the opposite of Kent's intention in scale and tone: he saw the room as being in green and gold with white. And here one can visualise even more clearly how iconography and decoration worked hand in hand under the guidance of Venus in the centre of the ceiling. Round her appear Jupiter, Juno, Apollo and Cybele representing the Elements, with Apollo's mask on the tablet of the chimneypiece flanked by his sunflower. Kent's pantheon inspired or echoed some of the pictures on the walls, which were of such subjects as *The Judgement of Paris, Venus and Cupid, Acis and Galatea,* all by Carlo Maratti, the greatest living master when Kent first arrived in Rome, and *Apollo and Daphne* and *Bacchus and Ariadne* by Giuseppe Chiari, whom Kent had known in Italy and who also painted pictures for Thomas Coke, eventually set up as the overmantels in the Saloon at Holkham. Again, as in the Saloon, Kent tied all the elements of the room together through the details. Thus, the cupids' heads at the turns in the beams of the ceiling recur in the broken pediment of the original overmantel frame (now in the Green Velvet Bedroom).

Who supplied the green velvet and when is not recorded, but there is an estimate of the material required and that shows 521¾ yards were needed for all the rooms that Sir Robert had in hand. That probably explains why the material today appears to be in two lots, one being slightly bluer than the other.

The room was furnished with two settees, twelve chairs and four stools, the frames being carved and gilded and the covers being of green velvet edged with gold lace (or braid, originally silver-gilt). It is not known who made them, but whereas the Saloon chairs were made by a carver who was not a chairmaker, these were made by a chairmaker who was also a carver. The masks on the top rails and the arms are distinctly Kentian and it is tempting to suggest that they are by someone like Benjamin Goodison, who was emerging in the late 1720s as a leading maker of carved and gilded furniture and was to produce pieces in a Kentian style. However, it is impossible to think of comparable chairs by him. Another, and to my mind more credible, alternative is William Bradshaw, who again was getting going in the years when Houghton was being furnished and he provided chairs as well as being a cabinet-maker, upholsterer and tapissier. In the mid-1730s he supplied chairs of a similar monumentality to Chevening, in Kent, and about 1740 appears to have made more than one set of chairs for Ditchley. Between the windows is a pier glass with a broken pediment that matched the overmantel and a key moulding round the glass that is repeated in the frame of the table beneath it. The latter has horns of plenty and garlands meeting in a lion's mask. The table top is lapis lazuli.

If the balance has changed in the Drawing Room, in the Velvet Bedroom there has been virtually no change (Fig. 15). The room is dedicated to Venus, Goddess of Love and Sleep, and that is expressed in the ceiling, the frieze, the tapestries, the green velvet and the design of the bed. The ceiling, unlike those in the preceding rooms, is painted not in grisaille but in colours, albeit soft ones, evidently at Sir Robert's insistence. It shows *Aurora Rising.* The frieze takes up the idea of cupids' heads in the Drawing Room, but they are given wings and they are repeated in the chimneypiece. The tapestries depict *The Love of Venus and Adonis* after Francesco Albani and were woven in Brussels (Fig. 16). Walpole used much more tapestry at Houghton than we would expect today but, although Gobelins tried to persuade him to buy tapestry for them in 1727, this was the only set specially woven for the new house, so that it fits precisely with the centres of the three main panels in the corners of the room, with borders of two panels joining on to the carved and gilt moulding of the chimneypiece, while the bottom corners relate to the scrolls of the window architraves.

At the beginning of the eighteenth century state beds, as the most spectacular and costly pieces of furniture in a house, often had complicated silhouettes with elaborate drapery and trimmings, but in the middle of the second

Fig. 15 Green Velvet Bedchamber

Fig. 16 Green Velvet Bedchamber, east and south walls

Fig. 17 The Marble Parlour, detail of differently veined and coloured marbles

decade they began to be simplified, as can be seen in Queen Anne's cut velvet bed made for Windsor Castle. Kent's green velvet bed at Houghton follows that approach, consisting as it does of a canopy in the form of an architectural entablature with a deep fringe with bundles and relying for its effect on the contrast of the green velvet and the very fine but still restrained enrichment in gold lace, with silver beneath showing through. The trimming picks out the entablature and the base as if they were architecture in wood, and forms a frieze with Apollo's sunflower as well as bordering the curtains. Then, within the bed the pedimented bedhead springs up into a double shell, making it into Venus's triumphal car. The gold trimmings and the way they are used is very extravagant, and happily on this occasion Sir Robert failed to destroy the bill from the suppliers of the trimmings, Turner, Hill and Pitter. They charged no less than £1219 3*s.* 11*d.* in 1732. With the bed are more of the chairs of the design used in the Drawing Room. The only other piece of furniture in the room is the lacquer chest, one of several in the house that were in the principal bedrooms.

The more one looks at the room, the more there is to enjoy in it, down to such subtle points as the way the friezes of the doorcases repeat those in the Drawing Room but are then changed in the room beyond; and the way the brown and gold borders of the tapestries seem to be echoed in the carved and gilded detail of the doors.

Next door is what in the eighteenth-century was always called the Vandyke Dressing Room, after the Mortlake tapestries woven after the full-length early Stuart portraits. The panels of James I and Anne of Denmark are signed and dated 'FP fecit 1672' for Francis Poyntz. The set is supposed to have belonged to Sir Robert's father. Here in 1745 was a glass table, presumably the one with the arms of Sir Robert engraved into the back of the looking-glass plate (cat. 49), an Indian cabinet and a silver filigree cabinet (probably the one attributed to Pierre Golle and now in the private rooms). The chairs match those in the Bedroom and Drawing Room.

There is a small lobby between the Dressing Room and the Embroidered Bedroom and off that leads a service stair, so that servants could move about behind the scenes without the company noticing.

The Embroidered Bedroom contains the bed of oriental needlework that must have been ordered very soon after the Garter was conferred on Sir Robert, because it arrived in time for the Duke of Lorraine's visit in 1731. Unlike the Erddig bed, where the Chinese embroidery seems to have been cut for the bed rather than designed for it, the Houghton bed, like the Calke Abbey bed (Derbyshire), must have been made up to take embroidery that had been specially designed for it, with drawings sent to the East. The backcloth is a particularly fine design, with the Walpole arms and the embroidered motifs standing out against the creamy-white quilted ground and the mouldings picked out in a light green braid. The curtains are worked with trees of life, flowers and birds.

The seat furniture in this room is the finest part of a large set, with frames of walnut and gesso and covered in more of the green velvet. The line of the chairs is particularly good, but with a date closer to 1715, it is possible that they were ordered by Sir Robert as part of his improvement to the old house at about that time and then recovered to suit the new house.

Originally, the room at the northeast corner of the house was to be another bedroom, but Sir Robert decided to devote it to his smaller pictures. The pictures are shown in a design, now in the Ashmolean Museum, which shows all four walls as well as the ceiling; recently a drawing has been discovered at Houghton that also shows a picture hang (cat. 56). It was presumably because of the pictures that Kent painted the ceiling with a teasing *Minerva fending off Envy* with a shield bearing the Walpole arms, the painting being almost in grisaille. Originally the walls were hung with more of the green velvet, and the seat furniture has always been part of the walnut and parcel gilt set. Again, Kent tied the room together through the repetition of motifs, for here the shell on the chimneypiece answers those in the frieze and the ceiling and is picked up in the shells on the overmantel frame.

The last of the parade rooms is the Marble Parlour; in many ways the most remarkable of all the interiors at Houghton. In the 1720s it was a novel idea to have a dining room as part of the main run of rooms in a house, and it is interesting that one of the earliest known is the one at Ditchley, planned by Gibbs in 1720 but not fitted up until the late 1730s by Henry Flitcroft: that was the largest of the rooms in the great apartment. It was Gibbs who first suggested the idea of the Marble Parlour at Houghton, because his plan shows access for servants from the landing of the north staircase behind the chimneybreast; it is conceivable also that the use of pilasters in the room goes back to him, because they appear in many of his rooms.

Kent took up Gibbs's notion both here and at Raynham, where he completed the dining room by 1732. There he treated the inner end of the room as a triumphal arch, an idea that Lord Burlington also used rather differently in the hall at Northwick Park, Avon. The use of marble at Houghton, however, must surely be Kent's idea (Fig. 17). But it was only quite late on that it was decided to commission another overmantel relief from Rysbrack for the chimneypiece, because earlier schemes surviving in the house show a great achievement of the Walpole arms. There is a payment for 'Swan ye carver' coming to Houghton in 1732–3, when the chimneypiece was taken down and the bas relief and chimneypiece were put up again. The order is superbly expressed in different marbles, black for the skirting, black and yellow for the dado, with white for the mouldings and capitals and violet for the shafts of the columns. The walls are lined with a white marble with grey veining, with slightly stronger veining on the chimneybreast and white for the chimneypiece and overmantel. The sense of shadow in the recess is exaggerated by the marbles, white with grey veining for the walls, pilasters in violet and the string course in grey with yellow. The tables have more black veining in the legs as well as black feet, and violet with white for the frames. What is so surprising is that the marbles are even used for the two 'invisible' doorcases that face each other behind the chimneybreast.

Fig. 18 Michael Rysbrack's figures of Peace and Plenty *c.*1726–8; over the east door in the Stone Hall

As might be expected in an eating room the theme of Bacchus and Bacchic motifs occur not only in the painted panels of the ceiling, but in the ribs of the ceiling, the friezes of the entablature and of the doorcases, in the chimneypiece and overmantel, and into the pier glass and table between the windows on the east wall (Fig. 19). But Kent also knew how to economise: the carving below the dado rail might be presumed to be gilded, like the rest of the enrichment, but, in fact, it is ochre paint, which is only apparent on close inspection. As in the Drawing Room, the colours of the ceiling continue into the decoration, with the original chairs having gilded frames with eagle arms and green damask covers. They are the only example I know of gilded chairs in a dining room, but were they made for the room? I had assumed that they were, but the detailing of their legs and top rails has a slightly earlier feel than the Green Drawing Room chairs although, if made for the room, should date from a year or so later. Also, the way the leg rises into the seat and the carving on the corner of the legs is not unlike details on the walnut chairs with yellow caffoy covers described in 1745 that now turn out to be by Thomas Roberts. That is not only interesting in itself but shows that Roberts worked on the main floor as well as supplying the caffoy. However, again, Roberts is a puzzle, because it has been impossible to work out a connection with his well-known namesake who died in 1714 and his son Robert recorded between 1714 and 1729. Given the scale of the Houghton order it is odd that he has not been found anywhere else.

Not only is the Marble Parlour the first dining room, but it has the earliest great table. Seldom opened up to its full size, it can be seen in old photographs. When Sir Thomas Robinson stayed at Houghton in 1731 the room was not finished, so it is not known where they dined, but he said, 'We were generally between 20 and 30 at two tables, and as much cheerfulness and good nature as I ever saw where the company was so numerous. Young Lady Walpole and Mrs Hamond, Sir Robert's sister, were the only two ladies. Sir Robert does the honours of his house extremely well, and so as to make it perfectly agreable to everyone who lives with him.'

What is, of course, missing from the room today is a display of Walpole plate, great sideboard dishes, sets of silver waiters for glasses and almost certainly an epergne for the table, and so on, which surely Kent would have counted on for special occasions, particularly since he was so interested in designing silver. None of Sir Robert's plate has survived at Houghton, but there is evidence of Kent's imaginative approach to it in the variety of vessels he has incorporated in the frieze and ceiling. An earlier Kent design for the room, dated on the back 1728 (cat. 58), engraved in Ware's *Designs of Inigo Jones* of 1731 (with the recesses empty), shows the marble tables with displays of plate of different dates together with a pair of sconces that have been found in the house and recently restored for use here. Representations of plate at that date are exceedingly rare, so it is impossible to know whether Kent visualised displays on the side tables at each end of the room as well as in the recesses, possibly silver gilt at one end and silver at the other. If he did it is surprising that the frames of the tables have no carving or gilding, whereas the pier table is gilded. The taps in the marble tables are a reminder that there would probably have been two cisterns, possibly of silver, one on a table for washing glasses and one on the floor to hold bottles.

Fig. 19 The Marble Parlour, pier glass and table

The second floor, or attic storey, as it was called in 1745, is brilliantly planned for comfort and privacy, with none of the bedrooms opening directly off the two main staircases and with most of them opening off L-shaped corridors that run behind the north and south walls of the staircases. There are four principal bedrooms at the corners of the house, with single rooms adjoining them on the north and south sides of the house and four small rooms on the west side and two large ones on the east side.

Several of these rooms were hung with tapestry which survived *in situ* until after 1892. The Family Bedroom, for instance, was hung with Mortlake panels of the *Seasons*, as

Fig. 20 The Staircase, showing William Kent's *Meleager and Atalanta c.*1727–31

can be seen from an old photograph, (these have been conserved recently). Tapestry is also mentioned in three bedrooms on the second floor in 1745, but the subjects are not recorded until 1888. There were five panels of scripture subjects in the North West Corner Room and Teniers subjects in the Yellow Damask Room or South West Corner Room, but, alas, six lots of tapestry were sold at Christie's (24 June 1902, lots 132–7). These included five panels of Mortlake *Seasons*, four panels of peasants carousing after Teniers, with the arms and crest of Walpole, two panels of Mortlake *Hero and Leander*, three panels of Flemish *Triumph of Cupid* and five panels of Flemish *Acts of the Apostles*. There is no record of these hanging at Houghton, but Le Blon of the Gobelins factory did try to interest Sir Robert in a project to weave the *Acts* in three different sizes. There also survives a set of 'painted dimothy hangings' or *toiles peints* after Watteauesque subjects in a bedroom on the West Front. The North West Bedroom also still retains its original oriental painted taffeta hangings and bed listed in 1745.

There is always more to see at Houghton. At the end of the 1792 inventory Horace Walpole wrote down '106 rooms & outhouses completely finished at Sir Robert's death no part was left unfinished, but the Chapel, the Church being so near the house'. And as a visitor noted in 1741, 'they can make up at an hour's warning 110 beds'.

5
The Planting of the Park

Tom Williamson

HOUGHTON HALL, and the treasures it contains, filled eighteenth-century visitors with wonder – or envy. But most were equally impressed by the magnificent landscape that surrounds it (Fig. 21). The park at Houghton has a complex history, which – like that of most other country house landscapes – cannot be understood in isolation from the story of the house that it surrounds, and complements.

Sir Robert Walpole originally intended to make drastic alterations to the existing manor house at Houghton before deciding, some time in 1720, to build a completely new building, on a site a few metres to the east. The gardens shown on the detailed earliest map of Houghton, surveyed by Thomas Badeslade in 1720, were thus designed to complement the original house: not surprisingly, the principal walks and vistas shown on this plan foçus on its site, rather than on that of the new hall. Badeslade's plan (Fig. 23), and that prepared by Colen Campbell in 1722 and published in volume III of his *Vitruvius Britannicus* in 1725 (Fig. 22), both show a garden typical of the first decades of the eighteenth century (Houghton MSS, Map 1: Campbell, 1725). It was formal in style, and strongly influenced by current French ideas, but simpler in design than gardens of the previous century: without complex parterres, and dominated by trees, grass and gravel (Williamson, 1995, 35–45). The main garden area lay to the west of the hall and consisted of a broad axial walk, lined with topiary bushes. This was flanked by turf borders and, behind, by low terraces. Beyond these, to north and south, were densely planted 'wildernesses': that is, areas of ornamental woodland and shrubbery dissected by hedged paths. That to the north was the largest and most complex, containing both straight walks (arranged in the form of a St Andrew's cross) and narrower, more serpentine paths, as well as a number of geometric clearings. Immediately in front of the hall, the axial walk broadened into a grass *plat* or lawn, the precise shape of which is shown slightly differently on the two plans. Sir Matthew Decker remarked in 1728 how 'The gardens in which you go out of the salon, and where will be a fine Portico... have a very fine prospect over the park towards a hill or rising ground; before it a large grass

Fig. 21 Houghton Park from the air. The parish church of St Martin marks the site of the village cleared by Sir Robert Walpole in the late 1720s. New Houghton is in the foreground.

platt fit for a bowling green, then a large gravel walk, on each side grass plattes, as also two fine woods of oak and beech hedges extremely handsomely cut out in divers walkes and pleasant arbours' (Cornforth, 1987, 164). And four years later Sir John Clerk of Penicuik described how 'On the garden side there is a large parterre all of green

Turff with a gravel walk round on each side of this a large Wilderness very handsomely laid out & the trees and hedges being of hornbeam are come to a great height' (Scottish Record Office, GD 18/2107).

We do not know precisely when all these features were established. Work on some scale was clearly going on in the gardens during the late 1710s. Fulke Harold, who was in charge of them, was paid a total of over £800 for various purchases, and for labour, in the three years between 1718 and 1721 (Yaxley 1988, 92). An undated design for the gardens among the Gough manuscripts in the Bodleian Library has been attributed to the famous designer Charles Bridgeman (Willis, 1977, 86, 180): but he only appears to have become involved at Houghton in the late 1720s, and no less an authority than Horace Walpole attributed the design of this, 'One of the first gardens planted in this simple though still formal style', to one 'Mr Eyre an imitator of Bridgeman' (Walpole, 1784, 54).

Beyond the gardens lay an extensive deer park. This was probably created in the later seventeenth century and was extended around 1720 from approximately 90 to approximately 120 hectares. It occupied terrain which is at most only gently undulating: the ground to the east of the hall rises gradually, but that to the west is, for the most part, dead level. The park's design, as depicted by Badeslade and Campbell, was dominated by a complex mesh of avenues, the largest of which, ranged east–west, was axially aligned on the house. The design of gardens and park was closely integrated, for the alignments of the *allées* in the former were continued as avenues running across the latter, implying that views out from the one to the other were not entirely obscured by high walls. Badeslade's map suggests that the garden was enclosed by a wall, but this may have been a low feature, or else punctuated by ironwork grills. More interestingly, Campbell's plan suggests that the northern boundary of the garden, at least, was bounded by a ha ha (later maps show a ha ha on the western side, too, although only that on the north still survives today). Campbell's plan, it is true, is as much a proposal as a depiction of reality: but by 1731, certainly, Sir Thomas Robinson was able to describe how the gardens were 'fenced from the Park by a *fosse*, and I think very prettily disposed' (Historic Manuscripts Commission, 15th report, Appendix, pt 6, 85).

Work on preparing the site for the new hall began in 1721 and work had largely been completed by 1735, a fairly short time scale for an enterprise on this scale. Edmund Prideaux's illustration of about 1725 (cat. 15) shows the new house, standing within the maturing gardens, at a time when the present domes were being built.

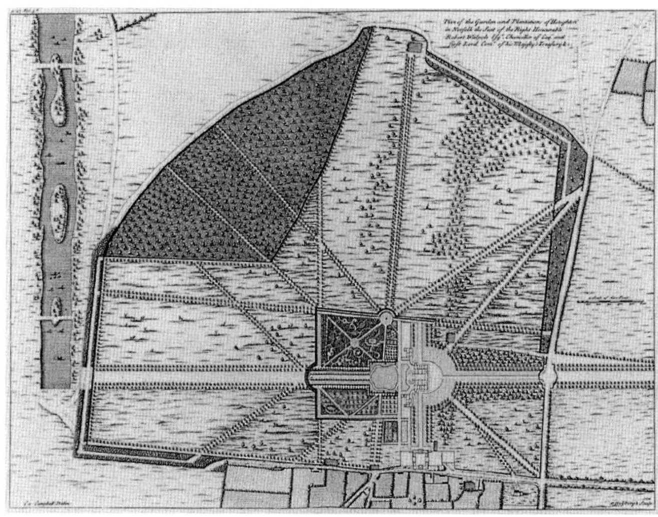

Fig. 22 Colen Campbell, plan of Houghton; this is in part a survey, in part a proposal for rebuilding the hall and altering the grounds. From *Vitruvius Britannicus* (1725)

A building as magnificent (and as politically important) as this demanded a suitable setting, and plans to enlarge the park seem to have been made even before its construction was begun. When Matthew Decker visited Houghton in 1728, and rode around the park, Robert Walpole showed him 'what was done already, and what more is designed'. The former included new plantations which extended 'now much beyond the park in several squares on each side of the avenue, and when these are grown so far that the deer can't hurt them, then the park is greatly to be enlarged, and it will have a most magnificent wood, from all the prospects of the house' (Cornforth, 1987, 164). The blocks of woodland flanking the axial avenue to the west of the park are, in fact, already shown on Thomas Badeslade's map of 1720, so the plan to expand was clearly well advanced at the time Decker was writing.

Decker's account implies that there was an intention to extend the park *westwards*: but when expansion did occur, in the years around 1730, it was in other directions: to the southwest, the east, and the southeast. To the south expansion was blocked by Houghton village, which was therefore removed, and replaced with a neat 'model' settlement, New Houghton. This was probably the first complete purpose-built estate village in England. The foundations for the first of the new houses were dug in July 1729, and by 1730 painters were priming doors and windows here, although the old village was not finally demolished until after 1732. Extending the park in this direction also necessitated the demolition of the stables which, according to Sir Thomas Robinson in 1731, were 'very large and [have] been finished about 13 years ago': 'not only as they are

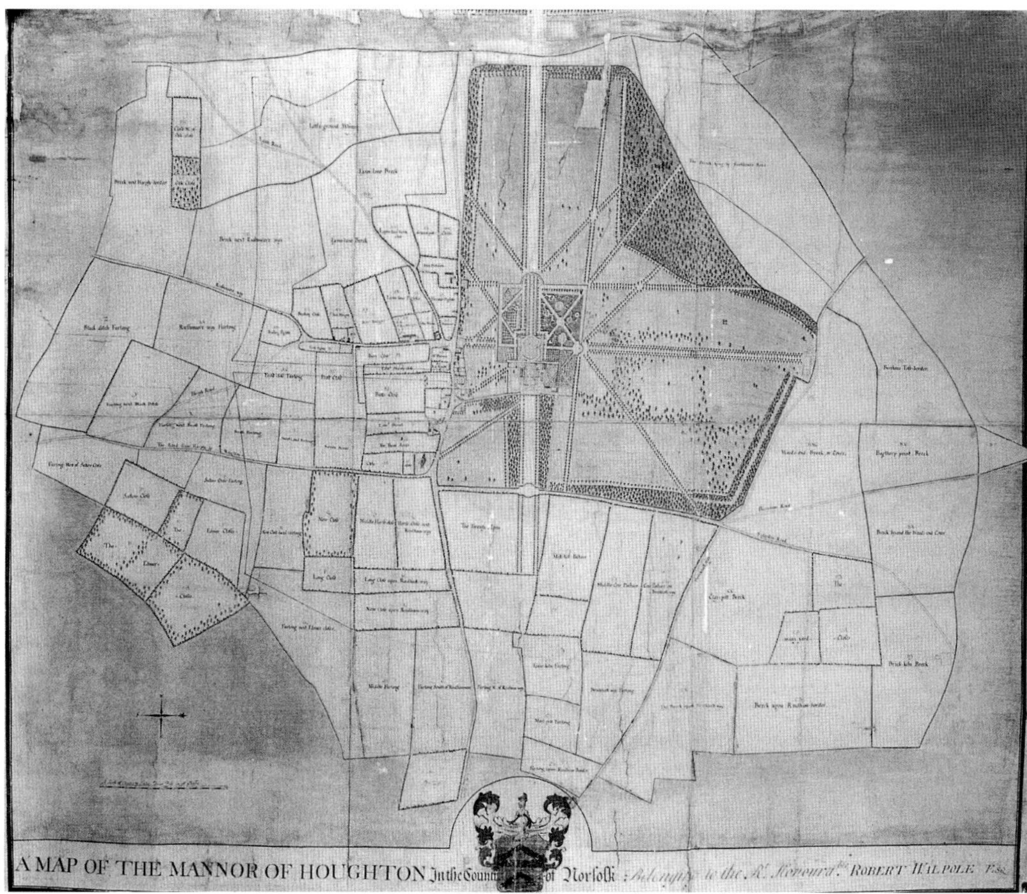

Fig. 23 Houghton Park, as shown on Thomas Badeslade's map of 1720

very ill built, but stand in the way of one of the most agreeable prospects you have from the house' (Historic Manuscripts Commission, 15th report, Appendix, pt 6, 85). To the east the old park had been bounded by a north–south public road, flanked by a perimeter belt: its line, and that of the bank protecting the western side of the plantation, today survives as prominent earthworks in the parkland turf. As a result of these changes, by around 1735 the park extended over an area of no less than 200 hectares.

Architecture in Britain in the 1720s was, in a sense, moving ahead of landscape design: Palladianism did not yet have an equivalent in gardening, and it is clear that there was some uncertainty over precisely what form the landscape laid out around the hall should take. The original plan seems to have been simply to enlarge the park to a suitably magnificent size, and to extend the existing mesh of avenues within it. This, at least, is what is implied by an undated proposal of about 1725 in the Houghton archives (Houghton MSS, Map 23). By the late 1720s, however, such a plan was losing its appeal. A larger park was clearly considered essential: but ideas about how the space within it was to be ordered were changing. In 1728 Decker was shown by Walpole, 'His further design of planting and placing his woods for the avenues which will be very long and large upon three sides of the house' – while in 1731 Thomas Robinson described how Charles Bridgeman and Walpole showed him: 'The large design which is the present undertaking: there are to be plumps and avenues to go quite round the Park pale, and to make straight and oblique lines of a mile or two in length, as the situation of the country admits of. This design will be about 12 miles in circumference' (Historic Manuscripts Commission, 15th report, Appendix, pt 6, 85).

The proposals thus somewhat obscurely described seem to tally with the grandiose design illustrated by Isaac Ware in the first edition of his *Plans, Elevations, and Sections... of Houghton in Norfolk*, published in 1735. This shows a radically different layout to that depicted by Badeslade, Campbell or on any other map of the 1720s: a massive yet simple design which included a vast perimeter ride flanked by block plantations, some in the form of military bastions. Gone is the dense mesh of avenues shown on the earlier maps, and in its place a much simpler, more monumental layout had been established. The eastern and western vistas from and towards the house were now simply implied, by block planting; while to north and south of the house wide,

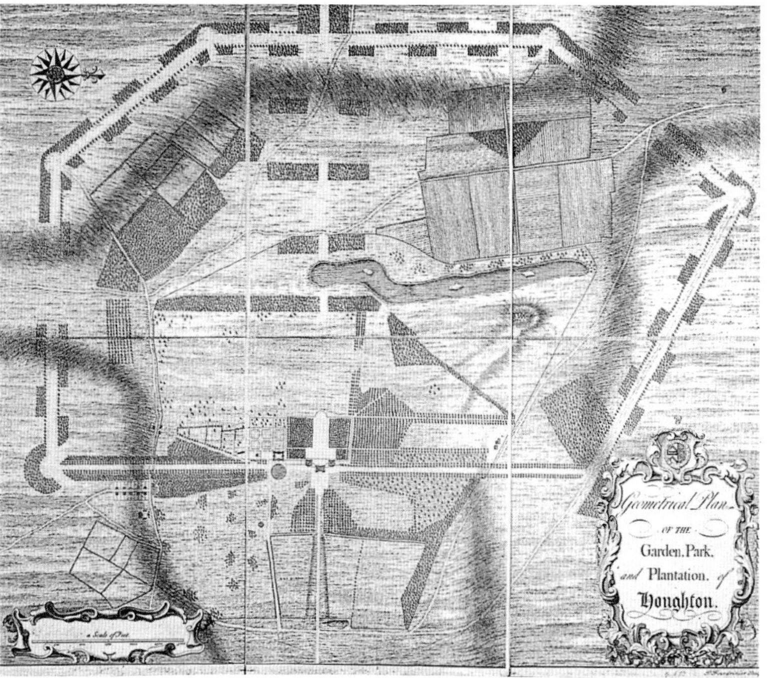

Fig. 24 Isaac Ware, plan of Houghton Park from *Plans, Elevations, and Sections of Houghton Hall in Norfolk*. First published in 1735, the engraving reproduced here is the republished version of 1764, and shows the cutting excavated by Sir Robert to the east of the house in the 1740s.

double-planted avenues framed the façades of the hall. Only four of the earlier avenues still survived, and three of these now ran through densely planted woodland, as indeed did the main avenue framing the north front of the house. The result was a simpler, starker layout; and one in which the principal avenues no longer focused on the walks and *allées* in the garden, but on the house itself. It is this pattern of planting which forms the basic structure to the Houghton landscape today (Fig. 24).

The Ware plan is not entirely reliable as evidence for the layout of the Houghton landscape in the middle decades of the eighteenth century, however: in spite of the fact that it was republished, with only minor alterations, in 1760 and 1784. More of the avenues from the earlier design were, in fact, retained than the map indicates: in particular, that running from the gardens, north-westwards through the park, survives to this day, and in the nineteenth century became the new north drive. In addition, there is no evidence that the external belt, with its distinctive bastions, was ever created. No trace of them appears on any subsequent map or plan, in the Houghton archives or elsewhere. More trustworthy in this respect, at least, are two undated maps, probably drawn up around 1735, which may have been intended as a guide to those responsible for implementing the planting proposals (Fig. 25) (Houghton MSS, Maps 27, 28).

Trees still growing in the park indicate that those used in the Bridgeman-period avenues were different from those employed in the earlier design. The latter are best represented in the present north drive avenue, just referred to: massive sweet chestnuts with girths in the region of six or seven metres, planted at intervals of about six metres centre to centre and with an avenue width of about nine metres. A scattering of individual trees from other avenues also survives, and these again are sweet chestnuts. The new avenues planted in the vast and brooding landscape of the 1730s were wider than those in the previous design, and used different species. Although these avenues are now principally composed of nineteenth- and twentieth-century trees, there is a handful of survivors from the original planting, and these make it clear that these replacements perpetuated the original composition. The main northern avenue is composed of beech (four trees survive from the original planting), as was that running north from the western termination of the garden towards the Water Tower. The southern avenue, in contrast, was planted with oak. Here, more of the original specimens have survived among the later replacements; a number of others, standing slightly back from the present lines, show that it was originally double-planted.

The fate of the elaborate gardens to the west of the hall during the 1730s is unclear. Ware's plan, and its subsequent reprints of 1760 and 1784, suggest that the central axial gravel walk had been removed and the complex *allées* within the wildernesses filled in, so that two simple geometric blocks of woodland framed a vista across a featureless lawn. If this was the intention, it was almost certainly never carried out. A number of plans and maps in the Houghton archive drawn up in the 1730s agree in showing the survival of the basic pattern of paths and *allées* here, while as late as 1745 a visitor to the hall described the gardens as 'not new, but neat and on the fore side of the house' (Houghton MSS, M 24). Horace Walpole in 1761 recalled nostalgically 'Those groves, those allees, where I have passed so many charming moments' in the years between 1742 and 1745 (Lewis, 1937–83, IX, p. 349). Right up until Robert Walpole's death in 1745, therefore, the essential layout of the geometric gardens appears to have been maintained, although there were no doubt many changes in detail.

The two undated maps from the 1730s (although not for some reason the Ware plan) show what is today one of the most striking features of the Houghton landscape. The Water Tower is a substantial classical structure, probably designed by Lord Pembroke, which served the mundane purpose of housing the tank that supplied the new house with water (Bowden-Smith, 1987). Its overall design echoes, to some extent, that of the hall: with its three-bay façade of slender Tuscan columns, rusticated ground floor and blank arches, it too represented a carefully considered expression of the new Palladian credo. It formed a striking focus for the vista, framed by a wide beech avenue, running northwards from the western end of the garden area.

While the broad lines of the design that emerged in the late 1720s and 1730s are thus clear, one or two aspects remain mysterious. In particular, the two 1730s maps and the Ware plan all show a serpentine lake just beyond the western boundary of the park, lying partly across the great western vista. This feature also appears on a number of earlier plans associated with alterations to the Houghton landscape: that published by Colen Campbell in 1725; and the undated plan of about 1725 in the Houghton archives. Later maps depict a number of ponds, the 'Wash Meres', in the low clayey ground here. It is difficult to believe that these were ever linked to create a continuous sheet of water. Only three large ponds survive in the area today. Various other small, disconnected and currently dry pits can be found within the adjoining areas of woodland. An undated plan of the early or mid-1730s shows a number of excavations in the area, together with the site of a brick kiln and a structure labelled 'barrow mens' house' (Houghton MSS, Map 4). Presumably the excavations were primarily intended to produce clay for bricks (for the internal walls of the house, as well as for garden walls) but there was clearly an intention to create a lake here, in the only part of this sandy estate where such an attempt might have had any real chance of success. But the deposit of boulder clay occupying this low-lying area is, in fact, thin and discontinuous: all Sir Robert's will and money could not triumph over the 'genius of the place', and successive visitors commented unfavourably on the absence of a lake at Houghton. The situation was only partially redeemed by the fact that one of the pits which could successfully hold water – that now known as St James' pond – lies in the middle of the western vista from the hall and – at least from the level of the piano nobile – supplied the required glint of water in the middle distance.

Work in the park did not cease with the new planting of the early 1730s. Indeed, undated memoranda in the Houghton archives indicate continuing activity into the 1740s. There are references to the establishment of new trees in the park, including sycamore and substantial quantities of Scots pine; and to the management of newly planted trees, especially through 'heading' – that is, removal of the leading shoots when the tree is semi-mature in order to create a low-branching, dense crown: 'The chest-

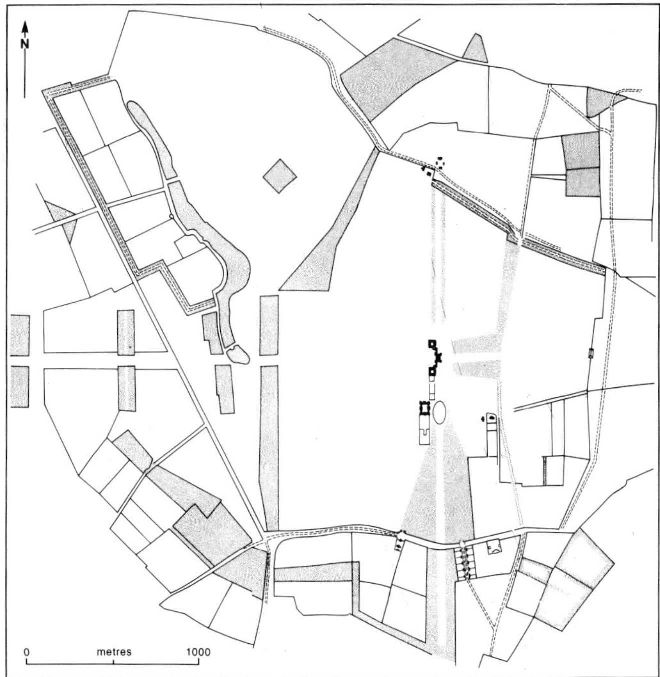

Fig. 25 An undated map of *c.*1735 (redrawn) showing that the design in Isaac Ware's plan was only partially executed

nut trees that are started on the north side of the park to be headed' (Houghton MSS, Red Box 33). There are also references to the pruning of evergreen oaks in the park: no examples of this antiquity now exist at Houghton, but the use of this alien tree, with its strong Italianate associations, is paralleled at nearby Holkham in the same period.

More radical interventions in the landscape were also being entertained in the late 1730s. In particular, attention turned to the somewhat foreshortened vista to the east of the house. In 1737, two proposals were drawn up for what appears to be a massive, terraced, amphitheatre-like feature, to be excavated into the sides of the low hill here (Houghton MSS, A53, A54). Both plans are difficult to interpret; neither was executed, and instead an undated memorandum of about 1740 signals a different solution to the problem: 'Item the matter of the removing of the hill to be decided'. A cutting was indeed opened up here, probably in 1742, and is illustrated on Ware's revised plan of 1760. It forms a striking feature of the landscape today. Proceeding along the East View away from the hall the natural level of the ground rises only very gradually. The cutting thus begins, at about 150 metres from the house, as a rather minor feature. At a distance of about 250 metres it is much more substantial, nearly 50 metres wide and some 15 metres deep. It has a somewhat untidy appearance, particularly towards its eastern end, and it is possible that it was abandoned half-completed on Sir Robert's death in

1745. The earth taken from the cutting was used to form a series of mounds. The most massive, to the north, covers the ice house; four smaller ones are today, and probably always have been, planted up as clumps. Others, still smaller in size, are scattered around the vicinity and these look like grassed-over spoil heaps, further indication perhaps that the project was abandoned rapidly in 1745. The vista was intended to open up views towards the woods around Raynham, the seat of the Townshends, Walpole's political allies: much of the land in between was owned by one or other family. The desired effect, however, could only be enjoyed from the state rooms on the piano nobile, and not from the basement, and to judge from various rough calculations which survive in the archives this was always the intention. The prospect was to be enjoyed from the floor of the house devoted to 'taste, expense, state and parade'.

The landscape of Houghton was in all probability the work of Charles Bridgeman, the leading landscape designer for the Whig élite in the 1720s and 1730s. It is true that direct evidence for Bridgeman's involvement is lacking in the surviving archives at Houghton, but the testimony of Thomas Robinson is supported by various other scraps of information: thus, for example, we learn that Bridgeman visited Wolterton (where he was also involved in the design of the grounds) in 1735 *en route* from Houghton (Peters, 1991, p. 27). Bridgeman's involvement at Houghton in the late 1720s and 1730s would hardly be surprising. He was then at the height of his career, having succeeded Henry Wise as Royal Gardener to George II and Queen Caroline in 1728 (a post he was to hold until his death ten years later). Houghton certainly exemplifies the kind of vast yet simple geometric landscapes created by Bridgeman (Willis, 1987). His designs continued the trend already established at the great houses in the first decade of the eighteenth century, towards a less cluttered form of geometric gardening. Grass *plats*, gravel paths and wildernesses replaced complex parterres; avenues and geometric vistas were extended far into the surrounding estate; and the design of house and landscape were closely integrated. The simplified geometric grandeur of Houghton invites comparison with Bridgeman's work at Stowe in Buckinghamshire or Wimpole in Cambridgeshire.

Yet whatever the nature of Bridgeman's contribution, it is important to emphasise, as many of the contemporary accounts do, the active involvement of Sir Robert himself in the genesis of the design. Moreover, we should note that the 'Bridgeman' landscape incorporated a number of features from the earlier, seventeenth-century design (the gardens and some of the avenues laid out around the earlier hall), and itself soon underwent further modifications which included, *inter alia*, the excavation of the great eastern cutting. The landscape, that is, owed as much to the owner as it did to the designers he employed: and it expressed his personal and political requirements, as well as the social assumptions and aspirations of his class.

The house and its landscape were closely linked. The great, four-square arrangement of avenues and vistas provided a setting for the house, emphasising the austere simplicity, as well as the alien grandeur, of its construction. But they were also a frame that determined the character of the views out from its rooms into the surrounding estate land, the importance of which is clearly indicated by the phenomenal efforts made to improve the view to the east. Yet it is worth emphasising that, had Walpole been prepared to build his house on a slightly different site – a few hundred metres to the northeast for example – long views could have been obtained in all directions. This he did not do: some imperative – unwritten, perhaps unexpressed – ensured that the new house was built as close as possible to the site of the ancestral home of the Walpoles. Houghton Hall may have been the key, the pivotal point in the new landscape: but its own location had been decided many centuries before.

This imperative to residential continuity did not extend to the rest of the population of Houghton. Their homes were destroyed and they were rehoused in a new settlement, quite peripheral to the new landscape and invisible from the house. The new village is composed of two rows of near-identical houses neatly and rationally arranged either side of a street. Plain, largely featureless, their standardised form represented both the suppression of the individuality of the inhabitants and their dependent status. The regularity of the plans and façades – more than an echo here of stripped-down Palladianism – was very different from the rambling disorder which, to judge from the evidence of the surviving maps, had characterised the old village. The houses expressed, in physical form, the conformity and discipline expected of the villagers.

What is striking is the peculiar thoroughness with which the remains of the old village were obliterated. Archaeological traces are limited to a few low banks that mark the line of the main east–west street, as shown on Badeslade's map of 1720. Such meagre survivals are in marked contrast to other settlement remains that exist within the park, to the north of the hall. Here, cut through by the north drive, there is a marked hollow way flanked by a series of well-preserved crofts; traces of a 'back lane' survive to the east. These classic settlement remains (among the best in Norfolk) form part of a wider relict landscape preserved in the parkland turf, including former open-field headlands and the ditches of former field boundaries (some of which are associated with ancient oak pollards). Towards the south, the village remains and the hollow way gradually fade as the hall is approached. Here they have clearly been deliberately levelled, so as not to interrupt the smooth expanse of turf around the house. There seems little doubt that, originally, they would have extended southwards to link with the east–west street cleared by Sir Robert; the latter, in other words, represented the rump of what had originally been a much larger settlement with a plan like an inverted T. The medieval predecessor of the present hall must have stood roughly halfway along this lost northern street. What is less clear is when this section of Houghton village was abandoned. A tithe list of 1578/9 indicates that the parish then contained a population of eighty-two people living in twenty households (excluding the Walpoles) (Yaxley, 1988, p. 83): suggesting that it was then more or less the same size as in 1720, and that the main phase of contraction had occurred earlier. This was typical, for villages cleared for emparking in the eighteenth century had usually experienced a high degree of previous contraction. The contrast between the flattened, scarcely-visible remains around the church, and the prominent earthworks to the north of the hall, is noteworthy. The latter, long-abandoned (and probably long-forgotten) when the park was laid out in the years around 1700, were not subject to the kind of ferocious levelling endured by the former.

By the mid-1730s only one building of the old village remained standing – the parish church of St Martin. It would, given the legal status of parish churches, have been very difficult to move, and it was moreover the burial place of generations of Walpoles. It survived as one of the few fixed points in a changing landscape. Yet it did not remain unaltered: instead, it was effectively appropriated by the new landscape. A new tower was erected in a whimsical gothick style (a number of alternative designs in this mode were prepared, and are preserved in the Houghton archives). In fact, the whole western wall of the church was rebuilt, and a new entrance made – with the tower acting as a porch. The existing south door was blocked, and converted to a window; the north door was sealed and the porch converted into a vestry; the windows were all renewed; and the entire building encased in a new flint facing (Fenner, 1988). The designer may have been William Kent, although Thomas Ripley is also a possible candidate (Yaxley, 1994). This, then, was the landscape of supreme political power in the 1730s: formal, precise, geometric yet essentially simple, with even the number of ornamental buildings kept to a minimum. The gothick church and the Palladian Water Tower seem to have been the only ones constructed, although there is evidence that others were planned. It was the hall itself which was, in an important sense, the principal 'garden building'.

Sir Robert Walpole died in 1745, leaving his son Robert with debts of over £40,000. It is hardly surprising that the latter appears to have added little to the Houghton landscape, although a small grove of cedar and pines, and one or two other small plantations, may have been established within the park (Broome, 1865). He was succeeded on his death in 1751 by George, 3rd Earl of Orford, then twenty-one years old. According to his uncle, Horace Walpole, the estate continued to go downhill, and in the 1760s and 1770s was in a very bad state, with 'the water house built by Lord Pembroke tumbling down; the garden a common; the park half covered with nettles and weeds; the walls and pales in ruin... ' (Lewis, 1937–8, IX, p. 349). Walpole's gloomy description is, however, almost certainly an exaggeration, tinged with nostalgia for a time when Houghton was at the very height of fashion. Some planting seems to have continued during the years immediately following George's accession; two outlying woods, Remberly Hill and Washmere Plantation, were established in 1755 and 1756, 'The Mount' (perhaps the ice-house mound) was planted in the same year (Broome, 1865). Nevertheless, to judge from maps made at the end of the century, comparatively little was done to the surrounding parkland in the half-century or so following Sir Robert's death. The 'Bridgeman landscape' survived intact, vast and sombre, growing slowly to maturity.

During the nineteenth century there were further changes: the establishment of a new avenue (rather clumsily laid out in relation to the rest of the landscape) in the West Park; the creation of new drives; and much new planting, including additional clumps. The gardens to the west of the house went through numerous changes. And embellishments continue to this day, with the West Park, under arable cultivation for much of the present century, currently being returned to grass and replanted. Nevertheless, the basic structure of Sir Robert's landscape still dominates Houghton park, and has been maintained over the centuries through careful replanting. Here, better than perhaps anywhere else in England, we can catch the flavour of landscape design in this crucial, final phase of the geometric tradition.

6

Sir Robert Walpole: The Prime Minister as Collector

Andrew Moore

SIR ROBERT WALPOLE was a discerning collector, and visitors to Houghton in the 1730s were almost without exception deeply impressed by both the house and its contents. The one exception was Edward Harley, 2nd Earl of Oxford, a staunch Tory, who considered it 'neither magnificent nor beautiful, there is a very great expense without either judgment or taste' (Harley, 1732, p. 160). Horace Walpole returned to Houghton some fifteen years after his father's death and commented: 'the surprise the pictures gave me is again renewed – accustomed for many years to see nothing but wretched daubs and varnished copies at auctions, I look at these as enchantment. My own description of them [*Aedes Walpolianae*] seems poor – but I shall tell you truly – the majesty of Italian ideas almost sinks before the warm nature of Flemish colouring! Alas! Don't I grow old?' (to George Montagu, 25 March 1761, Lewis XI, p. 348). In 1739 George Vertue had no doubt of the importance of Sir Robert's collection: 'Houghton Hall Sr Robert Walpoles fine and rare Collection of Paintings statues Busts &c the most considerable now of any in England' (Vertue, I, p. 6).

Fig. 26 Luca Giordano, *The Cyclops at their Forge c.*1660; oil on canvas, 192 x 151.5 cm (SHM 188); hung in the Saloon at Houghton in Sir Robert Walpole's time

It is, however, not a straightforward task to chart the development of the Prime Minister's collection which grew through the gifts and agency of friends, family and diplomats as well as those buyers acting on his behalf at auctions. Sir Robert himself appears to have attended auctions and bid at times. The growth of his collection was at its most rapid during the 1720s, as building at Houghton itself progressed. However, Sir Robert's active art collecting predates the laying of Houghton's foundation stone by at least five years.The earliest recorded purchases are two landscapes by Jan Griffier Senior (?1645–1718), bought 1 April 1718 for £15 5*s*. (CUL Account Book 20A, 1714–18). These, one a view of a seaport (SHM 6892), were, by 1736, hung as overdoors in the Green Velvet Bedchamber at Houghton. It is instructive to review the catalogues of the leading London art sales, in particular for the 1720s and 1730s. Robert Bragge and Andrew Hay, two prominent dealers of the period, can be found buying for Sir Robert, as can others, including Horace Walpole and John Howard, a framemaker and dealer.

Sir Robert was usually represented at the major collection sales, whether those of prominent aristocratic families, leading London dealers or those artists whom he had patronised, notably Grinling Gibbons and Charles Jervas. Not all of the works purchased by Sir Robert at the London sales went to Houghton; some were dispersed throughout Sir Robert's London addresses. When Horace Walpole's friend and correspondent Horace Mann (1701–86), British envoy at Florence, enquired in June 1743 as to whether the new picture gallery at Houghton would in fact denude the various rooms at Houghton, Horace responded: 'so far from unfurnishing any part of the house there are several pictures undisposed, besides numbers at Lord Walpole's at the Exchequer, at Chelsea, and at New Park. Lord Walpole has taken a dozen to Stanno, a small house about four miles from hence, where he lives with my Lady Walpole's vice regent [the singer Hannah Norsa]' (to Mann, 10 June 1743).

One of the earliest records of Sir Robert's collection is a bill presented to him by John Howard. Howard purchased a good number of paintings at several sales during the first half of the century (*c.*1710–45) and included among his clients Sir Robert Walpole, the 2nd Duke of Devonshire and Lord Effingham. Among the Cholmondeley manuscripts now at Cambridge University Library is a bill for which Howard received payment on 20 January 1721. This lists twenty-eight paintings, ten of which are unattributed, and is an indication of Sir Robert's early taste as a collector. At least eight are Netherlandish works, eleven are still life, animal or hunting scenes and about the same number are Italian and French School paintings. The final item is 'for inlargeing yor. Hon^rs Picture and preparing of it for Mr. Wooton £1-10-00; for a frame carv'd & gilt with gold to y^r Hon.^rs. Picture over the Chimney & Glass £33-00-00'. This elaborate frame could well have been for the 'Hunting Piece, Sr Robt in Green, Col^n Churchill in the middle' that hung in the Hunting Hall at Houghton in 1736 (see cat. 6) and had been commissioned from John Wootton less than six months earlier.

Most of the paintings mentioned in Howard's account were among those that never reached Houghton and were sold after Sir Robert's death, either in 1748 or 1751. Some, however, could be identical to paintings listed in the *Aedes Walpolianae*, notably 'a picture of Horses by Wovorman £03-12-00' – presumably *A Stud of Horses* by Wouvermans, which later hung in the Common Parlour at Houghton. Two battle pieces by Bourgignon (Jacques Courtois 1621–76) which now hang in the State Hermitage Museum, St Petersburg (SHM 1182, 1752), were formerly at Houghton and could well be the 'battle of Bourgnanion over a bridge... Ditto the companion' mentioned by Howard. However, there were two battle pieces by this artist in one of the 1748 sales (Houlditch MSS, month unknown, day 2, lots 50, 51). Howard's account, rather than providing solid provenance details for paintings known today, is best taken as an early indication of Sir Robert's taste. The bill totalled £95 *6s. 2d.* in framing costs, including '46 brass nails gilt with gold'. The account also lists works attributed to Paris Bourdon, Breughel, David de Coninck, de Heem, Melchior d'Hondecoeter and Willem van der Velde. Sir Robert, it seems, had yet to develop his taste for mythological, allegorical, religious and historical works. The majority of these works later hung in The Treasury, Whitehall.

John Howard appears to have started to bid at auction on behalf of Sir Robert in 1722. He was at the sale of Henry Bentinck, Duke of Portland, that year and purchased lot 67, *Old Woman Reading* by Ferdinand Bol. This later hung in the picture gallery at Houghton, described by Horace Walpole as 'An old Woman reading, an extreme fine Portrait, by *Bol*, bought at the Duke of *Portland's* Sale, when he went Governor to *Jamaica*' (SHM 763). According to Horace Walpole, Jacob Jordaens's *Self-Portrait with parents, brothers and sisters* (SHM 484) also came from the Duke of Portland's collection, although it is not listed in the Houlditch manuscript copy of the sale catalogue (NAL). This was an important early acquisition for Sir Robert and was recorded by George Vertue as at the Treasury, Whitehall, in 1722. Painted about 1615, the family group shows the painter's parents, Jacob Jordaens and Barbara Wolschaten, the painter himself with a lute and seven brothers and sisters. Small angels hover above, representing the souls of family members who had died very young. The painting features in William Kent's project for the decoration of the south wall of the Saloon at Houghton, about 1725 (see cat. 39).

Sir Robert was an active purchaser at two other important picture sales in 1722. 'Mr Walpole' purchased a total of seven works at the house sale of Mr van Huls. This was presumably Robert Walpole himself, but could have been a member of the family acting on his behalf. He bought two landscapes with figures attributed to Breughel for £10 (lots 206 and 207). He also purchased two paintings by Luca Giordano (1634–1705), the *Birth of Elizabeth* and *Her [Elizabeth's] confirmation*. Variously described in the Walpole inventories, these are presumably the *Birth of the Virgin* and its companion the *Presentation of the Virgin in the Temple,* which later hung in the Carlo Maratti Room at Houghton. Horace Walpole describes them in his *Aedes*: 'These two are finish'd Designs for two large Pictures, which he painted for the fine Church of the *Madonna Della Salute* at *Venice*.'

Sir Robert also acquired from van Huls paintings of the Holy Family by Johann Rottenhammer (1564–1625) and Williberts, both of which later hung in the Cabinet at Houghton (Walpole, 1747, p. 64). The seventh picture

Fig. 27 John Wootton, *Hounds and a Magpie*, *c.*1720s; oil on canvas, 128 x 152 cm (SHM 9781); hung in the Breakfast Room at Houghton in the time of Sir Robert Walpole

purchased from Huls was *A Noble Palace* attributed to Hendrick van Steenwyck II (*c.*1580–*c.*1649). November that year saw the collection sale of Grinling Gibbons; Horace Walpole records four major acquisitions from the Gibbons collection, notably Luca Giordano's *The Cyclops at their Forge* (lot 87, Fig. 26; see cat. 37), but also the two vast canvases by Francesco Mola, now in the Academy of Arts, St Petersburg, and a *Concert of Birds*, now recognised as by Frans Snyders (see cat. 5).

It is possible that it was in 1723 Sir Robert acquired paintings from the collection of the financial speculator, John Law (1671–1729). It was at this time, according to George Vertue, that the King bought six paintings from Law, while 'many more paintings was brought over' by him from the Continent. According to Horace Walpole, Sir Robert owned two paintings formerly in the collection of John Law. One of these, Francesco Albani's *Baptism of Christ* (SHM 29), was a fine example which hung in the Saloon at Houghton. John Law was a highly colourful character, having fought a duel and escaped from prison before leaving for the Continent where he pursued a number of financial schemes. He became controller-general of French finance in 1720, only to be dismissed from office four months later. One might expect to find ministerial gifts in Sir Robert's collection from such a man, but this seems not to have been the case. No record of the Albani survives before 1744, while the second painting from Law's collection, a *Holy Family* attributed to Giovanni Bellini, is recorded in the Yellow Damask Bedchamber at Chelsea in 1736.

Rather more specific for the year 1723 is a bill of £82 4s. from Sir Godfrey Kneller (1646–1723), paid for Sir Robert by Edward Jenkins on 22 June (Cholmondeley MSS, Accounts 22, p. 37, CUL). This is quite a considerable sum and could relate to a number of portraits by Kneller in Sir Robert's collection. Sir Robert hung five portraits by Kneller in the Common Parlour: *Grinling Gibbons* (SHM 1346), *King William III* and *King George I* (later both Gatchina Palace, destroyed), *Joseph Carreras* (cat. 13) and *John Locke* (SHM 1345). Kneller's resplendent full-length portrait of *George I* continues to hang today in the position Sir Robert himself desired, as the single painting in the Library at Houghton. One last portrait by Kneller survives at Houghton, that of *Charles, Lord Viscount Townshend*, hung in Walpole's day in the Supping Parlour. Kneller's account, paid barely eighteen weeks before the artist died, probably relates to work carried out over a period of time.

The difficulty in tracing the Prime Minister's methods in gathering together a collection fitting both to his office and his desire to be fully recognised as a leading gentleman of taste and refinement, lies in great part in his wilful destruction of swathes of correspondence (see cat. 16). A few letters to Sir Robert survive from the period December 1723–February 1724, written by the spy John Macky (Cholmondeley MSS, CUL). Macky was sent by Robert Walpole to the Austrian Netherlands, ostensibly to buy paintings, but secretly to monitor the Jacobite postal network at Brussels. To curry favour with Walpole, Macky had sent him a manuscript version of his spying activities, which was later published. On 2 December 1723 Macky was in Louvain and wrote, 'I hope you are returned to London, you have your pictures and that they please you'. A group of letters over the next few weeks reveals that Macky and one 'M. Jaupain' were responsible for purchasing the four great market scenes by Snyders earlier that year (see cat. 65). George Vertue records that Sir Robert paid £428 for these 'capital pictures' (Vertue, III, p. 18).

The correspondence with Jaupain is revealing, as it provides evidence that Robert Walpole took an active interest

Fig. 28 Anthony Van Dyck, *The Holy Family (Rest on the Flight into Egypt)*, 1630; oil on canvas, 215 x 285.5cm (SHM 539); hung in the Saloon at Houghton in Sir Robert Walpole's time

in art-historical issues relating to his collection. He attempts to ascertain who painted the figures and on 5 February 1724 Macky provides a provenance for the set: 'In one of your letters to Mr. Jaupain you seem to doubt the figures in the Markets to be of Rubens, but I can prove by the Journals of the familly of Vallegas that the Marquis took both Rubens and Snyders into his house in the reign of Phillip the third where they jointly painted those Markets and they never were out of that room till the death of Comte St. Pierre 130 years after.' This provenance is at variance with the traditional source for this series as having been commissioned by Antoine Triest in Bruges. Macky also offers to purchase another Snyders for Walpole: 'I saw at Michelin a large picture of Sneyders composed out of your four markets and finely disposed which will serve as a chimney piece to the Room where you hang the others. I can have it for near thirty pounds and its of the same master.' It is not clear whether this suggestion was taken up by Sir Robert.

Sir Robert appears to have had some dealings with the Scottish art dealer Andrew Hay. He was certainly at Hay's sale in 1725, buying lot 73, Pietro da Cortona's *Abraham, Sarah and Hagar*, for £215, and lot 62, Romanelli's *Hercules and Omphale* for £44 2*s*. (SHM 1601). It was in 1725 that Walpole secured possibly his greatest prize, the collection of mainly full-length portraits by Sir Anthony Van Dyck, originally formed by Philip, 4th Lord Wharton (see cat. 26). Horace Walpole describes the collection as of 'twelve whole lengths, the two girls, six half lengths and two more by Sir Peter Lely; he paid an hundred pounds each for the whole lengths and the double picture, and fifty pounds each for the half lengths'. John Howard may well have played a part in the negotiation. Late in 1722 or early 1723 Vertue twice saw 'out of the frames at Mr. Howards' the eleven whole lengths, 'the two girls' (*Philadelphia and Elizabeth Wharton*, SHM 533) and the portrait of William Laud, Archbishop of Canterbury (SHM 1698).

John Howard continued to enjoy a close contractual relationship with Sir Robert, being called upon to provide frames, but also to help with the hanging and occasional rearrangement of the paintings. A bill from Howard dated 1729 survives at Houghton and lists a number of small frames completed. It is notable for the sum of £28 charged 'for a very Large Rich Archetrive frame carv'd & guilt wth Gold with all the ornaments to a picture by Peter de Carton'. This was presumably the frame for the large *Abraham, Sarah and Hagar* bought at Hay's sale in 1725 and destined for the Yellow Drawing Room at Houghton. John Howard also recharges his costs for 'the joyner for hanging up several pictures and changing their places – 00.02.00.' (see cat. 16)

Howard's account also reveals a charge of eighteen shillings 'for a frame carv'd and guilt with gold to Master Haurris picture by Mr. Howgarth', and that he had 'pay'd Mr. Howgarth for Master Haurris picture' five guineas on 10 October 1729. This confirms that Sir Robert had commissioned William Hogarth to paint a portrait of his youngest son, Horace, aged just ten. This is the portrait, now in a private collection, which shows the young Horace pointing towards the numeral X on a sundial to indicate his age. This dates the commission to 1727–8 and confirms what has hitherto been only a traditional identification of this early Hogarth portrait (exhibited London 1987–8, no. 54).

It is the case that the Prime Minister actively supported contemporary artists. His commissioning of William Hogarth was just one small act of patronage associated with the development of his collections. Among portraitists, Charles Jervas (*c.*1675–1739) in particular was a favourite and he was employed not only as an artist in his own right, but – equally important – as a copyist. At times Jervas would provide commissioned portraits and copies of family portraits for Sir Robert to present as gifts. On 20 October 1725 Jervas was paid £21 for 'your half length for Mrs. Hamond' and ten guineas for 'your Lady, a copy'. Ten guineas was a standard price for a half-length copy (Cholmondeley MSS Vouchers 1725, CUL). A large number of copies by Jervas after paintings in Sir Robert's collection appear in Jervas's collection sale in 1739/40.

Another artist to receive Sir Robert's direct patronage was Ranelagh Barrett (active 1737–68). Barrett (or Barwick) was an extremely successful and skilful copyist who painted at least eight copies after paintings in the collection of Sir Robert. These are recorded by George Vertue in 1742, who recounts that Barrett 'by this particular of Coppying justly, especially in Colouring gaind him the reputation which got the Favour of Sr. Robt. Walpole – who gave him leave constantly to be in a room at his house which became a well situated office for Barret, who had much business and employment there, for persons of Quality &c and others. so long as Sr. Robt. livd in the treasury office' (Vertue, III, p. 112). This form of patronage also manifested itself at Houghton with the sheltering of Jan van Huysum's brother (see p. 138). The artist John Ellys sometimes acquired paintings on Sir Robert's behalf, notably Van Dyck's magnificent *Holy Family* (Fig. 28; see cat. 4).

Sir Robert's interest in contemporary painting was not exclusive to that of English artists. He appreciated the decorative work of continental painters and acquired at least two paintings by Watteau (1684–1721) not long after the artist's death. The most eloquent of these, *The Artist's Dream* (private collection), may have been purchased for Sir Robert by his eldest son Robert while he was in Paris, direct from Jacques Langlois, the painter-dealer on the Pont Notre-Dame. It subsequently hung in Lady Walpole's dressing room at Downing Street but never reached Houghton, being sold in 1748 (Houlditch MSS, day 2, lot 62) to Mathew Ducie, Baron of Moreton. Either Sir Robert or his son Robert purchased a second painting by Watteau, the *Sulking Woman* (SHM 4120). It is not included in the 1736 inventory of Sir Robert's collections and so could have belonged to either of them before being sold by the 2nd Lord Orford in 1748 (Houlditch MSS, day 2, lot 52). Bought for three guineas by Horace Walpole, the picture then hung at Strawberry Hill, subsequently reaching the State Hermitage Museum, St Petersburg, by a completely different route from those sold to Catherine the Great in 1779 (Washington, DC, 1984, no. 46).

Another sale from which Sir Robert made important purchases was that of the 1st Earl of Cadogan (1675–1726) where he bought two Bacchanals attributed to Rubens (1726/7 day 1, lot 36; day 2, lot 81). Horace Walpole records in the *Aedes* that Rubens's *Moonlight Landscape with cart overturning* (Fig. 30) also came from Lord Cadogan's collection, but it was not included in the 1726/7 sale. Horace cannot always be regarded as correct. There is certainly some confusion in the *Aedes* as to which paintings were included in the collection sale of the 'late Earl of Halifax'. Horace correctly records Sir Robert's purchase of Gaspar Poussin's *Landscape with a cascade and sheep* (1739/40, day 3, lot 87, now SHM). However, he assigns Andrea Sacchi's *Venus bathing, with Cupids* to this sale, whereas in fact it was purchased that same year from Charles Jervas's collection sale (1739/40, day 6, lot 401).

A key supporter for the Prime Minister was James Waldegrave, 1st Earl of Waldegrave (1685–1741). In 1730 Waldegrave was appointed Ambassador and Minister-Plenipotentiary at Paris, in succession to Sir Robert's brother Sir Horatio Walpole. He presented Sir Robert with a fine work by Jacopo Bassano, *Christ laid in the Sepulchre* (SHM 1573), but also was instrumental in helping Sir Robert acquire in 1734, the imposing *Holy Family with Ss Elizabeth and John the Baptist* by Nicolas Poussin (cat. 52). Sir Robert wrote to Lord Waldegrave on 21 March 1734/5: 'I will give 400 for your Picture [which] is I believe the highest price that was ever given for a Picture of Poussin, if yr Lordship will give yrself the trouble to offer that, I cannot believe that they will refuse it'. On 21 August that year Sir Robert wrote again: 'the Picture came yesterday to my hand in perfect good order. It is impossible not to be pleased with it, I thank your Lordship for persuading me to buy it...' (Waldegrave MSS, copy by Coxe, Cholmondeley MSS 2469, CUL).

Horace Walpole records a number of significant gifts to Sir Robert in the pages of the *Aedes*. These were not exclusively paintings, and the bronze cast of the *Borghese Gladiator* by Hubert Le Sueur (*c.*1595–*c.*1650) was the gift of Thomas Herbert, 8th Earl of Pembroke (1656–1733). This was placed in the spectacular setting of William Kent's staircase, supported by a tempietto. An acquaintance in common between Sir Robert and Pembroke was Sir Robert's Norfolk neighbour, Sir Andrew Fountaine (1676–1753). Fountaine was 'said to have purchased for Sir Robert Walpole some of the finest paintings in the Houghton Collection' (Beatniffe 1795, p. 219). Sir Andrew Fountaine helped to catalogue the Pembroke Library at Wilton and placed a sculpture at the foot of his own staircase at Narford Hall, *Vulcan chained to the Rock* by Claude David (now Victoria and Albert Museum).

James Brydges, 1st Duke of Chandos (1673–1744) gave Sir Robert *Bathsheba bringing Abishag to David* by Adrian van der Werff (SHM 1064). Chandos commented in 1724 that Sir Robert was 'making a noble collection' and proposed to approach him to see if he would care to acquire a set of 'Raphael cartoons', which were too large to house at Canons, Middlesex, 'at cost price which was as I remember 1200 pounds, though the virtuosi judge them worth an abundance more' (to M Gibson, Lothbury, 30 March 1724, Baker and Oxford 1949, p. 83). Sir Robert evidently declined the offer, if it was ever made. Chandos owed much to Walpole's good will.

This was also the case with Charles Churchill (d. 1745), the natural son of General Charles Churchill (1656–1714), who was for thirty years member for Castle Rising, Norfolk, through the influence of the Walpole family. He himself had an illegitimate son, also Charles, by the actress Anne Oldfield, who married Sir Robert's natural daughter, Maria. It was Charles Churchill who, in the summer of 1720, encouraged Sir Robert to take up John Wootton (Fig. 27) before he became 'otherways imployed' (16 August 1720, Cholmondeley MSS 803, CUL). Churchill presented Sir Robert with a gift of an architectural scene, described by Horace Walpole as 'a kind of a street with various marble palaces in perspective, like the Strada Nuova at Genoa'. This hung in Downing Street in 1736, attributed to Giulio Romano.

Another beneficiary of Walpole's influence was Benjamin Keene, the eldest son of Charles Keene, a merchant and alderman who was Mayor of King's Lynn in 1714, and his wife Susan Rolfe. Through Sir Robert's influence Benjamin Keene (1697–1757) was appointed agent for the South Sea Company at Madrid where, in July 1724, he was promoted to British Consul. Again through Walpole's influence, Keene became Minister Plenipotentiary at Madrid in 1727. He was much criticised in Parliament and by the press for his double role of British Minister and South Sea agent. Keene was recalled only in 1739 on the declaration of war between England and Spain. It seems likely that he brought with him the *Virgin and Child* attributed to Murillo and painted on black marble, which Horace Walpole describes as a present to Sir Robert (Walpole, 1747, p. 64) and which is first recorded in the Cabinet at Houghton, in 1744.

A second painting came as a gift to Sir Robert by way of the Iberian peninsula. James O'Hara, 2nd Baron Tyrawley (1690–1773) was appointed Envoy-Extraordinary to the Court of Portugal in 1728, where he remained as ambassador until 1741, despite at least one attempt to seek promotion from Lisbon (29 Sept. 1734, Cholmondeley MSS 2342, CUL). He too appears to have returned to England with a mark of his esteem for Sir Robert. In this case he presented the Prime Minister with a portrait of Edward VI (SHM 1260). According to Horace Walpole, it was formerly in the royal collection and included in the Commonwealth dispersal sales of Charles I's collection. The small panel was discovered in Lisbon by Baron Tyrawley, who gave it to Sir Robert at some point before 1744, when it too hung in the Cabinet at Houghton. At that time attributed to Holbein, it may now be better identified as an English school variant of a Flemish school painting that remains today in the Royal Collection.

Gifts made to the prime minister were usually magnificent examples of their kind. One such was *Moses in the Bulrushes* (SHM 1251), a large canvas by Eustache Le Sueur

Fig. 29 Anthony Van Dyck, *Sir Thomas Chaloner*, 1630; oil on canvas, 104 x 81.5 cm (SHM 551); hung in the Common Parlour at Houghton in Sir Robert Walpole's time

(1616–55) who was as admired in the early eighteenth century as was Nicolas Poussin. This hung in the Hall at Chelsea in 1736 and was subsequently destined for the picture gallery at Houghton. The painting was the gift of John Montagu, 2nd duke of Montagu (?1688–1749) who in 1725 became Grand Master of the Order of the Bath.

An important and consciously appropriate gift came from Sir Joseph Danvers, the son of John Danvers, who was the nephew of the distinguished soldier connoisseur Henry Danvers, Earl of Danby (1573–1644). The gift in question was Anthony Van Dyck's portrait of Henry Danvers in Garter robes (SHM 545) which was hanging in the Corner Drawing Room at Houghton by 1736. This was the only full length of a Garter knight in Van Dyck's oeuvre and was therefore both a fitting and flattering addition to Sir Robert's collection of full-length portraits by the artist (see also Fig. 29); in 1726 Sir Robert himself became the first commoner Knight of the Garter since 1660. The portrait is a sumptuous example of Van Dyck's ability to harmonise and soften his colours.

Sir Robert himself gave presents. One of his grandest gestures is reputed to have been the gift of the magnificent portrait of Henry Howard, Earl of Surrey (?1517–47) the eldest son of the 3rd Duke of Norfolk, to the then Duke of Norfolk, premier nobleman in England. The enormous canvas, painted by an unknown artist about 1546, was in the Arundel sale of 1720 at Stafford House, where it was bought by Sir Robert. Family tradition states that he then gave it to the Duke of Norfolk. However, Horace Walpole records that this was the portrait sold by the 2nd Earl of Orford in 1751 (Houlditch MSS, day 2, lot 6, 'Howard Earl of Surrey, whole length Zuccaro', bought by 'Vertue £27 6*s*'). In a letter to Bentley (5 August 1752), Horace Walpole records that the painting was bought by the 9th Duke of Norfolk, presumably through George Vertue. In Sir Robert's collection until he died, it hung unattributed in the Hall at Chelsea in 1736. The portrait itself depicts allegorical figures holding shields that show the Earl of Surrey's royal descent through his father and mother. The portrait of the 'poet Earl' remains *in situ* at Arundel Castle, having been ceded to the nation in 1976.

Sir Robert Walpole does appear to have made a direct gift to William Cavendish, 3rd Duke of Devonshire (1698–1755). Still at Chatsworth today is Anthony Van Dyck's full-length portrait of Arthur Goodwin. A rich and influential Buckinghamshire landowner, Goodwin had married the daughter and heiress of Philip, Lord Wharton. Sir Robert had acquired the portrait as part of the Wharton collection and it is notable for its soft brown harmonising tones and characterful modelling of the sitter's features. It appears that Sir Robert had presented his gift before 1736, at which time the painting was no longer in his collection.

Towards the end of his life Sir Robert depended greatly upon his youngest son to help him develop his collection. Horace's travels abroad on the Grand Tour were an inspiration to Sir Robert and he longed to go abroad himself. His house and collection represented the contemporary English taste for the Grand Tour *par excellence*, yet he himself had never gone on the Grand Tour. On 25 March 1743 Horace informed Horace Mann that Sir Robert has said that 'if he thought he had strength, he would see Florence, Bologna, and Rome, by way of Marseilles to Leghorn. You may imagine how I gave in to such a jaunt. I don't set my heart on it, because I think he cannot do it'. Horace was right and his father died one of the greatest exponents of the English Grand Tour taste without ever having travelled abroad.

Fig. 30 Peter Paul Rubens, *The Waggoner (Moonlight Landscape with cart overturning)*, 1620; oil on canvas, 86 x 126.5 cm (SHM 480); hung in the Gallery at Houghton in Sir Robert Walpole's time

7
The Sale to Catherine the Great

Andrew Moore

THE STORY OF THE DISPOSAL of Sir Robert Walpole's collection of paintings stretches over three decades and is by no means an event limited to the private sale of the bulk of the finest of his Old Master paintings to Catherine the Great, Empress of Russia, in 1779. Just as Sir Robert developed his collection over nearly thirty years, it took a similar period for his sons and grandson to cope with the aftermath of his death in 1745.

Horace Walpole's fears for the estate were part of his motivation in compiling the *Aedes Walpolianae*. In August 1748 he wrote to Horace Mann and commented 'as my fears about Houghton are great, I am a little pleased to have finished a slight memorial of it, a description of the pictures...' (Lewis, 1937–83, XIX, p. 496). Horace spent his life lamenting his father's failure to secure Houghton from debt. Soon after Sir Robert's death Horace wrote to Horace Mann, 'his debts, with his legacies which are trifling, amount to fifty thousand pounds. His estate, a nominal eight thousand a year, much mortgaged... If he had not so overdone it, he might have left such an estate to his family, as might have secured the glory of [Houghton] for many years: another such debt must expose it to sale!' (15 April 1745, Lewis, XIX, p. 32).

Horace's words proved to be prophetic. His relationship with his eldest brother Robert, 2nd Earl of Orford, was strained, no more so than when Robert withheld from Horace his legacy of £5,000. In his letter to Horace Mann of August 1745 Horace Walpole lamented: 'I cannot with indifference see the family torn to pieces, and falling into such ruin, as I foresee; for should my brother die soon, leaving so great a debt, so small an estate to pay it off, two great places sinking, and a wild boy of nineteen to succeed, there would soon be an end of the glory of Houghton, which had my father proportioned more to his fortune, would probably have a longer duration...'

Horace Walpole's assessment of his father remained consistent through his lifetime. In 1745 he felt that Sir Robert's 'fondness for Houghton, has endangered Houghton' (see p. 15). In 1761 he wrote to Lord Montague of a visit to Houghton: 'I have chosen to sit in my father's little dressing room... where... he used to receive the account of his farmers, and deceive himself – or us, with the thoughts of his economy – how wise a man at once and how weak!' (25–30 March 1761, Lewis IX, p. 349). In 1783 he wrote in similar vein to Thomas Pownall, 'He had made Houghton much too magnificent for the moderate estate which he left to support it... his fondness for his paternal seat, and his boundless generosity were too expensive for his fortune' (27 Oct. 1783, Lewis, XLII, p. 81).

Among the first attempts to make the estate solvent seems to have been the 2nd Earl of Orford's sale of paintings, organised by the auctioneer Christopher Cock. On 4 May 1748 the antiquary William Stukeley (1687–1765) records a sale which is known through the survival of just one copy of the catalogue: 'Dr. [Edward] Milward carried me to Cock's auction room where there is a most magnificent show of paintings to be sold by auction... they are the pictures of Sir Robert Walpole, under the fictitious name of Mr. Robert Bragge. I have seen 'em at Sir Robert's house. Thus, fares it with power and grandeur...' (Stukeley, 1880, III, p. 5). The sale took place on 5/6 May 1748 and consisted of 125 lots, of which sixty were sold for a total of £851 11*s*. (Oxford, Bodleian Library, Johnson D 762).

This figure is slightly at odds with the account that was submitted to Lord Orford on 9 May by Abraham Langford on behalf of Cock (Cholmondeley MSS, CUL). Cock's account is revealing and records something of the business of the auction. John Ellis, as Lord Orford's representative, was paid £800 7*s*. 6*d*. for the paintings. Further expenses incurred by Cock included bringing the pictures from Chelsea and £47 1*s*. 4*d*. 'for sundry dinners at the picture sale'. The account includes a small sale of plate that had taken place the previous September by 'private sale' which had raised just £21 11*s*. The fact that the sale took place under the name of Robert Bragge suggests an initial effort of secrecy on the part of Lord Orford. A second sale was held that year with no such attempt at anonymity. This second sale is known only through a manuscript transcription made by Richard Houlditch, now in the National Art Library (Houlditch MSS, 86.00.18–19). Although we know nothing of the buyers at the 'Bragge' sale, the Houlditch manuscript does record the buyers at the second 1748 sale. These included familiar figures who had themselves acted as Sir Robert's agents or sold paintings to him – including Robert Bragge and John Ellys (or Ellis). Friends and relatives also made purchases: Horace Walpole, Sir Paul Methuen and Sir Thomas Robinson all purchased works at the sale. One pair of 'large piece[s] of Birds, hieroglyphical' by 'Hondicooter' was purchased by Bragge and transported up to the new country seat of Robert's Norfolk neighbour the Earl of Leicester, Holkham Hall, where they remain today (Moore, 1988, pp. 16–18).

In 1751 Robert Walpole, 2nd Earl of Orford, died, leaving his son George to inherit. The second Earl left little besides debts to his son, including his own in addition to those of Sir Robert. Horace Walpole commented: 'Indeed, I think his son the most ruined young man in England' (to Horace Mann, 1 April 1751). A third sale of Sir Robert's pictures, together with pictures belonging to the second Earl, was organised at Langford's auction room at Covent Garden, 13–14 June 1751: 'The genuine collection of Italian, Dutch, and Flemish pictures of... the Earls of Orford... brought from the Exchequer and Richmond Park' (*Daily Advertiser*, 13 June 1751). Horace Walpole lamented the situation to Horace Mann: 'We have already begun to sell the pictures that had not found place at Houghton: the sale gives no great encouragement to proceed (though I fear it must come to that!) the large pictures were thrown away; the whole length Vandykes went for a song! I am mortified now at having printed the catalogue. Gideon the Jew [Sampson Gideon, 1699–1762], and Blakiston [Sir Matthew Blakiston, *c.*1702–74] the independent grocer have been the chief purchasers of the pictures sold already – there, if you love moralising!' (18 June 1751, Lewis, XX, p. 261).

Horace became increasingly involved in attempting to sort out the family fortunes, becoming the most informed of the family almost despite himself. He discovered that the second Earl had mortgaged the Houghton estate for £23,000 (Horace to Lady Ossory, 1 Sept. 1773) and late in life summarised the situation as it was in 1751: 'my eldest brother had been a very bad economist during his father's life, and died himself 50,000 pounds in debt, or more...' (to Thomas Pownall, 27 Oct. 1783, Lewis, XLII, p. 81). Sir Robert's legacy was already very different from that envisaged by the chorus reputedly sung in honour of his line at the celebrated Houghton Congresses:

May Houghton long flourish to give us delight
May its masters be all great and good as the Knight;
May a race long succeed, like the place without faults,
That may tread in his paths, and keep full the vaults.

(Ketton-Cremer, 1948, p. 165)

George Walpole, 3rd Earl of Orford, is remembered today, mainly through the letters of his uncle Horace Walpole, as the 'mad Earl', although R.W. Ketton-Cremer provides a more rounded pen portrait in an essay published in *A Norfolk Gallery*, 1948. Horace's friend John Chute met him as a young man and was 'quite astonished at his sense and cleverness' (Ketton-Cremer, 1948, p. 166). He developed into a spendthrift character, happiest in the role of country squire and succeeded the 1st Earl of Buckinghamshire as Lord Lieutenant of Norfolk in 1757. He also played a leading part in raising and organising the Norfolk Militia at the outbreak of the Seven Years War. Two major bouts of mental illness in 1773 and again in 1777–8, were readily labelled as insanity, possibly for want of any more informed diagnosis.

The 3rd Earl of Orford was not entirely without artistic sensibilities. His diary recording a voyage round the Fens in the summer of 1774 survives, and this reveals a sensitive command of language and cultural reference even when describing roistering exploits. As they passed by Benwick 'a number of children, crossing together near a neighbouring cottage (a school), added to the simplicity of the scene, which had much the appearance of some of the best Flemish landscapes' (White, 1868, p. 66). On a number of occasions George Walpole reveals an awareness of Old Master painting: 'at sunset we joined the Fleet. The few clouds to the west at a great distance were tinged with a beautiful pink colour, edged with silver: Claude Lorraine hath alone succeeded in imitating these roseate tints' (White, 1868, p. 90–1). George would have been familiar with three fine examples of Claude's work at Houghton (Fig. 32), one of which was not to be included in the sale to Catherine the Great. George's visual awareness was by no means limited to the landscape: at Ramsey 'we found the sex much handsomer, and the town better situated and built than any other we had seen in the Fens. The girls had many of them guido faces, with fair hair and good shapes, with expression and life in their countenances' (White, 1868, p. 98).

The possible sale of the Houghton paintings was evidently on the family agenda throughout this period. In March 1754 Horace Walpole learnt of the death of Margaret Tuckfield, the mother of Margaret, Countess of Orford: 'My Lord Orford's grandmother is dead too; and after her husband's death [not until 1767]... has left everything to her grandson... and the Houghton pictures may still be saved' (to Horace Mann, 28 March 1754, Lewis, XX, p. 418). However, it is the case that Horace Walpole himself for a time believed that the sale of the Houghton paintings was the only course of action if the family debts

Fig. 31 Rembrandt van Rijn, *Abraham's Sacrifice*, 1636; oil on canvas, 193 x 132 cm (SHM 727); hung in the Gallery at Houghton in Sir Robert Walpole's time

Fig. 32 Claude Lorrain, *Morning in the harbour, the Bay of Biscay*, *c.*1649; oil on canvas, 97.5 x 120 cm (SHM 1243); hung in the Gallery at Houghton in Sir Robert Walpole's time

Fig. 33 Nicolas Poussin, *Moses striking the Rock*; oil on canvas, 123.5 x 193 cm (SHM 1117); hung in the Gallery at Houghton in Sir Robert Walpole's time

were to be paid off. He was impressed at the way the art market was raising significant sale prices at auction in 1758 and wrote to Horace Mann, 'I want to paint my coat and sell it off my back – there never was such a season – I am mad to have the Houghton pictures sold now; what injury to the creditors to have them postponed, till half of these vast estates are spent, and the other half grown ten years older' (10 May 1758, Lewis, XXI, p. 200). Mann responded encouragingly: 'I think you would be in the right to profit of the season to sell the Houghton pictures. If they cost 100,000, by the proportion which Sir Luke Schaub's sold for and the emulation of the rich bidders, one should hope to get three times that sum for them. The present possessor does not seem to value them, and in a generation or two his heirs may get them again for half their first cost!' (3 June 1758; Lewis, XXI, p. 208).

Horace later chose to overlook his assessment at that time. The question of the Houghton pictures arose once more in the summer of 1773. John Manners (1730–92), the illegitimate son of Lord William Manners (1697–1772), proposed to Horace Walpole that he would seize the Houghton pictures, which he had heard were worth £60,000 in exchange for the £9,000 he had lent the 3rd Earl of Orford: 'the vulture's throat panted for them all – what a scene is opened! Houghton will be a rookery of harpies – I doubt there are worse scenes to follow, and black transactions!' (to Lady Ossory, 11 June 1773, Lewis, XXXII, p. 121).

That summer Horace was impelled to visit Houghton. On his return to Strawberry Hill he wrote a long letter to Lady Ossory recounting something of his feelings. Fond as he was of Houghton, he was horrified to see the condition into which the third Earl had allowed it to fall. He found it 'half a ruin, though the pictures, the glorious pictures, and furniture are in general admirably well preserved. All the rest is destruction and desolation! The two great staircases exposed to all weathers, every room in the wings rotting with wet; the ceiling of the gallery in danger...' On this visit Horace mentions the presence of copyists at work making drawings for John Boydell (see Gregory Rubinstein's essay, p. 65). It does appear to be the case that John Boydell's publishing project was intimately connected with the plans to sell the collection, even though the interest of the Empress Catherine was to be at least five years into the future. Boydell himself must have been aware of the developing discussions to sell the paintings. Horace, meanwhile, evidently regarded the project in a positive light.

Horace was still interested in the idea of selling the Houghton pictures when the merchant and banker Sir George Colebrooke (1729–1809) sold his paintings by auction in April 1774. In response to the Colebrooke sale, Horace's mental arithmetic led him to value the Houghton pictures at £200,000 (to Horace Mann, 1 May 1774, Lewis, XXIII, p. 569). It was three years later that, on 28 April 1777, John Wilkes, MP for Middlesex, gave a speech in the House of Commons answering Sir Grey Cooper's motion 'that the petition of the trustees of the British Museum, together with the general state of accounts... be referred to a committee of supply'. Wilkes advocated acquiring the Houghton pictures, 'one of the first collections in Europe' (see p. 152). Horace Mann wrote to Horace Walpole of his approval of the proposal and asked 'was it a thought of his own, or suggested to him by anybody?' (16 May 1777, Lewis, XXIV, p. 304). It is unlikely that Horace Walpole suggested the idea to Wilkes; although they were acquainted Walpole 'saw no wit' in Wilkes (to Montagu 16 Oct. 1765, Lewis, X, p. 180). By the spring of 1777 the question of the family pictures was quite evidently subject to metropolitan debate and rumour, and no doubt the auctioneer James Christie was already formulating his own plans (see p. 154).

By the autumn of 1778 a deal was struck between George Walpole and Horace Walpole and his brother Sir Edward, whereby both brothers renounced their claim to the inheritance of Houghton. In return Horace was secured £4,000 plus interest and his house at Arlington Street, worth £3,000. Almost immediately George Walpole set about the sale of the Houghton pictures, contracting James Christie to value the collection (see p. 154). On 18 December 1778 Horace Walpole wrote to Mann in Florence, 'The mad master has sent his final demand of forty-five thousand pounds to the Empress of Russia...' (Lewis, XXIV, p. 427).

Horace Mann was understandably puzzled by his friend's apparently sudden rejection of the idea of the sale. He commented in reply, 'I thought you had formerly advised Lord Orford to sell his pictures. I am sorry he should do it, if you disapprove of [it], but the sum for which he has offered them to the Empress of Russia seems to be vastly inferior to what I had always heard them valued at. I wonder that the King does not purchase them. One should be tempted in some cases almost to wish that there was authority lodged in some hand to prevent such mad owners from dissipating their patrimony and injuring their descendants' (16 Jan. 1779, Lewis, XXIV, p. 434).

Horace Walpole explained his change of attitude in the following terms: 'It is very true, I did desire the pictures should be sold, as I preferred his paying his grandfather's and father's debts to false splendour – but this is not the case now. As he is not legally obliged, he does not think of acquitting his father's debts; and as he has compounded his grandfather's unsatisfied debts for fifteen thousand pounds, he does not want forty thousand. In short, I am persuaded that the villainous crew about him, knowing they could not make away clandestinely with the collection in case of his death, prefer money, which they can easily appropriate to themselves...' (to Mann, 11 Feb. 1779; Lewis, XXIV, p. 441). Horace Walpole had, in fact, acted honourably throughout his dealings with his nephew. He could, for example, have declared George a lunatic and the estate would have been placed in Chancery and thus remained intact. However, the income from Lord Orford's court positions would have been lost and the honour of the family gravely diminished. It was a great sadness to Horace that now the sale was at hand the market was not what it had been five years previously.

There was a further delay when, as Horace Walpole records, Giovanni Baptista Cipriani (1727–85) was called in to give a second opinion concerning the valuation. Cipriani was a historical and decorative painter who had recently completed a decorative scheme for Lansdowne House (now Philadelphia Museum of Art, McFadden Bequest). A teacher at the Royal Academy, Cipriani appears to have called upon the future President of the Royal Academy, Benjamin West (1738–1820), to help him with the task. It is unclear as to precisely why they became involved, but both artists proved to have connections with the third Earl. One of West's pupils was George Farington, whose meticulous watercolour copies of the family portraits at Houghton still survive in the family (private collection). Farington had been copying paintings on behalf of Boydell since at least the autumn of 1774 and was one of the Earl of Orford's companions on his Fenland excursion that summer. Farington could well have added his recommendation of West to that of Cipriani.

Cipriani himself proved to be a favourite with Lord Orford. Once the sale of the Houghton pictures was finally complete, the third Earl commissioned Cipriani to paint a series of three vast decorative canvases in the Neo-classical style (sold Christie's 20 April 1990, lots 53–5). The paintings, *Philoctetes on Lemnos* (1781), *Castor and Pollux* (1783) and *Oedipus on Colonus* (undated) were hung by the third Earl in the cavernously empty Saloon alongside the portrait of Catherine the Great that he received as a gift from the Empress in 1780 (see p. 153). The Neo-classical subjects were akin to those hung at that time in the Saloon at Holkham Hall, the newly completed Norfolk country seat of Thomas William Coke, Earl of Leicester. Lord Orford also acquired other works by Cipriani as well as vast paintings of tropical and rare birds by Philip Reinagle RA (sold Christie's 20 April, 1990, lots 57–9).

It appears that James Christie, West and Cipriani must have conferred to agree the final valuation of £40,555. A list of pictures showing this total value, once in West's possession, is now in the W.S. Lewis Library, Farmington, Connecticut. The correspondence between Christie and Lord Orford's agent Carlos Cony makes it clear that certain pictures were not finally included in the valuation, and a number of draft lists, notably in the University Library Cambridge, the Fitzwilliam Museum (see cat. 20) and the British Library, show differences. The collection sold to the Empress did not include the family portraits or the statuary.

It is not certain at precisely what point the interest of the Empress Catherine was aroused. The idea of conducting a private sale with the Empress was evidently in the air in the autumn of 1778. On 12 November the coin collector and antiquary Matthew Duane (1701–85) wrote to Carlos Cony from Lincoln's Inn, 'I met at Bath, the Reverend Dr Arnold King, who transacts business for The Empress of Russia; he assured me that the Empress has expressly signified to him lately that she cannot buy any pictures, medals &c' (Norfolk Record Office, BL VI b). The following April Horace Walpole received the inaccurate message that the pictures had indeed been sold: 'I have been told today that they are actually sold to the Czarina – sic transit! (– mortifying enough, were not everything transitory)!' (to W. Cole, 23 April 1779, Lewis, II, p. 158).

We learn from the *Gentleman's Magazine* of 31 July 1779 that the paintings had been 'viewed by the Russian Ambassador, who sent over a list of one hundred of them to the Empress which are valued at £40,525'. In fact Lord Orford had discussed the matter with the Ambassador himself in November 1778, and it was this meeting that caused him to appoint James Christie to value the pictures at Houghton (C. Cony to J. Christie, 26 Nov. 1778, Norfolk Record Office, BL VI b). Catherine's ambassador to the Court of St James at this period was Aleksei Semonovich Musin-Pushkin (1732–1817). He and his wife Ekaterina were familiar anglophiles at court over a fourteen-year period. The negotiations with Lord Orford were among the last Musin-Pushkin undertook on behalf of the Empress before being recalled in 1779. With the outbreak of the American War of Independence and the increas ingly strained relations with France, diplomatic relations between Britain and Russia became strained and the Houghton sale was secured just in time from Catherine's point of view and it was time for Musin-Pushkin to be replaced by the new ambassador, Ivan Matveevich Simolin (1720–99).

Fig. 34 Salvator Rosa, *The Prodigal Son*, 1640s; oil on canvas, 253.5 x 201 cm (SHM 34); hung in the Gallery at Houghton in Sir Robert Walpole's time

During the 1770s, in particular, the Empress Catherine had succeeded in acquiring some major European collections, thanks to the diligence of her ambassadors and her own insatiable desire to collect on a grand scale. Catherine regarded art collecting virtually as a matter of state policy, recognising the ability of major collections to consolidate and enhance the authority and international prestige of her empire. It was Catherine who commissioned the building of a special pavilion to house a collection of 225 pictures bought in 1764 from the Berlin merchant, Johann Ernst Gotzkowsky (1710–75). The new pavilion was called The Hermitage and it was to this core collection that Catherine set about adding not simply individual acquisitions but entire collections. The Empress did not rely simply upon her own taste but that of a panoply of advisers, most notably Denis Diderot, Baron Friedrich-Melchior Grimm and her ambassador to Paris and later The Hague, Prince Golitsyn. She also corresponded with Voltaire and invited numerous artists to work in St Petersburg. Among the most notable of the collections she acquired were those of Count Heinrich von Bruhl (1769), Prime Minister under Augustus III, King of Poland and Elector of Saxony. It must have seemed most appropriate to negotiate for another prime-ministerial collection ten years later.

In March 1773 Josiah Wedgwood and his partner Thomas Bentley were approached by Alexander Baxter, an agent of the Russian government in Britain, who had recently been appointed consul. The result was the magnificent imperial service made of Wedgwood's celebrated creamware decorated with monochrome views of Britain. Houghton was notable for its absence among the East Anglian views which included Wimpole, Holkham and Norwich Castle. Wedgwood 'lamented the approaching fate of the Houghton collection of paintings' in a letter to Bentley of 18 September 1779, and drew bleak inference from the news: 'Everything shows we have past our meridian, and we have only to pray that our decline may be gentle, and free from those sudden shocks which tear up empires by the roots, and make the most dreadfull havock amongst the wretched inhabitants. Russia is sacking our palaces and museums, France and Spain are conquering our outposts, and braving us to our very doors at home...' (Finer and Savage, 1965, p. 239). While Wedgwood may be judged as simply overreacting, his response is the reverse side of the coin of which Catherine II had long since recognised the value.

Horace Walpole had made one last attempt to save the Houghton pictures by appealing directly to the King through his cousin, Francis Conway, Marquis of Hertford, the Lord Chamberlain, who sent a letter on to Windsor on behalf of Horace, but to no avail (Hertford to HW, 2 Aug. 1779, Lewis, XXXIX, p. 337). Horace finally acknowledged the completion of the sale in a letter to Horace Mann of 4 August 1779: 'The sum stipulated is forty or forty five thousand pounds, I neither know nor care which...' (Lewis, XXIV, p. 502). One more irony came ten years later when a fire gutted the picture gallery at Houghton: 'One of the wings of Houghton... is burnt down... As the gallery is burnt, the glorious pictures have escaped – or are rescued, to be consumed in a wooden palace on the first revolution at Petersburg' (HW to Lady Ossory, 12 Dec. 1789, Lewis, XXXIV, pp. 87–8).

Two questions remain, which Horace Walpole could not be relied upon to answer: how important was the Walpole Collection to the growing museum at the Hermitage and to what degree did Catherine negotiate a bargain? In the first instance, Sir Robert's was the quintessential collec-

Fig. 35 Jan van Huysum, *Vase of Flowers*, 1722; oil on canvas, 79 x 60 cm (SHM 1051); hung in the Cabinet at Houghton in Sir Robert Walpole's time

tion of the early eighteenth-century English gentleman of taste. Rich in works by Dutch and particularly Flemish artists, it was also well representative of the French and Italian schools. It included a number of masterpieces and many full-scale works, which continue to enrich the walls of the Hermitage today, most notably major works by Rembrandt, Rubens, Van Dyck, Maratti, Poussin and also Giordano, Guido Reni and Snyders. The arrival of the Walpole Collection in St Petersburg marked the end of an important phase in the development of the Hermitage collection. Sir Robert's pictures effectively consolidated the Empress's collections and even included a few paintings by English masters, such as William Dobson's *Abraham van der Doort* (SHM 2103), Sir Godfrey Kneller's portraits of Grinling Gibbons (SHM 1346) and John Locke (SHM 1345) and John Wootton's *Hounds* (SHM 9781).

It is not entirely clear just how much the Empress did pay for the Houghton Collection. Although Benjamin West and Cipriani confirmed a valuation of £40,455 for those pictures that were sold, William Cole recorded in his copy of the *Aedes Walpolianae* that the Empress paid only

Fig. 36 Peter Paul Rubens, *Hélène Fourment c.*1630–32; oil on panel, 186 x 85 cm; Gulbenkian Museum, Lisbon; hung in the Cabinet at Houghton in Sir Robert Walpole's time

£36,000 (see cat. 19), a figure roughly consistent with that of £36,610 given in a manuscript inventory, dated 30 July 1779 (British Library, 1486 d.l.). Gerald Reitlinger, in *The Economics of Taste: The Rise and Fall of the Picture Market, 1760–1960* (1961), cites the Houghton sale as a perfect cross-section of picture values in the mid-eighteenth century. The Empress is recorded as having spent £150,000 in total on the six collections she purchased between 1764 and 1779, including the Houghton Collection, which was by far the largest acquisition of an individual picture collection. Cole's copy of the valuation lists a total of 181 pictures. Among the highest valuations placed by Benjamin West, Cipriani and James Christie's colleague Philip Tassaert were those on Guido Reni's *Doctors of the Church* (SHM 59) at £3,500, Van Dyck's *Holy Family* (Fig. 28) at £1,600 and Rubens's *Mary Magdalen washing the Feet of Christ* (SHM 479) also at £1,600. These were high values for the period, but they were also high quality works that carried important provenances. The story attached to the Guido, for example, is told in the *Aedes*: 'After Sir Robert had bought this Picture, and it was gone to Civita Vecchia to be shipt for England, Innocent XIII, then Pope, remanded it back, as being too fine to be let go out of Rome; but on heering who had bought it, he gave Permission of its being sent away again. It was in the collection of the Marquiss Angeli' (Walpole, 1747, p. 70).

Although the Empress Catherine undoubtedly did purchase the collection at a bargain price, this was rather through lack of a realistic competitor on the market than through any undervaluing of the works themselves by West and his colleagues. Horace Walpole considered the collection overvalued by the time it came to be sold (to W. Cole, 12 July 1779), and the values do seem to bear him out for the period in question. Although the Van Dyck full lengths were only valued at £200 each or less, this was still twice what Sir Robert had paid for them. The French classicists were valued highly, presumably based upon the French market rather than the London salerooms of the time. Sir Robert's *Moses striking the Rock* by Nicolas Poussin (SHM 1177; Fig. 33) was valued at £900, his *Holy Family* also by Poussin (cat. 50) at £800. It is the case that the lists of values (published *Gentleman's Magazine* and also Chambers, 1829, pp. 520–39 with small variations to Cole's list) invariably reflect not only a recognition of the most important works but also the vagaries of taste. Sir Robert's belief in Carlo Maratti, while fully justified in his portrait of Clement IX (cat. 45) was not to stand up to the taste of the late eighteenth century. Artists' reputations continue to fluctuate, as do critical judgements of individual works. Nevertheless, it is sobering, for instance, that Sir Robert's two flower pieces by Jan van Huysum (Fig. 35) were valued at £1200 for the pair, while his superb Rembrandt, *Abraham's Sacrifice* (SHM 727; Fig. 31), was considered to be worth just £300.

The Empress had achieved an undoubted coup. When her adviser Baron Friedrich-Melchior Grimm informed her at one stage that he had heard that the Houghton Collection was no longer available, Catherine is reported to have replied: 'The Walpole pictures are no longer to be had, for the simple reason that your humble servant has already got her claws on them, and will no more let them go than a cat would a mouse' (Descargues, 1961, p. 42). By 1781, however, her collecting zeal had moderated and she wrote to Grimm, 'I renew my resolution to buy nothing more, not a picture, nothing...' (Waliszewski, 1894, p. 137). Her change of heart had come too late for Houghton. The Empress's name lived on in 'Czarina', a favourite greyhound bitch belonging to the 3rd Earl of Orford who took comfort in her many notable coursing victories in his later years.

8

The Genesis of John Boydell's *Houghton Gallery*

Gregory Rubinstein

THE CONTINUING EFFORTS of the publisher John Boydell (1719–1804) to establish in England a national industry of reproductive print-making to rival that of France constitute one of the more remarkable episodes in the history of British art of the second half of the eighteenth century. Boydell even, in the case of his *Shakspeare Gallery* project, went so far as to commission the history paintings that would provide his engravers with their prototypes; ultimately, that scheme was not a commercial success, but it won the publisher great acclaim as a patriotic promoter of a national school of history painting in the grand manner, the development of which was the fervent ambition of much of the English art establishment of the day. In general, however, the plates that Boydell published were not after works specifically commissioned for the purpose of being reproduced, but after paintings in established, aristocratic collections, and he produced a number of extensive compendia of prints of this type.

One such publication was *A Set of Prints Engraved after the Most Capital Paintings in the Collection of Her Imperial Majesty the Empress of Russia, Lately in the Possession of the Earl of Orford at Houghton Hall in Norfolk*, commonly known as *The Houghton Gallery*. The only example in John Boydell's massive output of an entire publication devoted to a single collection, *The Houghton Gallery* was undoubtedly the most sumptuous of his various highly ambitious print publishing ventures, though not numerically the largest. The 162 prints that make up this splendid collection were published, usually ten at a time, between 1774 and 1788, when they were gathered together into two folio volumes, each prefaced by a text catalogue based on Horace Walpole's *Aedes Walpolianae* of 1747: Volume I consists of an engraved frontispiece, a title-page and a dedication-page, followed by twenty-eight plates depicting 'plans, elevations, perspective views, chimney pieces, ceilings &c' of Houghton Hall (Fig. 37) and sixty prints after paintings in the collection; Volume II contains a further engraved frontispiece and title-page and sixty-nine prints after paintings (see cat. 74 and Rubinstein, 1991, pp. 23–7 for a full listing of plates).

The plates of *The Houghton Gallery* were executed in four different techniques (line engraving, mezzotint, stipple and aquatint), by no fewer than forty-five different engravers, only four of whom are represented by more than five plates, namely Richard Earlom (twenty-six mezzotints), Pierre Fourdrinier (twenty-four architectural line engravings), Jean-Baptiste Michel (fifteen line engravings and five stipples), and Valentine Green (fifteen mezzotints). As a result, the *Houghton Gallery* prints are extremely diverse in style, technique and authorship – and even date, given that several of them were re-issues of rather earlier plates – providing the opportunity for a number of illuminating comparisons. In addition, *The Houghton Gallery* marks the high point of the lengthy, if not always smooth, relationship between Boydell and Richard Earlom (1743–1822), the engraver of most of the largest and finest prints in the collection; this frequently underrated artist's virtuosity and stylistic development are both elucidated by an examination of his contribution to *The Houghton Gallery*.

Although there are precedents for extensive collections of engravings after paintings in a single collection – notably *Le Théâtre de Peinture*, the project supervised by David Teniers which resulted in the issue, beginning in 1658, of a large series of engravings after paintings in the collection of Archduke Leopold Wilhelm – *The Houghton Gallery* is more closely linked, in both title and concept, with one of Boydell's own earlier compendia, *A Collection of Prints Engraved after the Most Capital Paintings in England*. This publication spanned nearly a quarter of a century and was Boydell's main weapon in his continuing assault on the continental domination of the English market for engravings. In the early volumes at least, the *Most Capital Paintings* prints were unashamedly intended to appeal to as wide and as international an audience as possible. Following the example of William Woollett's hugely successful 1761 plate after Richard Wilson's *Destruction of the Children of*

Fig. 37 Pierre Fourdrinier after Isaac Ware, *Plan and Elevation of Houghton Hall*, 1735, Boydell I; the second architectural plate; engraving, 39.3 x 66.7 cm

Niobe, most of the prints were engraved in a thoroughly continental style of line engraving – many by French engravers – and a two-part French language catalogue of the set was even published in 1779 and 1783. None the less, the manner in which the project served as a showcase for British connoisseurship set the scene for Boydell's nationalistic programme of art patronage, which culminated in the initiation of the *Shakspeare Gallery* project in 1786.

This somewhat propagandist inclination was already clearly in evidence more than a decade earlier, in *The Houghton Gallery*. In the prospectus published on 25 March 1775 to accompany the first batch of *Houghton Gallery* prints (a copy of which is bound together with the 1752 edition of *Aedes Walpolianae* in the Cambridge University Library), Boydell stated that 'The Proprietor exerts his utmost Care to have the Work performed in a Manner which shall render it an Honour to our Country, a faithful Imitation of the Originals from which it is taken, and a Credit to every Artist employed in it'. Despite this, *The Houghton Gallery* is somewhat different in character from the early *Most Capital Paintings* volumes, most notably in the fact that although it contains many fine line engravings by French artists such as J.-B. Michel, Pierre-Charles Canot and Simon-François Ravenet the Elder (see cats. 48, 50, 54), rather more of the plates were executed in mezzotint: not counting the twenty-eight line engravings of architectural plans and elevations, which could hardly have been executed in any other medium, *The Houghton Gallery* contains sixty-one mezzotints, fifty-five line engravings, seventeen stipples and one aquatint. Although the choice of the type of print made after any particular painting was, as we shall see, often somewhat fortuitous, some broad patterns can be observed, reflecting widely held views of the particular strengths and weaknesses of each technique. Almost all the still-lifes and animal pictures, and also the large majority of the portraits, were reproduced in mezzotint, while all the landscape prints and almost all the genre pieces were line engravings. In the category of prints after religious, historical and mythological pictures there is a fairly even balance between the numbers of mezzotints, line engravings and stipple engravings.

Within the group of mezzotints, the majority are by Richard Earlom or Valentine Green, but many other leading mezzotinters of the day are also represented, including members of the so-called 'Irish group', who dominated mezzotint engraving in England in the third quarter of the eighteenth century (see cats. 37, 67). Mezzotint, a somewhat quicker and cheaper medium than line engraving, had for some reason never found as great favour with continental collectors as it had in England (hence its soubriquet 'manière anglaise'). Moreover, as mezzotint plates would have been incapable of supporting the large print runs necessary for wide foreign circulation, its extensive use in *The Houghton Gallery* shows that the publication was aimed at a rather narrower, more domestic audience. This is borne out by Boydell's promise in the prospectus that 'the Subscribers shall have the First Impressions' and that 'no more than Four Hundred complete sets shall be printed'. Thus, *The Houghton Gallery* marks a fascinating moment in Boydell's publishing career, executed as a rather specialised product for the domestic market, but at a time when Boydell's position was at its very strongest: his vast foreign trading activities had not yet been disrupted by war and revolution, and the ultimately crippling *Shakspeare Gallery* scheme was still in its early days.

Mounting uncertainty over the future of the Houghton Collection was undoubtedly a major factor in the initiation of Boydell's project to publish *The Houghton Gallery*. The decision to sell provoked a national outcry, and the fate of the Houghton pictures was even debated in the House of Commons: in 1777 John Wilkes proposed that they be purchased by the nation as the basis for a National Gallery, to be housed in a purpose-built gallery within the grounds of the British Museum (see Whitley, 1928, I, p. 326). Extremely interesting in the light of this parliamentary debate is a drawing in the collection of the National Portrait Gallery (see p. 151), which is traditionally described as a portrait of John Wilkes by Richard Earlom. If the attribution and identification of the subject are indeed correct, might this not have been a preparatory drawing for the frontispiece engraving that would surely have been included by Boydell in *The Houghton Gallery* had Wilkes been successful in his attempt to save the paintings for the nation? By July 1779, however, the sale of the Houghton pictures to the Empress of Russia was completed, and shortly thereafter, the paintings were shipped off to Russia.

Boydell's project to publish engravings of most of the paintings at Houghton was already well under way by the time of Horace Walpole's traumatic visit to Houghton in 1773; Walpole related how sometimes he 'stole from the steward and lawyer I carried with me, to peep at a room full of painters, who... are making drawings from the whole collection, which Boydell is going to engrave' (letter of 1 Sept. 1773; Lewis. 1937–83, XXXII, p. 142). Although it was perhaps more usual at this time to send a painting from which a print was to be made to the engraver's or publisher's premises for the purpose, in cases when this was not convenient artists were frequently dispatched to the paintings to make highly finished intermediate drawings. Very few such drawings are known today – as copies, they have been more susceptible to loss or incorrect attribution – but in their own time they were certainly valued, not only as records of specific compositions but also as works of art in their own right. For example, Earlom's preparatory drawing for his own print of *Agrippina landing at Brindisium with the Ashes of Germanicus* after Benjamin West fetched £61 19*s*. 6*d*. at auction in 1771 (Christie's, London, 23 April, lot 76), a price that only a minority of 'original' oil paintings could have surpassed at this date.

The preparation of drawings of this type also frequently served as the starting-point for an engraver's career, the case of Richard Earlom once again providing a good example. Earlom, who was to engrave many of *The Houghton Gallery*'s best plates, first worked for Boydell nearly a decade earlier, as a draughtsman preparing intermediate drawings for *Most Capital Paintings*; his name is one of the four listed in the introduction to the first volume of *Most Capital Paintings* as having made the drawings for this collection. (In addition to the nine prints Earlom engraved for *Most Capital Paintings*, I, II, at least thirty-four more, engraved by others, were based on his drawings – twenty-five with acknowledgement.) Earlom's early accomplishment as a draughtsman is demonstrated by the ten-year sequence of premiums and prizes which he was awarded by the Society of Arts, beginning in 1757, when he was only thirteen years old. The author of his obituary wrote in *The Gentleman's Magazine* (XCII, Nov. 1882, p. 473) that 'in 1765 [Boydell] entertained so high an opinion of our young artist that he engaged him to make drawings from the celebrated collection of pictures at Houghton, most of which were afterwards beautifully engraved by him, in mezzotinto.' An exhibition of Boydell's drawings, held at 'Mr. Ford's Great Room in the Hay-Market' in 1770, included no fewer than fifty-eight by Earlom, all except ten of which can be connected with plates published by Boydell, fourteen of them engraved by Earlom himself. Of those engraved by other artists, however, more than a third did not acknowledge Earlom's contribution: Francesco Bartolozzi, Simon-François Ravenet, François-Germain Aliamet, James Mason, John Hall and John Browne all produced plates based on Earlom's drawings without mentioning the draughtsman's name on the plate, even though it would not have been in any way unusual or inappropriate to have done so. Furthermore, various plates that bore the 'Earlom del[t]' credit when first issued were subsequently re-issued without it: *The Houghton Gallery* contains four re-issued plates from *Most Capital Paintings*, three of which, though otherwise unchanged, lack the acknowledgement of Earlom's draughtsmanship that they had borne when first issued. Such an inconsistent approach to the crediting on the plate itself of the artist who prepared the intermediate drawing for a print, though frustrating for the modern researcher, is fairly typical for the period. This is particularly so in the case of re-issued plates, in which substantial parts of the text areas would have to be re-engraved for republication; when, for example, Robert Dunkarton was reworking a plate for Boydell's firm in 1800, he felt it necessary to consult the publishers concerning 'how much of the present publication must be left' (Note of 13 Dec. 1800, to Mr Harrison of Boydells's firm; Free Library of Philadelphia, Lewis Collection of Autographs of Engravers). In this context it is interesting to note that, while nearly half of the plates of *The Houghton Gallery* (72 out of 162) record the name of the artist who prepared the intermediate drawing, when a portion of Boydell's collection of drawings including many of these same sheets was auctioned at Christie's in 1792 (30 April/1 May), the draughtsman's identity was only recorded in the case of two of the 136 drawings offered.

Three artists are credited on the *Houghton Gallery* plates as having prepared these intermediate drawings: Joseph and George Farington (on twenty-six and thirty-five plates, respectively) and Josiah Boydell (on eleven). An entry in Joseph Farington's diary, written on 15 September 1794 but describing a visit to Houghton some twenty-one years earlier, seems to support the view that these three were the only artists sent to Houghton in 1773 in specific connection with the project to publish *The Houghton Gallery*, despite Bruntjen's assertion (presumably derived from the passage in the artist's obituary quoted above) that Earlom was also sent to Houghton at this time (Bruntjen, 1985, p. 45). The drawings that Earlom had previously made after pictures at Houghton all appear, however, to have been included in an earlier sale from Boydell's collection, at Christie's on 22–3 April 1771, and would therefore no longer have been available at the time *The Houghton Gallery* was in preparation. Thus Earlom had to base his *Houghton Gallery* mezzotints on new intermediate drawings prepared by the Faringtons, despite the fact that he had himself made drawings after a number of paintings in the collection some ten years earlier – drawings that had been used by other engravers in the preparation of plates for *Most Capital Paintings*, and then sold. Few, if any, of the intermediate drawings for *The Houghton Gallery* are known today, although a copy in the Victoria and Albert Museum (VAM E. 1052–1966) after the Houghton painting known as *Teniers's Kitchen* is probably Joseph Farington's intermediate drawing for plate 22 in the first volume of engravings. A large, perhaps even complete, set of these drawings is, however, known to have been on display at Boydell's shop in 1786, and also at the Shakespeare Gallery in 1790, together with many drawings for *Most Capital Paintings*.

One of the few plates that Earlom himself executed for *Most Capital Paintings* was also the fourth plate from this collection, re-issued in *The Houghton Gallery*. Originally published in 1766, *Jacob burying Laban's Images*, after Sebastian Bourdon (cat. 53), was one of Earlom's earliest prints, and its inclusion in *The Houghton Gallery* alongside several masterpieces of his mature career permits a comparison between two very different approaches to the use of mezzotint, and also affords an excellent opportunity to examine the development, as well as the high points, of Earlom's technique in this medium. In 1766 Earlom's first six plates were published. One is an extraordinarily free etched rendition of the head of Christ from Salvator Rosa's *Prodigal Son* at Houghton; this was probably executed at the same time as Earlom's intermediate drawing for Ravenet's engraving, published the following year. (*Most Capital Paintings*, I, pl. 41; one of three plates re-issued (on 1 Aug. 1781) for *The Houghton Gallery* (II, pl. 32) without acknowledgement of Earlom's draughtmanship). Two other 1766 plates (after Rosa's paintings of *Jacob wrestling with the Angel* and *David and Goliath*, in the Duke of Devonshire's collection) were also executed in pure etching, but the remaining three plates from this year incorporate some mezzotint. As can be seen from the print after Bourdon, Earlom's use of mezzotint in these first essays is very rudimentary, all the forms and much of the tone of the image being defined by etched lines. The mezzotint has been applied relatively evenly, and Earlom has made little use of the richness of tone that the medium is capable of providing, a quality he was later to exploit to the full.

The use of mezzotint to provide a very general, almost wash-like tone behind an etched design could, of course, be extremely effective in other contexts, notably the reproduction of drawings executed in pen and wash; this was precisely the technique that Earlom employed in almost all of his three hundred engravings after the *Liber Veritatis* of Claude, the first of which were published in January 1771. For the reproduction of paintings, however, Earlom swiftly discovered that a subtler combination of etching and mezzotint was more effective, fine etched lines being used to clarify and define the forms within a composition, and intricately worked, rich mezzotint providing the tones. Two plates from *The Houghton Gallery* reproducing a pair of extremely similar fruit pieces by Michelangelo da Campidoglio (SHM 2485, 2486), one executed in 1779 by Josiah Boydell (Boydell, II, 45), the other some three years earlier by Richard Earlom (Boydell, I, 41), illustrate very clearly how different are the effects created by these two approaches to mezzotint engraving (for reproductions see Rubinstein, 1991, Figs. 3–6). Close examination of a single vine-leaf from Boydell's print shows how the engraver defined not only forms but also patterns of light and shade using a system of etched dots and lines; just as in Earlom's much earlier plate after Bourdon, mezzotint has been applied and worked in a very general way to reinforce effects of shading produced by etched marks, an approach that totally ignores the medium's greatest strength, its potential for infinite variations of continuous tone. In a similar area within Earlom's print, etching is far more sparingly used, and the mezzotint ground far more intricately worked, producing a livelier, more textured surface, beside which Boydell's leaf looks crude and flat.

In Earlom's finest prints the sophistication of the engraver's method of combining etching and mezzotint is even greater. The etched basis for the famous *Flower Piece* after van Huysum (Fig. 38) is extremely complex, yet by no means defines all the forms found in the finished print (cat. 55). Unlike the early print after Bourdon, which Boydell was able to offer in his 1803 stock catalogue in two versions, with or without mezzotint (priced at 5*s*. and 2*s*. 6*d*. respectively), the etching is here entirely complementary to the mezzotint, and neither could conceivably stand alone. Earlom was not, as Nagler claimed, (IV, p. 52), the first to make extensive use of etching in conjunction with mezzotint; some half a century earlier George White had done so with considerable success. Nor was the practice unknown in Earlom's own time, but in general those late-eighteenth-century engravers who employed this combination of media tended (as did Josiah Boydell in the print discussed above) to use the etching in a much more evenly distributed way, for two reasons: the first was that it was widely held that mezzotint was not a strong or precise enough medium to render forms adequately; the second was that the ink-holding capacity of the mezzotint burr is notoriously short-lived, so the number of good impressions from a pure mezzotint plate is severely limited. If, however, the forms of the composition and the chief areas of shading are all defined by etched or engraved lines, then tolerable impressions will be produced even after the mezzotint has deteriorated somewhat, and the print run can be greatly extended. This mixed-media mezzotint technique was to have its heyday in the later nineteenth century after the advent of steel-facing, which greatly slowed the flattening of the mezzotint surface; even in the mid-eighteenth century, however, the essential principles of this technique were fully understood and fairly widely employed.

Earlom's rather different approach to the combining of mezzotint and etching marks him out from most other engravers of his day, and constitutes both his strength and his weakness as a mezzotinter. The great disadvantage of employing a compositionally incomplete system of etching is that as the mezzotint element wears and the etched lines become increasingly prominent, the tonal and compositional balance of the print are very rapidly disrupted. Also, since many details of composition and lighting are defined in mezzotint rather than etching, the wearing of the mezzotint burr causes considerable loss of variety and depth. But although Earlom's plates undoubtedly wore less satisfactorily than those of many other engravers, in fine early impressions the effects produced by his characteristic use of intricately worked mezzotint are truly spectacular. To reproduce and translate the richly varied textures and hues of van Huysum's *Flower Piece* in either pure mezzotint or etching with subsidiary mezzotint tone would have been impossible.

It was claimed by both Nagler and Wessely that Earlom employed a mezzotint rocker with greater tooth density than those used by his predecessors or contemporaries, allowing him to produce a greater depth of tone and richness of texture in his grounds (Nagler, IV, p. 52; Wessely, 1886, p. IV). Comparison of Earlom's plates with those of Valentine Green, James MacArdell, Dunkarton and others does not, however, support this theory: the places where individual rockings stray over the edge of the ground reveal that all these engravers employed rockers with similar tooth densities. The richness of effect and sense of surface texture is created rather through the extremely subtle way in which Earlom worked his mezzotint ground. In comparison with a print such as Earlom's sumptuous mezzotint after Van Dyck's portrait of James Stuart, 2nd Duke of Richmond (1773; illus. Rubinstein, 1991, Fig. 10), Valentine Green's reproduction of a similar portrait by Van Dyck for *The Houghton Gallery* (Fig. 39) is workmanlike but uninspiring. The very sparing disposition of highlights that characterises Earlom's print, which captures and emphasises the opulent sheen of Van Dyck's surfaces while also allowing for the inevitable increase in harshness that results from the elimination of colour, is largely absent from Green's much more literal translation.

As Hubert von Herkomer put it, 'To find the black and white that, as it were, underlies the colour, needs a sensitive eye' (Herkomer, 1892, p. 92), and the key to Earlom's greatest successes lies in his acute understanding of how to

Fig. 38 Richard Earlom after Jan van Huysum, *A Flower Piece*, 1778, Boydell, I, 59; preliminary etched-only state, 55.7 x 41.9 cm; Fitzwilliam Museum, Cambridge

render extremely subtle effects of light and shade in the medium of mezzotint, a talent that allowed him to capture the surface effects of fabrics, fruit or fur better than any of his contemporaries. In his best plates, the bravura passages of surface textures, with which he has replaced the visual variety provided in the original paintings by colour, are not exaggerated to the extent that they disturb the compositional harmony of the whole. Even in a print such as *Bathsheba bringing Abishag to David* after van der Werff (Boydell, II, 20), in which large areas of the composition are devoted to meticulously rendered fabrics, attention is not diverted from the figure group, and in *Mary Magdalene washing the Feet of Christ* (Boydell, I, 57), the dashing rendering of surfaces is crucial in capturing the drama of Rubens's painting. Another *Houghton Gallery* print after Rubens shows how Earlom was able to exploit the texture not only of the objects represented in a picture, but also of the very medium of the prototype; his *Meleager and Atalanta* (cat. 66) is a strikingly effective simulation of a tapestry cartoon, as well as a powerful and vigorous image. (This was, incidentally, the only double-folio size print in the collection, and was, at two guineas, twice as expensive as any other.)

Comparing Earlom's finest prints with those of Valentine Green (which are not, for the most part, to be found in *The Houghton Gallery*), the striking disparity between the various professional accolades and honours accumulated by each engraver during the course of their respective careers is hard to comprehend. Green was appointed official mezzotinter to George III in 1773 (only six years after his first mezzotint was published), subsequently received a similar appointment to Charles Theodore, Elector Palatine in Düsseldorf, and in 1775 became the sixth engraver ARA. Associate membership of the Royal Academy was not necessarily something that Earlom desired – many engravers of the day boycotted the Royal Academy in response to their continued exclusion from the ranks of the full Academicians – but he never held office in any other artists' organisation and, to judge by the paucity of references to him in Farington's diaries, remained a largely peripheral figure in the London art world of his time. This can partially be explained by the fact that Earlom was apparently a man of some independent means, who may not have been driven by the same commercial pressures as an artist such as Green, but at least as important a factor was undoubtedly the adverse effect of Earlom's highly sophisticated and individual manner of combining etching and mezzotint on the number of first-rate impressions that could be extracted from one of his plates. In comparison with the relatively consistent impressions to be had from a plate by other mezzotinters, such as Green, Earlom's prints show dramatic variations in terms of wearing, and some of the less complimentary assessments of his abilities must surely have been unwittingly made on the basis of impressions from rather worn plates.

Fig. 39 Valentine Green after Anthony van Dyck, *Sir Thomas Wharton*, 1775, Boydell, I, 3, mezzotint; 52.9 x 35.4 cm

Earlom's distinctive technique lent itself to certain types of composition more than others, and in general he produced proportionately fewer prints after portraits than most of his contemporaries (see Rubinstein, 1991, p. 16). In its day, mezzotint was thought particularly appropriate for the reproduction of portraits (see, for example, Gilpin, 1802, p. 38) and two-thirds of the portraits in *The Houghton Gallery* were engraved in mezzotint, yet of the twenty-six plates Earlom executed for the collection, only three

Fig. 40 Valentine Green after Murillo, *The Assumption of the Virgin*, 1775, Boydell, I, 25; mezzotint, 50.3 x 35.6 cm

were portraits. Valentine Green's fifteen mezzotints – the second largest contribution in the medium – included seven portraits and seven religious pictures (Figs. 39, 40), while all James Watson's five mezzotints for *The Houghton Gallery* were portraits. In fact, *The Houghton Gallery* as a whole contains relatively few portrait engravings (only 30 of the 162 plates), and a group of seventeen mainly anonymous Walpole family portraits was not included, despite the fact that drawings had been made of them (nos. 137–153 in the 1790 Shakespeare Gallery exhibition of *Houghton Gallery* drawings). Earlom's substantial involvment in the project clearly reflects this emphasis on subject prints, although factors determining which paintings from the collection were included in the publication, by whom they were engraved and in what media were complex. In many cases, such decisions were made on grounds of expediency or necessity rather than aesthetic principle, and the result is that *The Houghton Gallery* is, for all its sumptuous exclusivism, rather a haphazard collection of prints. Take for example the two prints, published together on 1 September 1785, after the paintings of *Diana* and *Apollo* by Rosalba (Boydell, II, 43, 44): although the pictures are a matched pair the prints are utterly different in technique and effect, the *Diana* executed in stipple by Charles West while the *Apollo* is a line engraving by J.-B. Michel. The stipple technique, relatively rapid of execution, was increasingly employed as the series progressed, in prints such as the portrait of Hélène Fourment, by Louis Sailliar after Rubens (Boydell, II, 36, published 1 Feb. 1883, as Van Dyck; Fig. 41). Moreover, as the paintings themselves disappeared into Russia, Boydell clearly encountered great difficulties in compiling a suitably complete set of prints. In one case, the problem was solved by making a print from a nearly identical version of a Houghton picture in the Duke of Newcastle's collection (*A Game Market* by Earlom, after Snyders and 'Long John'; Boydell, II, 50), while another plate was engraved after a picture by Guido Reni in the possession of the Bishop of Bristol which was very similar to the one in the Houghton Collection (*The Shepherds' Offering* by J.-B. Michel; Boydell, II, 48).

In several other cases, the easiest solution was simply to re-issue earlier engravings, such as the four plates from *Most Capital Paintings* discussed above; indeed, it seems that Boydell tried to gather in *The Houghton Gallery* every plate in some way related to Houghton that he could lay hands upon, including plates that he had not himself originally published. The twenty-eight engraved plans and elevations of Houghton (see Fig. 37) had already been through at least two editions before their inclusion in *The Houghton Gallery*: they were first published in 1735 by their draughtsman, the architect Isaac Ware, and in 1760 were reissued, together with text from Horace Walpole's *Aedes Walpolianae*, by their engraver Fourdrinier. Even older were the three portraits after Van Dyck with which the collection ends, originally published by their engraver, Pieter van Gunst, in Amsterdam in 1716. How and when Boydell came by these plates is not clear, but since two of the three pictures were not otherwise represented in *The Houghton Gallery*, they were clearly worthy of incorporation. The portrait of Charles I had already been engraved in mezzotint by Josiah Boydell (Boydell, I, 48), but van Gunst's line engraving of the picture was nonetheless included alongside those of Queen Henrietta Maria, and Philadelphia and Elizabeth Wharton. This was not the only instance of the inclusion of two prints after the same painting. The first volume of *The Houghton Gallery* contains J.-B. Michel's 1775 engraving of *The Prodigal*

Son, after Salvator Rosa, but according to Boydell's introductory text this print did not do the painting justice, and in 1781 Ravenet's version from *Most Capital Paintings* was re-issued and included in volume II. The distinctly chaotic manner in which various older plates were included was a direct result of the length of time that *The Houghton Gallery* took to produce. In 1775 Horace Walpole lamented, 'alas! it will be twenty years before the set is completed. That is too long to look forward... people will be tired in a quarter of the time. Boydell, who knows this country, and still more this town, thinks so too...' (Lewis, 1937–83, I, p. 385). In fact, Boydell's own loss of interest in his project was probably the most important single factor; by the mid-1780s his attention was focused on the *Shakspeare Gallery* scheme, and seeing *The Houghton Gallery* through to the bitter end had ceased to be a high priority. Such a loss of momentum was entirely characteristic of the publisher's grand projects: *Most Capital Paintings*, which had begun life as a systematic catalogue, became an increasingly random compilation as the series progressed, the later volumes containing considerable numbers of previously published prints, occasionally re-issued, but usually just incorporated with their original publication details.

Despite its various inconsistencies, however, *The Houghton Gallery* creates a more impressive overall effect than any of Boydell's other collections of prints. This is partly due to the grandeur of the collection that it records, but as much as anything else it is the result of the exceptionally high quality of the majority of the plates, both line engravings and mezzotints, and in particular of Richard Earlom's contributions, which mark a watershed in the lengthy association between publisher and engraver and something of a pinnacle of achievement in the career of the latter.

Fig. 41 L. Sailliar, then believed to be after Anthony van Dyck, *Helena Forman*, 1783, Boydell, II, 36; stipple engraving, 57.9 x 39.2 cm

9
The Cholmondeleys at Houghton

Chloë Archer

THE CHOLMONDELEY PERIOD effectively begins with the death of George 3rd Earl of Orford in 1791. In his will he left Houghton and its estates to his last surviving uncle, Horace (1717–97), 4th and last Earl of Orford, owner of Strawberry Hill and noted connoisseur. The third Earl had stipulated that when Horace died the house and its estates should pass to his great-nephew George, 4th Earl and (from 1815) 1st Marquess of Cholmondeley, grandson of his aunt Mary Walpole (Fig. 42). At the time of Horace Walpole's death, Lord Cholmondeley was in Paris and the news of his inheritance was communicated to his agent in Cheshire by George Blount, his attorney in London:

'And now my dear Sir, I have to communicate what will surprize and delight you at the same time. What think you of our good Lord coming in for the Houghton estate after the demise of Horace Walpole. So it is for on the death of the last Lord Orford, it was found he had made a codicil to his last will bequeathing it in such a manner to Lord Cholmondeley' (Cholmondeley archives, Cheshire Record Office, DCH/X16).

However, the matter was not as straightforward as this might suggest. The provision for the house and estate to pass to Lord Cholmondeley and his heirs had been made both in Lord Orford's first will of 1752 and again in a codicil of 1776. However, in 1756 Lord Orford had made a second will leaving it instead to the Walpoles of Wolterton, the family of Sir Robert Walpole's brother. While the later codicil overrode this, the existence of the second will led the Walpoles to challenge the Cholmondeleys' right to inherit. As Timothy Brent, Lord Cholmondeley's agent in London observed, 'I think Lord Cholmondeley's title the best' but 'this... must and inevitably be a subject of litigation... I have written to Lord Cholmondeley very fully upon this business, but have avoided raising his expectations too high' (Cholmondeley archives, Cheshire Record Office, DCH/X16).

The Wolterton case contesting the validity of the 1776 codicil was finally heard at the Court of Common Pleas on 6 May 1796, when the jury found in favour of Lord Cholmondeley. However, on 1 July of the same year it became

Fig. 42 Pompeo Batoni, *George James, 4th Earl and later 1st Marquess of Cholmondeley* (1749–1827), 1772; oil on canvas, 76.2 x 63.5 cm; The Marquess of Cholmondeley

known to the family that Colonel Walpole (son of Lord Walpole of Wolterton) was pressing for a second trial. This took place on 7 February 1797 and the previous judgement was upheld, less than a month before the death of Horace Walpole on 2 March.

The contesting of the third Earl's will had not, however, been the only obstacle in the way of Lord Cholmondeley's inheritance at Houghton. While Horace Walpole had been left the house and land, it emerged that all the contents of the house were part of Lord Orford's personal estate. These were still spectacular, despite the sale of the finest of the pictures to Catherine the Great in 1779. However, since the third Earl had left massive debts of £87,000 the executors proposed selling the contents, which included the Kent furniture, Sir Robert's library and the family portraits. Horace Walpole, who did not possess the means to purchase them, was obliged to seek the financial assistance of his great nephew Lord Cholmondeley, who finally succeeded in securing them in July 1792 for £6,000. This sum was raised with considerable difficulty and it involved both selling his house Trent Place, near Enfield, Middlesex, and accepting a loan of £5,000 from his mother Hester, Lady Malpas. To further complicate the situation it was necessary that Horace Walpole should appear to be funding the purchase himself, since one of the executors of Lord Orford's will, the disreputable Robert Mackreth, and Lucas, Lord Orford's solicitor, both supported Colonel Walpole, who opposed the idea that Lord Cholmondeley should purchase the contents of the house while the will was still being contested. Lord Cholmondeley himself showed considerable courage in making such a substantial investment because the lawsuit had not been resolved at the time of purchase and he did not yet know for certain that Houghton and its estate would be his. As it was, two months earlier on 9 May 1792 Messrs Jaques & Sons of Savile Row had sold, by order of the executors, 'the superb sideboard and table service comprizing upwards of 10,000 oz, valuable and curious gold and silver watches, snuff boxes, trinkets, coins and medals, the property of the Earl of Orford Decd. including Sir Robert Walpole's official seal and another of his family arms; cornelian set in gold'. Some treasures had therefore already eluded Horace Walpole before he was able to satisfy the executors that he was in a position to buy the contents.

By 1796 the Cholmondeleys were already closely involved with the house and on 20 June 1796 Farington could record that Horace Walpole told him how 'Lord and Lady Cholmondeley have been a week at Houghton and are delighted with the place, and are to pass two months there in the autumn. [Horace Walpole] has told Lord Cholmondeley that while he lives he will keep the house in as good repair as he found it in, and that any alterations or additions Lord Cholmondeley may be disposed to make, he is welcome to begin them as soon as he pleases'. 'I may drag on,' said Horace Walpole, 'a year or two longer, but [in] that time I would not have an interruption to any schemes your lordship may have formed' (Garlick and Macintyre, 1978, p. 326). The house and the estate had by this time been put on a more secure financial footing and Horace Walpole's will of 1793 shows that in that year there were only two mortgages, amounting to £17,500. Three years later in 1796 they were said to be worth £500,000 with an income of £10,000 a year. Despite having inherited considerable debts when he succeeded to the title on the his grandfather's death in 1770, Lord Cholmondeley had himself managed to achieve a considerable level of prosperity, partly as a result of bequests from various relatives and also through a financially advantageous marriage in 1791. His wife, Lady Charlotte Bertie, had a fortune of £30,000, which produced an income of £1,400 a year. Thus he was able to maintain not only Houghton but also Cholmondeley Hall, his family seat at Malpas in Cheshire, which he had inherited at a time when his finances were in such a parlous state that Horace Walpole feared he would have to pull it down.

Lord Cholmondeley was a man of culture who had travelled extensively in Europe and was keenly interested in the arts. He had already exercised his taste in the pictures he had bought for his town house, which were described by a contemporary newspaper as 'excellent', and in the rebuilding of Trent Place. His purchase of the contents of Houghton shows his concern with the appearance of the interior of the house. The standard of the depleted collection gained by the addition of thirty paintings left to him by Horace Walpole specifically for Houghton. These included two views of Florence by Thomas Patch (see cat. 78) and a portrait of the Duchess of Gloucester by Allan Ramsay and two Walpole family portraits. The first Marquess almost certainly also brought some of his own family pictures from Cholmondeley Hall. As far as the decoration of the rooms was concerned, his lasting memorial is the White Drawing Room, formerly known as the Carlo Maratti Room after the works by this artist which used to hang here before the sale to Catherine the Great. In 1797 the Prince of Wales came to stay with Lord Cholmondeley, who at that time was his Chamberlain. Tradition maintains that he presented his host with the white silk that now covers the walls of this room. It is probably English, with a very early example of a French-inspired Neo-classical pattern, and transformed the room into a typically light late-eighteenth century interior, an effect augmented by the contemporary chandelier and the simple white dress worn by Lord Cholmondeley's wife in her portrait by John Hoppner which was to hang above the fireplace.

Apart from this *tour de force*, Lord Cholmondeley carried out other redecoration projects, the most important of which was the introduction of the Chinese wallpaper in the Cabinet Room in 1797. Structural work included the restoration of the Picture Gallery, Chapel and adjacent rooms in the North Office, that had been seriously damaged in a fire that took place in the winter of 1789. In the park impressive gates by Jean Tijou (*fl.* 1689–1712) were brought from Cheshire by the fourth Earl in 1799 and installed at the New Houghton entrance to the demesne. A Cheshire surveyor, Joseph Hill, was also commissioned to produce a survey of the Houghton estates which was completed by 1800. This was followed in 1805 by the remodelling of Cholmondeley Hall in the gothick manner. Rechristened Cholmondeley Castle, this became the permanent residence of the Cholmondeley family. From then onwards Houghton was only favoured with brief visits. However, some of these were evidently quite lively and involved entertaining. As the *Norfolk Chronicle* reports for November 1807, 'An entertainment was given by Lord and Lady Cholmondeley to upwards of 300 persons at Houghton Hall. The great hall was converted into a theatre for a performance of an opera...' (Mackie, 1901, p. 61).

Once the fourth Earl was installed at Cholmondeley he began to consider disposing of Houghton. An ideal opportunity came after the Battle of Waterloo when, on behalf of a grateful nation, Parliament made a grant to the Duke of Wellington to acquire a country residence in recognition of the services he had rendered to his country. His connection with Houghton went back several years and had begun, indirectly, when walnut from the estate had been used for musket stocks for his army. Similarly, walnut from Houghton had been used for Nelson's ships. The Duke visited Houghton with Marshal Blücher, the Prussian general, in 1814. The scene was described in 1865 by the Reverend Broome, Vicar of Houghton, in his book *Houghton and the Walpoles*: 'Some of the older villagers still remember the Duke's visit to Houghton in 1814, accompanied by Marshal Blucher, when they, and other villagers stopped the carriage, at a short distance from the South gates, unharnessed the horses, and drew it in triumph to the Hall.' (p. 23). Four years later it is recorded that the Duke came to Houghton again and on this occasion he is said to have carved his name on to one of the pillars of the colonnade. By 1815 the Duke's agent, Mr Benjamin Wyatt, had started to make enquiries about buying Houghton and wrote to him giving his opinion of the place: 'I consider Houghton to be a place of considerable magnificence; but I must confess that it has not the degree of grandeur which according to my ideas it ought to have as a national monument to your services, and as an example of the feeling which the nation bears towards you.' As negotiations continued, further reservations emerged, chiefly that Houghton was too far from London, secondly that the house would always be associated in the popular imagination with Sir Robert Walpole and thirdly that Lord Cholmondeley was asking too high a price. The Duke eventually settled at Stratfield Saye, Hampshire, in 1817. On 9 November 1816 the *Norfolk Chronicle* reported that: 'The wealth of Mr Watson Taylor, the purchaser of Houghton Hall, is immense. For the mansion, and a huge tract of land around, he gave the Marquis of Cholmondeley £350,000'. This story proved to be without foundation. (Mackie 1901, p. 141).

On his death in 1827, the first Marquess was succeeded by his eldest son, George (1792–1870). He, in turn, was followed by his younger brother William (1800–94). Neither spent any prolonged periods of time at Houghton, using it chiefly as a base for shooting, for which the estate has always been renowned. The account books for this period show that expenditure continued on repairs to estate property and some new cottages were built. Repairs and alterations were also made to the church of St Martin in the park. These included the restoration of the roof and the chancel arch and the addition of responds in the Early English style. In about 1850 the church was repewed and a large east window was installed in 1867. Both men took a particular interest in the schools on the estate and records exist of the sums they spent on employing teachers. There is evidence that they were considerate landlords and we know that during the 1840s the second Marquess paid for medical attention for tenants. The third Marquess was also a member of the Plymouth Brethren, which is said to have led him to close down all the pubs on the estate.

The contents of the house were kept intact, and it is clear from the 1843 guide to Houghton that a considerable number of additional pictures had been added to the collection, but it is not possible to determine exactly when this happened. The 1848 guide shows that during the years 1843–8 a considerable number of changes were made in the positioning of pictures in the house. During these five years approximately one third of the collection was redeployed. However, during the mid nineteenth century there was also considerable deterioration and the house and the estate began to take on a generally neglected appearance. This was vividly recorded by James Grigor in his book the *Eastern Arboretum* of 1847. He begins his account of Houghton as follows:

> In noticing this seat, we must refer chiefly to what it has been, not what it is; for there is now scarcely anything to interest the visitor, unless he contrast its present fallen condition with the unexampled grandeur it exhibited in bygone times. In this respect, it affords the richest materials for meditation. The entire building is standing; but it has assumed the sullen lifeless-like aspect of the cloister. Its halls are forbidden to the visitor, and their splendid and costly embellishments are mouldering away amidst damps and darkness. 'The right worshipful equipage' of the

Walpoles has dwindled down into a few menials, who seem scared at the appearance of a stranger: there is not even a regular gardener kept, and the party who officiates as such informs you that 'there may be some pine trees and other things in the park but he is not aware of any!' Almost everything else has gone in a like ration. The gardens are gone, the lawn is obliterated, – that very spot where those great statesmen, according to their own account, passed so many charming moments, is now handed over to some petty farmer to feed his cows on! The entrance-lodges, offices and stabling, with their stalls for a hundred horses are still here, but empty, – conspiring with other things to form a picture only of magnificent desolation. The very roads which conduct us to the hall which in the days of the Walpoles sparkled with the equipages of the great, are glutted with mud and almost impassable. Everything seems to have suffered by the long lapse of years' (Grigor, 1847, p. 192).

Despite recorded repairs to the lodges at the entrance to the park, these clearly presented a depressing picture. Grigor refers to a letter from Horace Walpole of 1773 which mentions horses in the garden of the house and 'banditti' lodged in every cottage and writes: 'Whether the offspring of the banditti aforesaid inhabit the cottage, we did not stop to enquire; if so, they are in perfect keeping with the buildings, for we know not of anything that so detracts from the general grandeur of this princely abode, as the paltriness of several of the lodges, and the shabby meagre appearance of the houses surrounding the enterance to the park' (Grigor, 1847, p. 197).

While allowing for some exaggeration, we do know that in 1835 part of the park had been ploughed up and that while some new planting had been carried out by the first and later the second Marquess the cedar and pine trees planted by the 2nd Earl of Orford were almost completely destroyed by a gale in 1860. It was around this time that the Cholmondeleys made another attempt to divest themselves of Houghton by offering it to the Prince of Wales (later Edward VII), who was looking for a country estate where he could enjoy the shooting, which was one of his favourite pastimes. Fortunately for the preservation of Houghton, he settled on the neighbouring Sandringham estate some seven miles away, which he bought in 1861. However, Edward and Alexandra, Princess of Wales, became quite regular visitors to Houghton and comments on their visits by the Reverend Broome, who was then living in the house, show that by the early 1860s the place was enjoying something of a revival. He reports that when the royal party visited on 22 October 1863 the Duke of Cambridge observed the 'great order and cleanliness' of the apartments (Broome, 1865, p. 25). It was shortly afterwards that two new water tanks were constructed to supply the house, following a prolonged drought in 1864.

Fig. 43 The Stone Hall, *c.*1900

Before the death of the third Marquess in 1884 the family had decided to let the house and estate to a succession of tenants. The first of these took up residence in 1888 and the last, the Countess of Strafford, relinquished the house to the Cholmondeleys in 1916. It is clear that during this period Houghton began to take on a considerably more prosperous appearance. Photographs taken around the turn of the century show well tended, elaborately laid out gardens around the house (Figs. 43, 44). They also record the Prince of Wales (from 1901 King Edward VII) taking part in shooting parties. Game books were consistently kept and it is clear that the Houghton estate could hold its own with Sandringham in this respect.

The inventories made when a new tenant took on the house provide valuable insights into its life and modernity. The one made before the first tenant moved in in 1888 shows that there had been no major alteration in the arrangement of the contents since the guide book of 1848. Only thirteen pictures had been moved from their positions as recorded at that date. The inventories and photographs show that electric light had been installed by 1900. In 1891 a sale catalogue lists contents from Houghton but it is clear these belonged to the first tenant. The same catalogue also shows that by this date many bedrooms also had a water-closet attached. The family did, however, dispose of a few elements of the interior decoration, including a number of tapestries, which were sold at the end of the century.

The Cholmondeleys had not given up the idea of finding a more permanent solution to the financial problems of Houghton and in 1886 a sale catalogue was published but no buyer was found. There was perhaps another attempt to interest the Royal Family in taking Houghton on, as a newspaper report of July 1901 informed its readers that the Duke and Duchess of Cornwall (also known as the Duke and Duchess of York and later King George V and Queen Mary) were to take up residence on their return from abroad. We do not know how much truth there was in this suggestion, but their country residence at the time, York Cottage in the grounds of Sandringham, was extremely cramped and inadequate for their growing family. This would certainly have seemed a very attractive alternative to Queen Mary who was known to have a hearty dislike of York Cottage, where her mother-in-law, Queen Alexandra, would visit her unannounced, to her intense irritation. Houghton, with its historic connections and outstanding interiors, certainly appealed to her, as was evident on her later visits to Sybil, Lady Cholmondeley, wife of the fifth Marquess. The same newspaper account and the Houghton archives both refer to various people, clearly sub-tenants, who also occupied the house at different times. These were said to have included the Earl of Wilton and 'a rich American, a Mr Bishop, who gave some magnificent parties and even entertained the King – as Prince of Wales – and the present Heir-Apparent'. It is clear that both the tenants and their sub-tenants only used Houghton periodically and then primarily for the shooting.

It is not surprising that Houghton should have been let during the late nineteenth century onwards, nor that an attempt should have been made to sell the house during that period. From about 1880 Britain was plunged into an agricultural depression, which lasted for some twenty years. This was caused largely by the importation of cheap corn from America, following a series of disastrous harvests, that the landed interest was no longer strong enough to block. The centuries-old belief that land was the only secure investment was finally shattered. As agricultural rents decreased, many large estates began to come on to the market. One does not have to look far to see the effects of this depression on other landowners. Norfolk as a whole

Fig. 44 The Garden, looking west, *c.*1900

was seriously affected, since land use was primarily arable. The Felbrigg estate belonging to the Ketton family provides just one example of the decay and neglect that frequently set in. Given the low income that such estates were bringing in at this time, it is easy to see why they might be difficult to sell. In any case, it was not at all unusual for country properties to be let during this period. Renting houses for the shooting was commonplace in the nineteenth century and Norfolk estates, which offered excellent sport, were in a particularly fortunate position to make the most of this source of income. It was also a period when to help compensate for the losses being suffered, many owners decided to sell some, at least, of the more important and valuable contents of their houses. Examples in Norfolk include the sale by Lord Amherst from the Didlington Hall library in 1909 and the disposal of part of the outstanding collection of maiolica, Limoges enamels and Nevers ware assembled by Sir Andrew Fountaine of Narford in the eighteenth century and sold through Christie's in 1884.

On the outbreak of the First World War, Houghton was still in the care of the Countess of Strafford. The army used it throughout the war, although soldiers did not occupy the main block of the house. The account books recall the Dorset Yeomanry being stationed there, and by 1918 there were certainly prisoners-of-war living at Houghton. By now Lady Strafford had left and at this point a new and exciting chapter in the history of the house was about to begin. In 1884 the 4th Marquess of Cholmondeley (1858–1923) had succeeded his grandfather but, like him, he had let Houghton and remained based at Cholmondeley Castle. He preferred racing to shooting and when in 1913 his eldest son and heir George, Earl of Rocksavage (later 5th Marquess of Cholmondeley), married Miss Sybil Sassoon he presented them with Houghton as their country home. The advent of Lady Rocksavage (as she then was) was of supreme importance to the future of Houghton, for not only did she bring immense dedication and style to the estate but she also had a very considerable fortune (Fig. 45). Her parents, Aline and Edward Sassoon, belonged to two of the richest and most prominent Jewish families of the nineteenth century, the Sassoons and the Rothschilds. By the time of Sybil's marriage they had both died and Sybil and her brother Philip were among the wealthiest people in England. The Houghton that the young Cholmondeleys moved to in 1919 had been well cared for by Lady Strafford, who is said to have told Lady Rocksavage to make sure that she looked after it properly when she relinquished her tenancy! Nevertheless, it required a considerable expenditure and they decided to concentrate initially on the interior of the house. At a date

Fig. 45 Sybil Cholmondeley, 1920s

when, in the words of *The Times*, 'all England seemed to be changing hands', this was an outstanding example of a strengthening commitment to inheritance. Their move to Houghton was in tune with a distinctive trend among some to retreat to old family seats and traditions following the horrors of the Great War. The Cholmondeleys were fortunate, too, that, unlike so many landed families, they had not lost their heir.

The 1920s was a period when there was a growing appreciation of eighteenth-century architecture, furnishings and decoration. The Cholmondeleys' enthusiasm for Houghton can be seen as part of this, as can Philip Sassoon's remodelling of eighteenth-century Trent Park which he had inherited from his parents and which by a curious stroke of fortune had once, as we have seen, belonged to the 4th Earl of Cholmondeley. Houghton was to benefit from their continuous care for a period of nearly eighty years. After the fourth Marquess's death in 1923, his widow lived on at Cholmondeley Castle until her death in 1939 and, on his marriage in 1947, the castle passed to Lord and Lady Cholmondeley's eldest son, Hugh, the future sixth Marquess. However, Houghton was only occupied for a period in the summer and for the shooting season. During the 1920s and 1930s Lord and Lady Cholmondeley were chiefly based in London and frequently travelled abroad. The fifth Marquess was a very keen and proficient polo player and they both excelled at golf and tennis, taking part in tournaments around the world. Regular visits were made to Cannes where they were important figures on the social scene, and in 1933 they purchased Le Roc, a villa which they rebuilt in the modern style. At Houghton repairs and modernisation of services continued and there was a flourishing community life on the estate. Gymkhanas and flower shows were held and bazaars raised money for the church-roof restoration fund as did tours of the house conducted by Lord Cholmondeley. With no pub in the village, a sports and social club was established in the stable block. In the 1920s and 1930s a film was shown once a week and every year there was a Christmas party. Football and cricket were played on pitches near the house, the cricket pitch being one of the finest in West Norfolk. Lord Cholmondeley was passionately interested in sport and believed that it should be made as freely available as possible. In the 1930s he took up an exercise system called the Margaret Morris Movement. He became a keen advocate of this and promoted it among the staff on the estate. This involved keep-fit exercises done to music, usually Schubert, at Houghton and Cholmondelely Castle. A newspaper headline from the *Daily Herald* of 25 April 1938 reading 'Houghton-le-fit shows the way' sums up his enthusiasm as he organised inter-village sporting competitions and opened new sports pavilions with his wife. At national level he became one of the prime movers and also Chairman of the Basic Physical Training Association, and later succeeded in establishing a permanent training course at Loughborough College. His other interests included a passion for cars, particularly Bugattis, and italic handwriting, a subject for which he established prizes at Eton, Winchester and Harrow.

During the Second World War Houghton was once again used by the army and the navy but, as before, the main body of the house remained closed to the forces and did not suffer the damage inflicted on so many other country houses. A variety of regiments were billeted there, as was the Royal Air Force for a period. Again a prisoner-of-war camp was established in huts near the stable block. It is also said that the fifth Marquess took advantage of the presence of the troops to drill them in the Margaret Morris Movement.

After their return from the war the Cholmondeleys renewed their maintenance and restoration projects at Houghton and estate life continued to thrive. The outside world was taking a growing interest in the house and its contents and there was a considerable increase in public appreciation, which had begun at the time of their return to Houghton after the First World War when a flurry of articles had first appeared in a number of national periodicals. Although Lord Cholmondeley did not particularly enjoy entertaining, there was a steady stream of visitors to the house and they never failed to be entranced, not only by the house and its situation but by the delight their hosts took in it. Lady Cholmondeley in particular had a very special understanding and appreciation of Houghton. The typical response of guests is summed up by an entry in Harold Nicolson's diary for 27/28 August 1952:

> We drive down from Yorkshire and reach Houghton at 4.45 warmly greeted by Rock (Lord Cholmondeley) and Sibyl. We have tea, and are then taken over the state-rooms. Everything is in superb condition, and added to the treasures of Walpoles and Cholmondeleys are Philip Sassoon's and pictures and carpets. I have never seen a house so perfect and self contained.
> We visit the garden and the long white room and gymnasium and the tennis court. This house really is a manifestation of Kent's genius. Every detail is a work of art – not a hinge scamped – the back of things are as perfect as the side that shows. Sibyl has beautiful objects of every sort that are displayed on the tables and add luxury to this amazing setting. Certainly the loveliest eighteenth century house that I have ever seen. It is touching to notice how Rock and Sibyl adore it. She is a wonderful guide, and shows the house in small doses at a time. (Nicolson,1968, p. 228)

In 1957 Nicolson's wife Vita Sackville West wrote to Lady Cholmondeley from Sissinghurst describing her response to Houghton: 'in some strange way you contrive to make its grandeur as friendly and easy as a cottage' (Cholmondeley archive, Houghton Hall, letters to Sybil Cholmondeley, 41).

Harold Nicolson's impressions emphasise the importance of the contents as a crucial factor in Houghton's impact. Lord and Lady Cholmondeley made gradual additions to these and in particular introduced a number of important pictures. These included three Sargent portraits: two of Lady Cholmondeley as Countess of Rocksavage, painted in 1913 (cat. 80) and 1922, and a portrait of 1907 of her mother, Lady Sassoon. Lady Cholmondeley was triumphant that she managed in 1975 to buy back the portrait of Joseph Carreras by Godfrey Kneller which had been sold by the 3rd Earl of Orford to Catherine the Great. The Holbein *Portrait of an Unknown Woman with a Squirrel and a Magpie* (now London, National Gallery), was brought to Houghton from Cholmondeley Castle where she had discovered it on a back staircase unattributed and ignored. However, the most spectacular influx of objects to Houghton took place in 1939, with the death of Philip Sassoon. He left the bulk of his outstanding collection of mainly French eighteenth-century pictures, furniture and other decorative art to his sister. The pictures included de Troy's *La Lecture de Molière*, Jean-Baptiste Oudry's *The White Duck* and an important Gainsborough, *Mr and Mrs Browne of Tunstall*, acquired by Mrs David Gubbay *c.*1947. Oudry came to Houghton in the early 1980s when Lady Cholmondeley sold her town house, 12 Kensington Palace Gardens, and those objects from Philip Sassoon's collection which had been there were brought to Houghton. Lady Cholmondeley also made a particularly important acquisition of contemporary art in 1918, when she bought William Orpen's *The Play Scene from 'Hamlet'*, the work with which he won the Slade School Diploma in 1897. Orpen had already become a friend of the Cholmondeleys and had painted her portrait in 1913, the same year that Sargent painted his *Lady Rocksavage* (cat. 80).

Inevitably there were also disposals that had to be made to contribute towards the upkeep of the house and estate. The cost of keeping servants rose after the Second World War and the number of both domestic and outside staff was considerably reduced, a trend that was universal in most great country houses. In the 1930s there were some sixteen permanent indoor servants. As the number of staff declined, the garden deteriorated, although in 1949 a grove of pleached lime trees in the French manner was planted next to the house. Land, too, was gradually sold off. Before the First World War the estate had consisted of about 6,475 hectares but this was reduced not long after the fifth Marquess took over Houghton and again following the agricultural depression of the 1930s with the sale of land to the Air Ministry. After the Second World War a large amount of land was sold to George VI and now forms part of Sandringham estate.

In 1968 the fifth Marquess died. His widow, now the Dowager Lady Cholmondeley, lived at Houghton until her death in 1989. She spent an increasing amount of time there, especially after the sale of her London house, and undertook two great restoration projects. The first, the rebuilding of the steps on the west front, which had been taken down and sold by the third Lord Orford, was completed in 1973 in memory of her husband. The second was the repair of the eighteenth-century water tower in the late 1980s. Lady Cholmondeley continued to entertain, and on a local level was actively involved with the King's Lynn Music Festival. Members of the Royal Family continued a long tradition of visiting from Sandringham and the guests at a magnificent party held to celebrate Lady Cholmondeley's ninetieth birthday included HM The Queen, HM The Queen Mother and HRH The Prince of Wales.

Fig. 46 Lord and Lady Cholmondeley at 12 Kensington Palace Gardens. A charcoal study by John Singer Sargent of Lady Cholmondeley when Countess Rocksavage (1912) stands on the easel.

The sixth Marquess, who died in 1990, was based at Cholmondeley Castle during his lifetime and his widow still lives there. Their son, the seventh Marquess, has continued the programme of maintenance and restoration begun by his grandmother at Houghton, and in order to fund this he was obliged to sell a significant proportion of the Philip Sassoon collection from Houghton in 1994. While some would argue that the importance of the country-house interior lies in the sum of its contents from all periods, these objects were not part of Walpole's original interior and were not consistent with his taste. Lord Cholmondeley continues to make acquisitions for the collection and is also undertaking the restoration of the garden. Houghton is set to survive, and thrive, well into the third millennium.

THE CATALOGUE

THE CATALOGUE of the exhibition *Houghton Hall: The Prime Minister, The Empress and The Heritage* (Norwich and London 1996–7) is divided into four sections: *Portraits of Sir Robert Walpole*, *A Tour of the House*, *The 1779 Sale to Catherine the Great* and *Houghton Today*.

In *A Tour of the House* fifteen rooms are featured, each with an introduction outlining the interior decoration and the contents of that room as originally conceived and executed in the time of Sir Robert Walpole. The names of each room are those recorded by Horace Walpole in his *Aedes Walpolianae* (1747); recent name changes are also given if applicable (e.g. the Breakfast Room is now known as the Gun Room). The present locations of paintings formerly at Houghton are given where known.

The introductions to each room are by Sebastian Edwards, as are the entries on architecture, furniture and sculpture (cats. 7–9; 15; 30–6; 38–44; 46–7; 49; 57–9; 69–70). The entries on paintings, prints, drawings and manuscripts are by Andrew Moore (cats. 1–6; 11–14; 16–21; 23–9; 37; 45; 48; 50–6; 65–8; 71–9). The entries on metalwork and ceramics and J.S. Sargent are by Chloë Archer (cats. 10; 22; 60–3; 80). Cat. 64, glass, is by Wendy Evans.

Measurements are height x width x depth unless otherwise indicated.

Portraits of Sir Robert Walpole

Fig. 47 John Eccardt and John Wootton, *Sir Robert Walpole and Catherine Shorter;* oil on canvas, 50.5 x 102.4 cm; The Lewis Walpole Library

The Prime Minister's face was one of the most painted of the period. Artists who were commissioned to paint Walpole included Michael Dahl (?1659–1743), Thomas Gibson (*c.*1680–1751), John Theodore Heins (1697–1756), Thomas Hudson (1701–79), Hans Huyssing (1685–1753), Charles Jervas (*c.*1675–1739), Sir Godfrey Kneller (1646–1723), Jonathan Richardson (*c.*1665–1745), Jean-Baptiste Van Loo (1684–1745) and John Wootton (?1678–1764). His patronage of these artists resulted in an explosion of commissions from amongst his family, friends and followers. Indeed, the multiplicity of Walpole's patronage may well have contributed to the failure of any one artist, including Hogarth, to capture the market.

Both Kneller and Jervas painted Sir Robert in his early thirties, but most of the portrait types of Walpole show him later in life, at best portly. George Vertue in 1738 refers to a portrait by Van Loo, whose 'great success is likenes, naturaly without flaterry – or raising the character, but in that its remarkable that Sr. Robert Walpole and the Duke of Grafton were done too grosely... but the generallity were allwayes pleasd with his likeness of portrait'.

Until his death in 1739, Charles Jervas was principal painter to the King. However, according to Vertue, Sir Robert 'so well likd and approvd of [Van Loo's] painting that had it not been for an Act of Parliament that prevented Forreigners of any Nation to have or enjoy places of salary in the Government, he would have presented him with the place of King's Painter'. It was Van Loo's painting of Walpole in the chancellor's robes, signed and dated 1740, that was among the Houghton paintings sold by George Walpole, 3rd Earl of Orford, to the Empress Catherine in 1779 (SHM 1130). Versions of this portrait today hang at Lyme Park, Cheshire and also Lambeth Palace, while shortened versions can be seen at Hampton Court, Chequers[1] and Chatsworth.[2] A half-length studio version is in the National Portrait Gallery.[3] A third type, derived from the prime version of Van Loo's portrait of Sir Robert remains in the Walpole family collection,[4] while a quarter-length version remains today at Houghton.[5]

When reviewing the many versions of portraits of Sir Robert Walpole that survive, it is necessary to recognise that certain types recur, notably those of Van Loo and Richardson. Richardson's depiction of Walpole's characteristic stance was so powerful that it engendered caricatures (see p. 13), and even Hogarth's painting of John Gay's *The Beggar's Opera* shows the character of MacHeath, popularly associated with Walpole, adopting a similar gait.

1 Government Art Collection

2 A third version was in the collection of the Earl of Rosebery, Dalmeny House, Lothian, sold Christie's, 5 March 1939, lot 88

3 NPG 70; a comparable version was sold Sotheby's, 17 Feb. 1982, lot 163

4 Private Collection. See Singh [1927], i, p. 146

5 A studio version, sold Christie's, 15 Dec. 1993, lot 16. Thanks go to John Guinness for information; see also Kerslake 1977, pp. 197–205

1 **Sir Godfrey Kneller**

Lübeck 1646 – London 1723

Sir Robert Walpole, 1710–15

Oil on canvas, 91.5 x 71 cm

Prov: commissioned as one of the Kit-cat Club portrait series by Jacob Tonson; presented to the National Portrait Gallery by the National Art Collections Fund, 1945 (NPG 3220)

Exh: London, 1820 (17)

Lit: Piper, 1963, p. 257

The National Portrait Gallery, London

This portrait is one of two principal images of Walpole before his first period of office as Chancellor and First Lord of the Treasury. (The portrait that shows him at his youngest remains at Houghton today. Painted by Charles Jervas *c.*1708–10, it depicts Walpole as 'Secretary at War to Queen Anne'.) This three-quarter length hung in the Little Breakfast Room at Houghton in 1736.

Kneller's portrait was painted for the Kit-cat Club, where gentlemen would meet to discuss politics, literature or the latest news. By 1700 the club, comprising most of the leading Whigs of the day, met at a tavern near Temple Bar, kept by Christopher Cat. When Walpole joined he was a rising young Member of Parliament. It was through the Kit-cat Club that Walpole could socialise with the leading managers of the Whig party. After the accession of George I the club met increasingly infrequently, but it was there that the young Robert Walpole learned the direct correlation between patronage of the arts (notably literary) and political patronage. Fellow club members included not only William Pulteney (1684–1764) and James Stanhope (1673–1721), but also such men of letters as Joseph Addison (1672–1719) and Richard Steele (1672–1729).

An important second portrait of Walpole by Kneller was formerly at Raynham Hall, Norfolk. Signed and dated 1716, this was warmly commended by Horace Walpole in a letter to Lord Hardwicke dated November 1772.[1]

1. Singh [1927], II, p. 217 (120); Christie's, 5 March 1904, lot 4. Now in the collection of St Michael's Mount (National Trust). A second version remains with the Walpole family (private collection); a third with the Cholmondeley family.

2 **John Wootton and Jonathan Richardson**

Snitterfield *c.*1682 – London 1764; London *c.*1665 – London 1745

Sir Robert Walpole, c.1726

Oil on canvas, 90 x 75 cm

Signed, lower right, 'J. Wootton'

Prov: Horatio, 1st Baron Walpole; by descent to present owner

Exh: London, 1984A (16)

Lit: Meyer, 1984, pp. 44–5

Private Collection

John Wootton's pre-eminence in England as a painter of sporting and landscape subjects during the first half of the eighteenth century was greatly strengthened by the patronage of Sir Robert Walpole. Walpole's commissions included several sporting subjects as well as his own portrait. This commanding image of Walpole shows him as a Ranger of Richmond Park, very much in the guise of Country Squire. Sir Robert's eldest son, Robert, was appointed Ranger in 1726, but it was Sir Robert who took advantage of the perquisites of the office. He rebuilt the Ranger's Lodge in Richmond New Park, where he set up his mistress, Maria Skerrett.

The composition was painted in conjunction with the portraitist Jonathan Richardson. Walpole's stance is particularly successful in suggesting a man of substance and stability at home in the well-ordered world of the English countryside. It is almost certainly the earliest of four main versions of the composition, although the precise circumstances of the commission are unknown.[1] Another prime version is at Houghton Hall today (Fig. 1), but no version is recorded in Walpole's own possession.

This portrait is included here in lieu of a number of hunting subjects by Wootton, which graced the walls of Houghton in Sir Robert's day. One that hung over the chimney in the Small Breakfast Room was *Hounds and a Magpie* (SHM 9781). This was one of three portraits of hounds by Wootton recorded in Sir Robert's collection in 1736: the others hanging at Grosvenor Street ('White Hound') and at Downing Street ('Two Dogs'). A fourth later hung in the Hunting Hall and was copied by Ranelagh Barrett (*fl.* 1737–1768).[2]

1 For other versions see Meyer, 1984, pp. 44–5

2 Boydell, II, 22; Barrett's copy sold Christie's, 8 Dec. 1994, lot 136

---

3 **Stephen Slaughter**

London 1697 – Kensington 1765

Sir Robert Walpole, 1742

Oil on canvas, 239 x 148 cm

Signed on plinth, centre left, 'Step^{n} Slaughter / Pinxit / 1742'

Prov: commissioned by Sir Robert for Horatio, 1st Baron Walpole of Wolterton; by descent to present owner

Lit: Musgrove MSS, Additional MS 6391, British Museum, 1797 ('Robert Walpole 1st E of Orford; in his robes as Chancr of the Excr'); Chambers, 1829, p. 218

Private Collection

Of the many portraits of Sir Robert Walpole this has generally passed unnoticed. It shows Robert Walpole at the end of his long and distinguished career, in his robes as Chancellor of the Exchequer, and was painted in the year he resigned from office and retired to Houghton.

Painted for his brother, Horatio, 1st Baron Walpole of Wolterton, this is an image calculated to record his achievements. He sits in a grand architectural setting, with parkland and statuary visible in the background. He wears his Garter Star and has his purse of office at his side. As the first Prime Minister since the Restoration he is remembered for his grasp of the financial and commercial aspects of government and for laying the foundations of free trade and British colonial policy.

A letter to Lord Walpole from his nephew Robert in Chelsea survives in the Wolterton archive, dated 6 August 1743. This refers to the delivery of 'the whole length picture of Ld Orford, together with the head which you bespoke for the Woodhouse family, set out this day for Norwich in the Waggon packd up in a large deal case. I have paid for them, the whole length I shall write to my Lord for... I can not say I think the head is so like as the whole length'.[1]

Stephen Slaughter was one of the last artists to be patronised by Sir Robert.[2] According to Vertue he 'lived abroad near 17 years at Paris and Flanders', returning to London in 1733. In 1744 he was to be appointed Keeper of the King's Pictures. George Vertue records that Slaughter was recommended to the post by the Duke of Kingston and confirmed in it by Charles, Duke of Grafton, the Lord Chamberlain. Slaughter attended the third Lord Orford's sale of Sir Robert's pictures in 1751, buying pictures attributed to Saftleven, Rosa da Tivoli, Viviano and Teniers.[3]

1 Now Norwich Castle Museum; purchased 1996

2 A seated three quarter length of Sir Robert by Slaughter, also dated 1742, is now in the Palace of Westminster. Slaughter also painted Walpole with his secretary Henry Legge, a version of which is now at the Treasury (Kerslake, 1977, i, p. 204).

3 13 June, lots 37, 43; 14 June, lots 19, 27

A Tour of the House

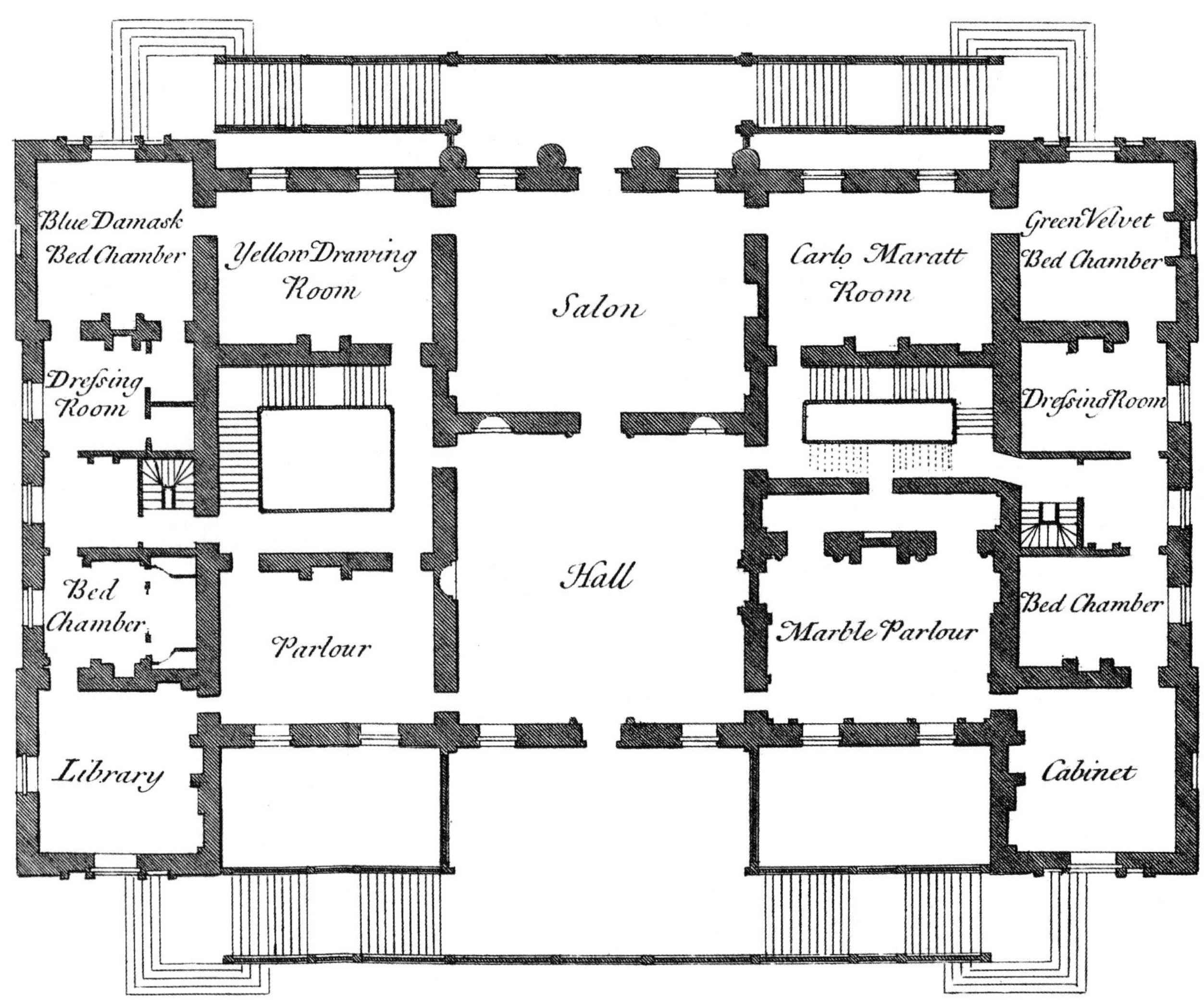

Fig. 48 Plan of The First Floor, from Horace Walpole, *Aedes Walpolianae*, 1767 edition

Fig. 49 The Arcade, 1986. This vaulted sub-hall runs the depth of the house. This was the formal entrance to the ground floor, where hunting parties would have gathered. Horace Walpole, in his guide to the house, *Aedes Walpolianae*, 1747, gives only a brief reference to this imposing space. Instead, he used 'the common approach' through the south door directly into the Breakfast Room.

The Breakfast Room

[The Gun Room]

The first room entered from the South Front door, the 'Common Approach', as Horace Walpole describes it, forms part of a suite of three rooms referred to by the 2nd Earl of Oxford as the 'Hunting Apartment'.[1] Visitors entering on the ground floor quickly discover that hunting is one of the predominant themes throughout the house, in both the decoration and choice of pictures. In these plainly finished, first few rooms the theme was merely alluded to in the subject matter of a handful of paintings.

The Breakfast Room still retains its white-painted panelling and is only distinguished by its Corinthian cornice. In Horace Walpole's *Aedes* he lists nine paintings here, including Wootton's *Picture of Hounds* (SHM 9781). Dominating the room must have been Frans Snyders's *Concert of Birds* (SHM 607) which was then attributed to Mario di Fiori, or Mario Nuzzi, bought from the collection of Sir Robert's favourite royal craftsman, Grinling Gibbons. Other paintings that must have appealed to their owner's sporting interests were a *Head of a Horse* by Van Dyck[2] and a *Greyhound's Head* by Jan Wyck.[3] These works, which hung alongside portraits of Sir Robert's grandfather, Sir Edward Walpole (who built the first Houghton), neighbour Viscount

Townshend and Mr Harold, the gardener (cat. 4), reflect the rather informal family character of these rooms of everyday use. The inclusion of this last portrait of one of the servants is unexpected, and might suggest a closer relationship between this particular servant and master than was considered usual.

The furniture in the room by 1745 shows that it was used more as an office than an eating-room, 'where tenants come to account', as Sir Matthew Decker recalled in 1728.[4] There were walnut chairs, some with leather covers, two tables – probably plain – and a bureau; perhaps the mahogany one that stands in the room today. As in most of the ground-floor rooms, both furnishings and decoration were suitably simple and robust enough to withstand the rigours of the local hunting set who regularly met and drank here. However, everything is as well made and finished as in the celebrated rooms of state above.

1 Harley, 1737/8
2 Sold Sotheby's New York, 11 Jan. 1996, lot 66 as Studio of Sir Peter Paul Rubens
3 Formerly Gatchina Palace, now untraced
4 Decker, 1728

4 John Ellys

*c.*1701 – London 1757

Fulke Harold, the Gardener c.1736–44

Oil on canvas, 71 x 53.5 cm

Prov: Sir Robert Walpole, at Houghton Hall by 1744; then by descent to present owner

Lit: Vertue, III, p. 95; Walpole, 1747, p. 39; 1792 MS Inventory (Houghton M24c)

The Marquess of Cholmondeley

It is comparatively rare to find the gardener responsible for the grounds of a great country seat being honoured by the estate owner with a commissioned portrait.[1] Fulke Harold (d. April 1754) was gardener to Robert Walpole from at least 1718 and was engaged in laying out the garden and park.[2] In 1744 Fulke Harold's portrait hung among family portraits, 'Below stairs In the Breakfast Parlour Over the Glass Old Harold y Gardener'.

Sir Robert Walpole's selection of John Ellys to paint Harold's portrait is illuminating. A pupil of Sir James Thornhill (*c.*1716), Ellys is said to have worked with him on the decorative scheme at Greenwich. Ellys later studied in the Vanderbank Academy and gained a foothold in London society as a painter of portraits in the Kneller tradition. It is not clear when Sir Robert became interested in Ellys, but it is likely to have been through Walpole's influence that he succeeded Philip Mercier as Principal Painter to the Prince of Wales in 1736.

George Vertue records that Ellys received the appointment of Master Keeper of the Lions in the Tower of London through the favour of Sir Robert. For this post he

received nine shillings a day for feeding 'the royal beasts'. Ellys advised Sir Robert and purchased pictures on his behalf. He was, for example, at the collection sale of Charles Montagu, Earl of Halifax, where he purchased 'A Landscape, Highly Finished', attributed to Gaspar Poussin on behalf of Walpole.[3]

Sir Robert also sent Ellys abroad to buy pictures. Vertue records a 'large picture of the Virgin and the Angells by Vandyke' bought for Walpole by Ellys for £800 in Holland. This is Van Dyck's *Holy Family* which was with M. Valkenburg, Rotterdam in 1731 (now SHM 539; Fig. 28).

1 The identification of this portrait with Harold is by family tradition. The portrait was copied by George Farington and identified then as of Harold (watercolour, private collection).

2 See Yaxley, 1988, p. 87; see also cat. 21.B

3 8 March 1739–40, lot 87; *The Cascade*, 58.5 x 84.5 cm, SHM 1206 (Walpole, 1747, p. 93)

5 **Richard Earlom, after Frans Snyders**

A Concert of Birds, published 1 December 1778

Mezzotint, etched letter proof, 41.2 x 57.8 cm

Inscribed, [arms in centre] 'John Boydell excudit 1778. Mario di Fiori pinxit. Richd Earlom Sculpsit. / A CONCERT OF BIRDS. / In the Breakfast Room at Houghton / Size of the Picture 4.^{F} 7^{I} by 7.^{F} 9$^{1/4}$ long. / Published Decr 1.st by John Boydell Engraver in Cheapside London'

Lit: Boydell, II, no. 3; Wessely, 1886, 139. With the full inscription, the title in closed letters. This impression printed in brown ink

The Hon. Charles Lennox Boyd

This is a late state, printed in brown, which is a particularly successful representation of a painting that in Sir Robert's time was believed to be by Mario Nuzzi, also called di Fiori (*c.*1603–73). This oil is, in fact, one of the best variants of a theme Snyders turned to on a number of occasions during his career.

Horace Walpole himself commented upon the original oil in a manner that suggests that he himself doubted the attribution to Mario di Fiori: 'a very uncommon Picture, for he seldom painted anything but Flowers; it belonged to *Gibbins* The Carver, and is four Feet seven Inches high, by seven Feet nine and a quarter wide.' The detailed depiction of the subject matter would certainly have appealed to Grinling Gibbons.

Fig. 50 The Hunting Hall, 1986, showing the late eighteenth-century, painted Chinese wallpaper

The Hunting Hall
[The Family Dining Room]

The sober appearance of this room was altered at the end of the eighteenth century, when the original deal panelling was hung with blue Chinese wallpaper, which remains today. The Hunting Hall served as the principal eating room on the ground floor and was used for both breakfast and dinner (still in the afternoon in Sir Robert's day). Sir Edward Harley, later 2nd Earl of Oxford, described a typical breakfast with Sir Robert: 'The next morning all go down and breakfast in the hunting parlour, where Horace Walpole's [Robert's brother] picture is... For breakfast every body calls for what he will; people do not all come at a time, which is wrong...'[1]

By 1743 the room was dominated by two paintings – *Susanna and the Elders* by Rubens (SHM 496) and Wootton's *Hunting Piece* (see cat. 6). These larger canvases could only have been hung at either end of the room, as the windows and large, rusticated chimneypiece dominate the long walls. Their choice suggests that this room was very much a male preserve. The chimneypiece is made from stone and has a high, segmental pediment that encloses a mirror. It is so out of character with the those on the upper floor that it lends further credence to the idea that Gibbs was responsible for the initial designs for Houghton (see John Harris, pp. 20–4).

Sir Robert's Norfolk Congresses must have eaten here, sitting at four tables on some seventeen or more walnut chairs with leather seats, of which several sets remain in the house (cat. 7). The tables are likely to have been plain trestles that could be removed when not in use. All three rooms in this corner of the house had painted floor cloths, a practical choice given the reputation for lengthy meals and hard drinking at Houghton.

Between this room and the Breakfast Room was the Supping Parlour, a slightly finer room where the Norfolk gentry probably met Sir Robert in private. Off the Hunting Hall to the north is the Arcade, a long vaulted room, that was sparely decorated and furnished. This was the formal entrance to the ground floor and the main circulation space for both family and servants. It fulfilled the purpose of both entrance hall and long gallery, a room now out of fashion, where family and guests could stroll and gossip in bad weather.

1 Harley, 1737/8

6 **Daniel Lerpinière, after John Wootton**

A Hunting Piece, 1 December 1778

Line engraving, 47.8 x 61.1 cm

Inscribed, 'A HUNTING PIECE In the Hunting Hall at Houghton size of the Picture 6 F by 8 F.3.I long. Wootton Pinxit. John Boydell excudit, 1778. D Lerpinière Sculpsit. Mr Thos Turner Sr Robt. Walpole Coll Charles Churchill. Published Decr 1st 1778, by John Boydell Engraver in Cheapside London.' With the Arms of Sir Robert Walpole in the centre, inscribed: 'Fari Quae Sentiat'

Lit: Boydell, I, 56

Exh: London 1984A (59)

The Trustees of the British Museum (1977-u-940)

This engraving is in reverse of the original painting and shows Sir Robert Walpole seated on a grey hunter between Thomas Turner and Colonel Charles Churchill. The latter was the illegitimate nephew of the Duke of Marlborough and a loyal friend and supporter of Walpole. The original oil may be dated to the early 1720s and lent the room in which it originally hung its name and ambience.

A large painting at Petworth House, Sussex, *Sir Robert Walpole at the Hunstanton Meet*, shows Sir Robert in a similar pose, but with Thomas Turner taking centre stage.[1]

1 An earlier engraving of the subject by G. Bickham junior is included in the portfolio scrapbook prepared by Horace Walpole in 1743 for his *Aedes Walpolianae*, now in the Metropolitan Museum, New York.

7 **Anonymous English craftsman, first quarter of the eighteenth century**

Side chair or back stool, c.1725

Walnut and beech frame, with replacement brown leather upholstery and brass decorative nails, 100 x 58.5 x 65 cm

Prov: probably supplied to Sir Robert Walpole, Houghton Hall; by descent to present owner

Lit: Cornforth, 1987A, p. 125

The Marquess of Cholmondeley

This is a typical example of the many walnut chairs with leather seats remaining in the 'hunting suite' today, which come from the seventy-odd mentioned in the basement storey in the 1745 inventory. These show minor variations on a simple, high-backed, cabriole-leg chair with pad feet: a conventional shape common at the time.

The choice of so many walnut chairs on the ground and the upper floors, when great quantities of the newly fashionable mahogany were being used throughout the house, seems rather outmoded; indeed, by 1745 there may have been set of twenty-two mahogany 'French elbow chairs' in the Coffee Room opposite the Hunting Hall. This may be explained, together with more dated details such as the C-scrolls on the inside of the legs, if these chairs were provided before the new Hall was completed. However, the design of these chairs is entirely suited to the everyday, hard use that all the furniture in these rooms must have been subject to. The choice of leather covers in both eating and reception rooms is equally practical. Almost all of these chairs have had their leather replaced, and they remain in use today. Early upholstery surviving on similar-style chairs elsewhere in the house has seamed, square-profiled edges to the seats, decorated with thin braid. This was probably in common use on many of the chairs before being replaced with the present close-nailed finish.

8 Anonymous English craftsman, first quarter of the eighteenth century

Small side- or chamber table, c.1725

Mahogany, pine and oak carcase with mahogany veneer, brass handle
74 x 87.5 x 57 cm

Prov: probably supplied to Sir Robert Walpole, Houghton Hall; by descent to present owner

Lit: Cornforth, 1987A, p. 125, fig. 5

The Marquess of Cholmondeley

Sir Matthew Decker commented on the great quantity of mahogany used at Houghton; 'This wood is so general used, that even the water closet is made of the same' (1728), and three years later Sir Thomas Robinson was again impressed by the 'vast quantity' he saw. This use extended to everyday furniture, such as this small chamber table, several of which survive in the house today. As Geoffrey Beard discusses above, mahogany was supplied to Houghton in plank-form from 1725, so it is likely that such furniture as this was made on site. It appears to have rapidly taken over from walnut as the predominant timber for plain furniture, as well as being used for almost all of the unpainted joinery in the house.

There are two types of these small, single-drawer tables, which were probably used as dressing tables in the bedchambers on both the ground and the second floors. Although not identified as such in the earliest inventory, they seem to correspond in number to the dressing tables listed in 1792, and are what Thomas Chippendale would later describe as a 'Chamber Table'.[1] This particular version displays the simple form and good construction found in so much everyday furniture at Houghton. It also has pleasing details such as the 'pinched' corners to the tops and scalloped lappets on the legs, details that prevent this ordinary furniture from appearing too utilitarian.

1 Gilbert, 1978, pl. 426

9 Anonymous English craftsman, second quarter of the eighteenth century

Spindle-backed elbow chair, c.1730–40

Mahogany, 95 x 63 x 61 cm

Prov: probably made for Sir Robert Walpole, Houghton Hall; by descent to present owner

Lit: Cornforth, 1987A, p. 126, fig. 8

The Marquess of Cholmondeley

There were twenty-four of these unusual mahogany chairs listed in the Arcade in the 1745 inventory. They take the place of the low Windsor chairs often encountered in secondary or more modest halls in early eighteenth-century inventories. Such chairs were robust enough for heavy use but could be made in finer timber than normally associated with their traditional country counterparts. For example, Lord Burlington had eight mahogany Windsor chairs in the lower tribune or sub-hall of his villa at Chiswick.[1]

The chair's overall shape owes much to late seventeenth-century predecessors; in particular its rectilinear, railed construction, crested top rail and the rather drooping scroll arms. In addition, the small, ball finials to the back are a development from earlier chairs. The rail back and box-like construction appears to derive from locally made East Anglian chairs, but in this example the details are refined. Instead of spindle-turned rails there are finely turned, miniature columns and the whole has much squatter proportions than similar country chairs, suitable for a well-padded squire's

seat. Other sets of near-identical chairs, probably dating from later in the century, are found in the long galleries at Blickling Hall, Norfolk, and Audley End, Essex.

The chair's lower stretchers with feet attached make them very stable. This detail explains why they are locally known as 'drinking chairs'. However, their overall design may be of early Italian origin. In Johann Zoffany's celebrated painting of the *Tribuna of the Uffizi*, (Royal Collection, Windsor) painted in Florence in the 1770s, the Hon. Felton Hervey can be seen sitting in a chair with very similar arms and feet.

1 Rosoman, 1986, p. 99

10 **Thomas Ridding**

fl. London 1699–1705

Group of ten items of pewter plate, c.1720

Three plates, diameter 24.5 cm; one plate, diameter 51 cm; two plates, diameter 46 cm; three dishes, diameter 24 cm; one oval tureen, height 24 cm, depth 26 cm

Each engraved with the Walpole crest and inscribed 'HONI.SOI.QUI.MAL.Y.PENSE'; stamped 'THOMAS / RIDDING', flanking a dragon and also stamped; Ridding' and 'X' beneath a crown

Prov: supplied to Sir Robert Walpole, Earl of Orford, for Houghton; by descent to the present owner. Thirty items from this group were sold Christie's 8 December 1994 (lots 121–5)

The Marquess of Cholmondeley

Thomas Ridding was made a Freeman of the Worshipful Company of Pewterers by patrimony, 22 June 1699. He was almost certainly the son of the pewterer Thomas Ridding of London, and started trading with him in 1705. These items were part of a much larger group originally at Houghton, and are referred to in the inventory of 1745. In the Store Room there were 'Forty six dozen and half of Pewter plates'. The 1792 inventory records 'In the press in the Maid's Room 49 round Pewter dishes 18 round ditto ... 4 old round dishes 36 Doz and 9 Meat Plates'. In the Cholmondeley archive at Cambridge University an account book (no. 22) lists sums paid to a pewterer called Ridding, during the period 1717–27.

Fig. 51 The Common Parlour, north and west walls, 1996, showing mostly walnut furniture typical of the family rooms on the main and bedchamber floors

The Common Parlour

This large but simply decorated room was the everyday eating room in the southern, family half of the 'Grand Story'. Unlike the Supper and Hunting rooms below, it is unclear quite how and when it was used in the eighteenth century. However, its position meant that it also acted as an ante-room to Sir Robert's own apartment, which consisted of his Library and Bedchamber beyond.

Beneath an uncoloured, Inigo Jones-inspired ceiling, the walls have light-coloured wainscoting. Ribbon and flower mouldings ornament the panelling, with occasional flourishes such as the volutes of the windows that sprout trails of husks at the bottom. The white paint is only relieved by the part-gilt pier-glass with carved drapery festoons above it, and by the unusual gilded drops of fruit and flowers above the chimneypiece. Horace Walpole mentions that the latter were made of pear-tree wood by Grinling Gibbons and that they framed Sir Godfrey Kneller's portrait of Gibbons. This description suggests that they might have come from the old house and were gilded at a later date.

The chimneypiece is made up of contrasting white statuary marble with purple-and-white Seravezza marble. The former is carved with a Bacchic libation urn, draped with oak-leaf swags, a reminder of the purpose of this room. Above, the frieze is filled with vine leaves.

The choice of paintings for the Common Parlour was a mixture – predominantly seventeenth-century portraits, mythological and genre subjects, but with some religious pictures. Eventually it included three paintings by Kneller; *William III* and *George I* and the Spanish poet *Joseph Carreras* (cat. 13). It is tempting to see such a picture hang as a deliberate attempt by Sir Robert to give his splendid but very new 'palace' a greater sense of history. The royal portraits can also be seen as a show of loyalty to the Whig ascendancy. (For a discussion of the picture hang of the Common Parlour see cat. 14.) These paintings may have been specially framed in the type of Kentian, eared frames shown as overdoors in Isaac Ware's cross-section of this room from his Houghton volume.

In the inventory of 1745 there were several tables and twenty-four walnut chairs (later described with leather seats), suitable for dining. The great giltwood chandelier in the room today may well be an original survivor from Houghton in its heyday, although it was not listed as hanging in this room.

11 Salvator Rosa

Arenella 1615 – Rome 1673

Portrait of a Man, 1640s

Oil on canvas, 78 x 64.5 cm

Prov: Sir Robert Walpole, Grosvenor Street, London, by 1736; Common Dining Parlour, Houghton Hall, 1744; by descent to George Walpole, 3rd Lord Orford; bought by Catherine II of Russia, 1779

Lit: 1736 MS; 1744 MS; Walpole, 1747, p. 46; Boydell, I, 40; Vsevolozhskaya and Kostenevich, 1984, pp. 249–50

The State Hermitage Museum, St Petersburg (SHM 1483)

Rosa, in common with Claude Lorrain, was especially popular with English collectors in the eighteenth century. Sir Robert Walpole was no exception and possessed two spectacular examples of this romantic artist's large canvases, both now in the State Hermitage Museum, St Petersburg. In the Gallery at Houghton hung *Democritus and Protagoras* (SHM 31) a later work that Horace Walpole described as 'in his fine taste'.[1] Another large and impressive canvas by Rosa, *The Prodigal Son*, dating from the 1650s, hung in the Gallery at Houghton. (Fig. 34)[2]

Rosa's few portraits are among his most successful works, often essentially romantic in character. This portrait has been thought to represent a brigand, but it was not given this interpretation until it was engraved in 1777 by J.-B. Michel for Boydell's *Houghton Gallery*, when it was entitled *A Captain of Banditti*. Filippo Baldinucci, the seventeenth-century biographer of Italian artists, reports that Salvator Rosa painted a self-portrait in Florence, wearing the costume of Pascariello, including torn gloves. Commissioned by one Girolamo Signoretti, the portrait later belonged to Cardinal Leopoldo de' Medici. Rosa was an amateur actor and the anecdote could indeed refer to this portrait in which the sitter wears an ill-fitting glove.[3]

1 'The Fate of the old man, & his sons trying to break the bundle of sticks 6.0 x 4.2¼', 1736 MS

2 SHM 34; oil on canvas, 253.5 x 201 cm

3 A fourth Rosa is Walpole, 1747, p. 64: 'Three soldiers: a fine little Picture... in his brightest manner'; Eng. Boydell, II, 60. George Walpole sold a further three paintings attributed to Rosa in 1751 (Houlditch MSS, 13 June, lot 20; 14 June, lots 43, 44)

12 Frans Hals

Antwerp 1580/85 – Haarlem 1666

Portrait of a Seated Man, c.1646–8

Oil on canvas, 68 x 56 cm

Signed with monogram

Prov: Sir Robert Walpole by 1736; by descent to George Walpole, 3rd Earl of Orford, by whom sold to Catherine II of Russia, 1779; bought from the Soviet Union in 1930 by M. Knoedler & Co. for Andrew Mellon; given by him to the National Gallery of Art, Washington, DC, 1937 (NGA 1937.1.71)

Lit: 1736 MS; Walpole, 1747, p. 46; Boydell I, 39; Slive, 1970, no. 167

National Gallery of Art, Washington, DC

Horace Walpole wrongly catalogued this painting as a self-portrait by Hals. This attribution stayed with the painting when it was engraved in reverse by J.-B. Michel in 1777 for John Boydell. The print also recorded the wrong measurements for the painting.[1] The title was first questioned by Bode in 1883.[2]

Horace Walpole regarded Dutch painters as servile imitators and 'drudging Mimicks of Nature's most uncomely Coarseness...' However, Frans Hals was sufficiently thought of in England by the middle of the eighteenth century to merit an anecdotal reference by George Vertue.[3] Horace Walpole revered him (erroneously) as the master of Kneller. The connection with Kneller presumably led to the decision to hang the painting in the Common Parlour with a number of Kneller's portraits, notably his fine portrait of Grinling Gibbons (SHM 1346).

1 Michel was working from a copy made for the engraver by George Farington.

2 W. Bode *Studien zür Geschichle der Holländischen Malerei*, Brunswick 1883

3 Vertue, II, p. 141

13 Sir Godfrey Kneller

Lübeck 1646 – London 1723

Joseph Carreras, c.1685

Oil on canvas, 72.5 x 63.7 cm

Signed, lower right; 'G. k.'

Prov: Sir Robert Walpole, Grosvenor Street, London, by 1736; by descent to George Walpole, 3rd Earl of Orford; Catherine II of Russia, 1779; sold 1854, by Nicholas I; Dr Ochotchinski, St Petersburg, by 1913; Baron Balthasar Ungern Sternberg; Dr E.I. Michel, London, 1972; bought by Lady Cholmondeley 1975

Exh: London 1971/B (no. 77)

Lit: Vertue, III, p. 44; Walpole, 1747, p. 46; Walpole, 1888, II, p. 205; Stewart, 1971, pp. 61–2; Boydell, I, 15

The Marquess of Cholmondeley

Kneller was the most influential society painter of his time. Having settled in England in 1676 he was soon taken up at court. His portrait of the Spanish poet Joseph Carreras dates from before the artist was appointed Principal Painter to William and Mary in 1688, and amply demonstrates his ability to interpret character and likeness with, in this case, a subtlety of palette that recalls the painters of the Venetian late Cinquecento. Horace Walpole commented in his *Anecdotes*:

A portrait at Houghton of Joseph Carreras, a poet and chaplain to Catherine of Lisbon, has the force and simplicity of that master [Tintoretto], without owing part of its merit to Tintoret's universal black drapery, to his own afterwards neglected draperies, or to his master Rembrandt's unnatural chiaroscuro.

George Vertue, too, esteemed this portrait highly: 'a bold head of Kneller one of the most capital.' Sybil Cholmondeley rightly regarded her purchase of this canvas in 1975 as a particular triumph, being the only painting sold to Catherine the Great to return to hang at Houghton.

14 Unidentified draughtsman

A plan of the picture hang in the Common Parlour, c.1742

Sepia and black ink on laid paper, 75.6 x 54 cm

Prov: Houghton Hall archive A/65; by descent to present owner

The Marquess of Cholmondeley

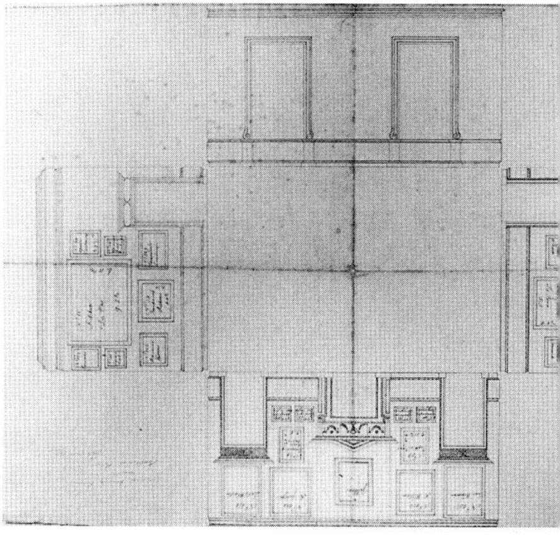

The plan shows a total of twenty-seven pictures covering the painted panelling, which matches the number recorded by Horace Walpole in his *Aedes*, compiled by 1743. In the *Aedes* Horace sometimes indicates the layout of the rooms, but usually specifies only the overmantels or overdoors. He rarely bothers to indicate left or right, south or north. Such details are, however, in the inventory of 1744.

There are a number of significant differences between the picture plan shown here and those recorded by Horace Walpole and the 1744 inventory. This plan does not show Sir Robert's *Venus bathing, with Cupids in a Car* by Andrea Sacchi (SHM 127), nor the *Nativity* by Carlo Cignani, nor Van Dyck's *Sir Thomas Challoner* (SHM 551) and a further series of portraits by Mor, Hals, Kneller, Rembrandt, Rosa and Rubens. At the same time the plan does show significantly more pictures for the Common Parlour than were hanging in 1736. One may conclude that this plan was made before the paintings from London came to Houghton after Sir Robert's resignation from office. It is one of a series of such plans surviving at Houghton (see also cats. 56, 69).

It is interesting to note that, despite subsequent changes, a certain continuity was preserved in the room. The portrait of Grinling Gibbons by Kneller (SHM 1346) hung in the Common Parlour from at least 1736, as did the Wharton family portraits of Anne Lee, later Lady Wharton, and Mrs Jenny Deering. The final ensemble of portraits of the European schools, together with two 'Cook's Shops' by Martin de Vos (SHM 610) and Teniers (SHM 586), were the focus of the Parlour Room. As befitted a dining room, two royal portraits graced the walls, those of William III and George I by Kneller.[1]

1 Both sold to Catherine II, 1779, these were destroyed during the Second World War when hanging at the Gatchina Palace.

Fig. 52 Sir Robert Walpole's Study, 1994

The Study

[The Library]

Sir Robert's Study, as the Library is referred to in the inventory of 1745, is a relatively small room in one of the corner towers of the house. However, its effect is quite imposing because of the way in which the bindings of the books are designed to enhance the architecture of the room itself. Opposite the Palladian window (as it appears from the outside) the mahogany presses rise and fill an arched recess, flanked by 'pilasters' of gilt spines. The bookshelves are all finely carved with architectural ornament and at the bases of the pilasters are concealed drawers with mahogany linings that still appear as new. Visiting Houghton in 1728 Sir Matthew Decker summed up the effect of this Library succinctly: 'in which are many valuable books bound, and so neatly and well placed that it makes a perfect picture.'

In many histories Sir Robert has gained a somewhat unjustified reputation as a workaholic who devoted any spare time to hunting and drinking. Such a neatly contrived library, where a missing book can ruin the effect, might seem to confirm this view. However, as J.H. Plumb has pointed out, he was in fact a well-educated man for the period, a colleger at Eton who went on to King's College, Cambridge, and the conventional yet scholarly collection of books reflected his genuine interests. The impressive way in which he displayed his library also reveals a pride in his father's academic reputation 'for study and learning extraordinary', for it contains many of his books as well.[1] Not surprisingly Sir Robert's name and that of his eldest son appear in the subscribers' lists of several of the most important architectural books of the day.

The Library is still dominated by Kneller's full-length portrait of George I, in a heavy Kent frame. This is the only painting in the room listed in Horace

Walpole's catalogue. Opposite it is a heavy-looking and rather old-fashioned writing table, which originally had a plainer companion piece. In spite of their size, there were also eleven chairs, later described as with blue damask. Given that we know that everyday business transactions took place in rooms below, the large number of chairs in this small room may mean that it served equally as an ante-room to Sir Robert's bedchamber, which is smaller still. Intriguingly, by 1745 there were also two telescopes made by Navine and Blunt; these conjure up images of the great builder and landowner of Houghton surveying his estate from the comfort of the Library.

1 Plumb, 1956, p. 82 (quoting *Lives of the Norths*, 1826 p. 304)

15 Edmund Prideaux

Norwich? 1693 Prideaux Place, Padstow 1745

Album of topographical views of England, c.1716–1727, open at a view of Houghton Hall from the west, c.1725

Pen and wash on paper, 26.7 x 40.6 cm (album size)

Inscribed, 'Houghton Rt: Hon: Sr: Robt: Walpole. Norfolk'

Prov: Edmund Prideaux, d. 1745; by descent to present owner

Lit: Harris, 1964, pp. 19–21, 29, 30; Harris, 1988, p. 6; Harris, 1989, p. 93; Yaxley, 1988, p. 92

P.J.N. Prideaux-Brune Esq.

The drawing shown is bound in a very early-surviving album of views of English houses made by the antiquarian and amateur draughtsman, Edmund Prideaux. He was the son of another antiquarian, the Dean of Norwich, Humphrey Prideaux. Edmund seems to have made several tours of England visiting various houses, many with family connections in Norfolk and the West Country (most notably Prideaux Place, Cornwall), drawing as he went. These views were subsequently bound into an album.

John Harris has dated Prideaux's view of Houghton under construction to around 1725, when completion of the first, southwest cupola, shown in the drawing, was commemorated in its pierced weather-vane. This would make this the earliest view of Houghton as built and it gives important evidence that James Gibbs's domes were original features and did not replace the Wilton-style towers that Colen Campbell drew in his engraving for *Vitruvius Britannicus*, III. It is clear from the drawing that the uncompleted house had a number of ordinary hipped roofs, placed directly above the cornice, presumably to make the house partially habitable during its ten or so years of construction.

In front of the western entrance is a temporary building that was probably the masons' lodgings, which is roughly on the site of the old house. The drawing also confirms the early layout of the formal parterre to the west of the house, leading to a wide double avenue, flanked by clipped yew or cypress trees. Behind the enclosing standard trees to either side appear the taller trees of the wildernesses and the chimneys of the wings of the house.

The presence of figures in formal dress may indicate that the house was occupied at this date or could merely be artistic licence. Generally, Prideaux's view is a little naive and tends to distort the proportions of the house. However, these technical limitations are likely to show that he was striving to record what he actually saw and that the details in the drawing are probably reliable.

---

16 Walpole Correspondence; manuscript letters, bills, etc

Prov: Sir Robert Walpole, then by descent to present owner

The Marquess of Cholmondeley

Although Sir Robert built himself a handsome library for housing his books, he made no provision for storing documents. The destruction of his papers began quite early in his career. On 19 June 1721 Jonas Rolfe, who was acting as his steward, wrote:

> I am writing to you in your honour's study where I have a thousand ungrateful companions the Mice who doe dayly dispoyle to youre papers, parchments and bookes, especially those bound in vellum which I could wish were put up in boxes or removed 'till some fitter place might be fixed up for them, the vermin having nibled holes and made free passages in to the drawers, they roame in such numbers 'tis impossible to think of destroying them unless the whole be removed; in the mean time what are yett untouched by them are very insecure...

Most of Sir Robert's papers must have been kept at his town house, first at Arlington Street, then Downing Street, or Chelsea. John Plumb has pointed out that it is possible that many were destroyed at the time of the Committee of Secrecy, which investigated his ministry with a view to impeachment, in 1742. Certainly, very few private letters survive and these are mostly early family letters. Nevertheless, the manuscript collection relating to Walpole, now in the care of the University Library, Cambridge, is extensive.[1]

The manuscripts that remain with the family are, by comparison, very few. Those still at Houghton offer material mainly on estate business, but do contain some bills and accounts, which inform this publication. A selection of these is:

A bill from John Howard, framemaker, to Sir Robert Walpole, 1729

Pen and ink on paper, 32.2 x 19.8 cm

Houghton archive, RBI, 45

Drawn up by Howard in 1729 in the sum of £78 1s. 2d., and was finally paid 16 June 1731.[2]

A letter from M. de Thoms to Sir Robert Walpole, Rome, 6 December 1737

Pen and ink on paper, 22.8 x 19 cm

Houghton archive, RBI, 44

De Thoms informs Sir Robert of a painting by Carlo Maratti, *The History of Rebecca*. He also offers 'the eight famous pieces done by Nicola[s] Poussin, of the Sacraments. The Duke of Orleans has eight which Poussin did after them, but these are better. They are in pawn at Prince Panfili's, who neither does understand them nor cares for them'. It is said Sir Robert made the purchase but that their export was opposed. The set was eventually bought in 1785 by James Byres for the Duke of Rutland of Belvoir Castle (*in situ*).

A bill to Sir Robert Walpole for work undertaken by William Hubert, 8 May 1730

Pen and ink on paper, 23 x 18.7 cm

Houghton archive, RBI, 47

William Hubert's bill, presented on 8 May 1730, was receipted by G. Hubert on 16 May 1730. The bill is for work including repairs to '4 Pair of French mettle Branches with oval Backs & masks finely Repaird: £16.0.0' and '8 Branches for the two Oval large Glass sconces finely Repaird at 17.6 each: £7.0.0'. It also includes 'A fine french lustre neatly Repaird, composed of french mettle & cristal cutt: £35.0.0'. The entire bill amounted to £92 4s. and indicates that Sir Robert was employing French metalworkers working in England.

1 Chinnery, 1953, p. 5
2 Moore p. 52

17 'A Catalogue of the Right Hon.ble Sir Robert Walpole's Collection of Pictures, 1736'

Autograph MS, thirty-six folios, 24.2 x 13.8 cm, bound into the author's copy of *Aedes Walpolianae*... 2nd edn, London 1752 (with extensive annotations)

Prov: Horace Walpole; Strawberry Hill Sale, 25–28 April 1842, Holloway (dealer); Willis (dealer); J.W. Ford (his sale, Sotheby's, 5–7 May 1904, lot 642); Francis Harvey; purchased J. Pierpont Morgan, 1904

New York, The Pierpont Morgan Library (PML 7586)

This manuscript catalogue is the earliest record of the collection of paintings Sir Robert Walpole had amassed by 1736. His collection was at that time housed at Houghton (120 paintings), Downing Street (154 paintings), Grosvenor Street (66 paintings), and at Chelsea (78 paintings). The process of amalgamating the collection at Houghton had taken place by the time Horace Walpole had compiled the first edition of his *Aedes Walpolianae*, 24 August 1743.

The manuscript makes it clear which paintings were hung at Houghton by 1736. At that time, for example, the four market scenes by Frans Snyders were hanging in the Saloon, as suggested in the plans of William Kent: only once the picture gallery was built could they be moved to make room in the Saloon for pictures brought from

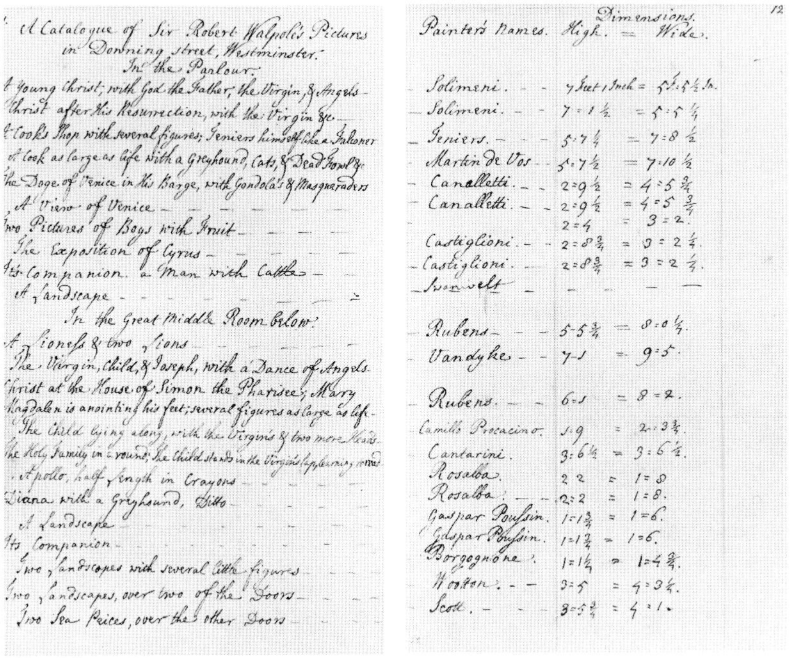
A Catalogue of Sir Robert Walpole's Pictures in Downing street, Westminster.

In the Parlour.

	Painter's Names.	Dimensions. High.	= Wide.
A Young Christ, with God the Father, the Virgin, & Angels	Solimeni	7 feet 1 Inch	= 5 f. 5 ½ In.
Christ after His Resurrection, with the Virgin &c.	Solimeni	7 = 1 ½	= 5 : 5 ¼
A Cook's Shop with several figures; Teniers himself like a Falconer	Teniers	5 : 7 ¼	= 7 : 8 ½
A Cook as large as life with a Greyhound, Cats, & Dead Fowl &c.	Martin de Vos	5 : 7 ½	= 7 : 10 ½
The Doge of Venice in his Barge, with Gondola's & Masqueraders	Canalletti	2 = 9 ½	= 4 : 5 ¾
A View of Venice	Canalletti	2 = 9 ½	= 4 = 5 ¾
Two Pictures of Boys with Fruit		2 = 4	= 3 = 2
The Exposition of Cyrus	Castiglioni	2 = 8 ¾	= 3 = 2 ¼
Its Companion a Man with Cattle	Castiglioni	2 = 8 ¾	= 3 = 2 ¼
A Landscape	Swanevelt		

In the Great Middle Room below.

A Lioness & two Lions	Rubens	5 - 5 ¾	= 8 : 0 ¼
The Virgin, Child, & Joseph, with a Dance of Angels	Vandyke	7 - 1	= 9 : 5
Christ at the House of Simon the Pharisee; Mary Magdalen is anointing his feet; several figures as large as life	Rubens	6 = 1	= 8 = 2
The Child lying along, with the Virgin's & two more Heads	Camillo Procacino	1 : 9	= 2 : 3 ¾
The Holy Family in a round; the Child stands in the Virgin's lap, leaning	Cantarini	3 : 6 ½	= 3 : 6 ½
Apollo, half length in Crayons	Rosalba	2 2	= 1 = 8
Diana with a Greyhound, Ditto	Rosalba	2 : 2	= 1 : 8
A Landscape	Gaspar Poussin	1 = 1 ¾	= 1 = 6
Its Companion	Gaspar Poussin	1 = 1 ¾	= 1 = 6
Two Landscapes with several little figures	Borgognone	1 = 1 ¼	= 1 = 4 ¾
Two Landscapes, over two of the Doors	Wootton	3 = 5	= 4 : 3 ¼
Two Sea Peices, over the other Doors	Scott	3 = 5 ¾	= 4 : 1

London. The character of the Green Velvet Drawing Room as planned by Kent was also well established as the 'Carlo Maratti Room' in 1736, although Sir Robert had yet to acquire the Maratti portrait of Pope Clement IX (cat. 45).

The two enormous canvases by Pier Francesco Mola, *Lucius Curtius jumping into the Gulph* [sic] and *Horatius Cocles defending the Bridge* (both now Academy of Arts, St Petersburg) hung in the 'Great Room above Stairs' at Downing Street. So too did 'twelve Water Colour Landscapes' attributed to 'Ritzi', presumably Marco Ricci (1676–1730).[1] The majority of the Wharton collection of portraits by Van Dyck was housed in the 'Great Room' at Grosvenor Street.

The final folios include a list of twenty-four 'Pictures bought since the catalogue was made'. These include Van Dyck's *Inigo Jones* (SHM 557) and Rembrandt's *Abraham going to sacrifice Isaac* (SHM 727). This manuscript survives to record a signal moment in the course of Sir Robert's very active career as a collector.

1 These were in addition to the total of 154 paintings cited above.

18 An Inventory of 'Pictures &c at Houghton 1744'

MS, seven folios, pen and ink, 18.5 x 30 cm

Prov: the Lytton family archive; the Cobbold family; on deposit to Hertford Record Office

Lord David Cobbold (Hertford Record Office, K 1547)

The particular interest of this 1744 inventory of the paintings at Houghton lies in the seventh folio, which contains the earliest known plan of the picture hang in the newly established Picture Gallery at Houghton. The handwriting accords well with that of the 1736 inventory and is likely to have been Horace Walpole's own inventory.[1]

Unusually, the picture plan includes some of the prices paid for certain paintings. The cost of Snyders's *Fruit Market* (SHM 596) is shown as £200; the two large canvases by Mola each cost £150; the *Adoration of the Shepherds* attributed to Palma Vecchio cost £300. Two paintings that hung on the north side of the gallery are costed. The first, *The Doctors of the Church* by Guido Reni (SHM 59) (which

Horace Walpole regarded 'the first in this collection') is noted as having cost £700. A similar pride of place was given to the second, Salvator Rosa's *Prodigal Son* (SHM 34), which cost £500. Another painting by Guido in the collection, *The Adoration of the Shepherds* (here called 'Child in the Manger'), also cost Sir Robert £500.

These prices may be compared with those paid by the Empress Catherine II in 1779. Catherine paid £1,000 for the group of four market scenes by Snyders; £400 each for the paintings by Mola; £250 for the Palma Vecchio; £3,500 for *The Doctors of the Church* and £400 for *The Adoration of the Shepherds* by Guido; £700 for Rosa's *Prodigal Son*. The 3rd Earl of Orford may be seen to have gained a return of £5,900 on his grandfather's outlay of £2,500, excluding inflation, on just seven pictures.

1 Of Murillo's *Ascension* (SHM 387) in the Saloon he writes: 'I call it the ascension of our Savour & have Ld Orford's Authority for it; but, 'tis commonly call'd the Assumption of the V.Mary tho indeed ye Figure is too young for sitter.'

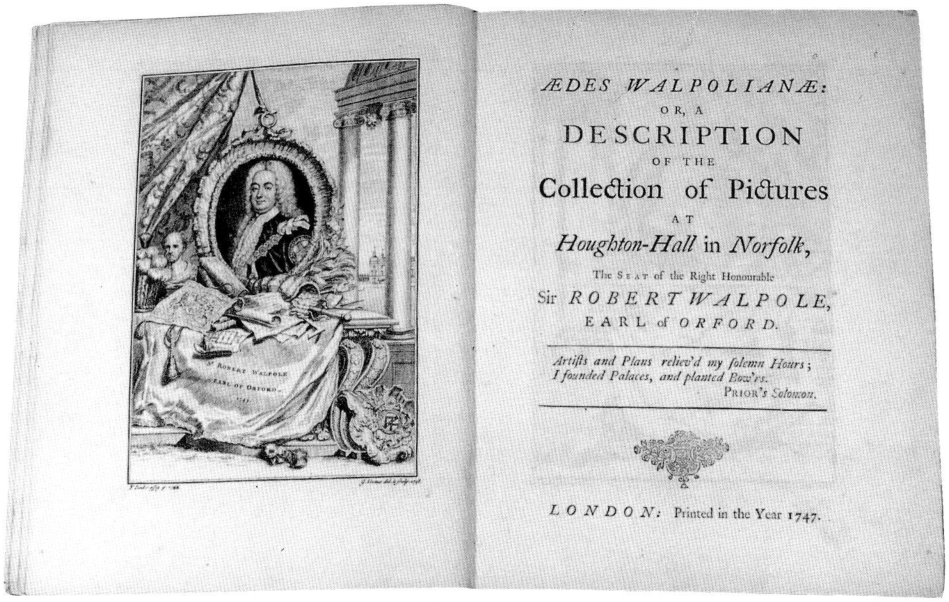

19 ***Aedes Walpolianae: or, a Description of the Collection of Pictures at Houghton Hall in Norfolk, The Seat of the Right Honourable Sir Robert Walpole, Earl of Orford***

Private edition, with manuscript additions in brown ink, 1747, quarto, 29.5 x 22.5 cm

Prov: William Cole (1714–82)

The Marquess of Cholmondeley

Horace Walpole's creation of Strawberry Hill, together with his characteristically critical views expressed later in life about the affairs of Houghton, have combined to overshadow his real affection for his father's Norfolk home. Indeed, Houghton was of seminal importance to Horace in the development of his early connoisseurship. The compilation and publication of his *Aedes Walpolianae* was the direct result of the experience gained on his Grand Tour (March 1739 – September 1741), during which he acquired works of art for both himself and his father; when Horace Mann finally received a copy he wrote to Horace from Florence on 20 June 1749 of Dr Antonio Cocchi's view, who 'was very sincere, and as you know he is a judge, I can't help telling you that he thinks the observations extremely just, is pleased with the idea of the whole as being quite new, and thinks it the best compendium upon painting that has been wrote, and that the characters of the great masters are most judicious'.[1]

In the summer of 1742 Horace Walpole visited Houghton and composed a 'Sermon on Painting' which was delivered before his father by his chaplain. This referred to several of the pictures at Houghton and was later published as part of the *Aedes Walpolianae*. The twenty-nine-page introduction, completed the following summer, was Horace Walpole's first published art criticism. Horace introduced his catalogue of the pictures at Houghton with some pride: 'There are not a great many Collections left in *Italy*, more worth seeing than this at Houghton: In the Preservation of the Pictures, it certainly excells most of them.' His judgements were coloured by the fact that he had never visited Holland and Flanders, but the entire publication, which included the 'Sermon', the 'Introduction', 'A Description of the Pictures' and a poem entitled 'A Journey to Houghton' by the Revd Mr Whaley, as well as an admiring dedication to Sir Robert, form a lasting memorial to the collection.

This edition includes, bound-in, a manuscript priced list of the Houghton paintings, provided 16 April 1779 by Thomas Lombe (1719–1800), an attorney at Cambridge who was also a collector. Horace wrote on 2 June 1779 to inform Cole that he would be pleased to receive Lombe's list as this was the first opportunity he had to view the values determined for their sale to the Empress Catherine. On 12 July Horace wrote at length on receipt of a transcribed copy of the list, 'I confess I think them much overvalued'. On page 122 Cole records that at one stage Henry Bromley, 1st Lord Montfort (1705–55) had tried to purchase part of the collection. Elsewhere he records that the Empress Catherine paid £36,000.

1 Horace Walpole may have been inspired by the first published catalogue of pictures in any English country house, Count Carlo Gambarini's *Description of the Earl of Pembroke's pictures*, 1731.

20 Horace Walpole's *Aedes Walpolianae*, 2nd edition, 1752, with manuscript notes, values and diagrams showing the position of the pictures at Houghton Hall before their sale, 1779

Printed book with manuscript additions, 29.5 x 22.5 cm

Prov: Sir Robert Hyde Greg; bequeathed by him to the Fitzwilliam Museum, Cambridge, 1953

The Syndics of The Fitzwilliam Museum, Cambridge

The importance of this bound-in edition of Horace Walpole's *Aedes Walpolianae* lies in a series of manuscript diagrams depicting the arrangement of pictures at Houghton in a number of key rooms. Four folios are devoted to the Picture Gallery and have particular interest in so far as they are not exclusively schematic. They attempt to capture, with simple flourishes of the pen, the Kentian frames in which the paintings were displayed and also measurements, architectural features and even the disposition of furniture about the gallery.

Six folios record prices for the paintings, which are likely to be on-the-spot attempts at valuing the collection. This could relate to an insurance exercise, but is more probably a record of an early valuation for sale of about 1778. As such, it may relate to the visit of Benjamin West and Giovanni Baptista Cipriani to advise the third Lord Orford.

A second bound-in edition of the *Aedes*, now in the collection of the University Library, Cambridge, also contains a manuscript valuation of the Houghton paintings. This is recorded as being Philip Tassaert's valuation, in a manuscript note 'copied from Mr. Christie's catalogue Nov. 9th 1824'. Philip Joseph Tassaert (1731–1803) was a painter, restorer and picture dealer who advised James Christie and was almost certainly the 'competent' who accompanied Christie to Houghton in November 1778.

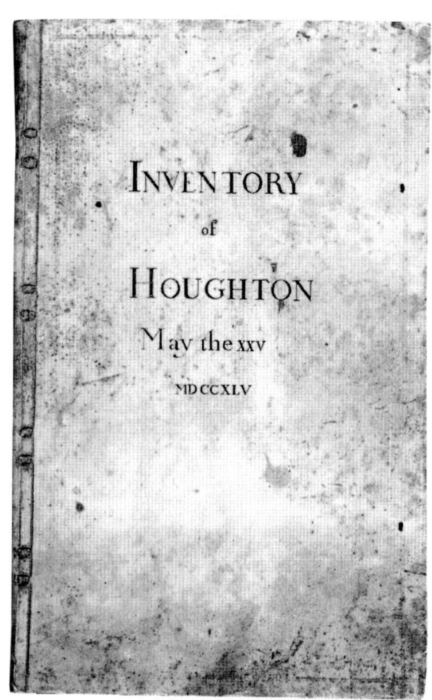

21 Inventory of Houghton, 25 May 1745

Manuscript folios, ink, bound in reverse calf, 32 x 21 cm

Prov: taken at Sir Robert Walpole's death; then by descent to present owner; Houghton archive M24h

The Marquess of Cholmondeley

The 1745 inventory of the contents of Houghton Hall on the death of Sir Robert Walpole is the most complete record of just how the furniture and contents were planned and graded in accordance with the importance of the rooms. The inventory reveals how Sir Robert's collection was dispersed throughout Houghton, with differing degrees of emphasis that directly correlate to the overall interior decoration of the house. In this respect it is a more revealing document than Horace Walpole's *Aedes Walpolianae*, which concentrates upon the paintings with only some attention to the architectural and decorative features of certain rooms. The 1745 inventory and the *Aedes*, when read in conjunction with each other, provide the most comprehensive survey of Sir Robert's active patronage of architects, artists and craftsmen that could possibly be surmised.

The inventory also records the 'Utensils in the Gardens, taken May the 4th: 1745' and 'Mr Harolds Utensils, taken May the 9th: 1745'. The latter included 'one little cart, and Water Tub on D°; Two Water Pott's; One Wheel Barrow; Two saws for Pruning and six chissels; One Hoe and two skuffle's; Three Picks and four Grub Axes; One Crab Apple Press for Verjuice; one foot plough'.

22 Paul de Lamerie

's Hertogenbosch 1688 – London 1751

The Walpole Inkstand, London 1729

Britannia Standard silver, 30.3 x 30 cm, weight 94 ounces

Prov: Sir Robert Walpole, 1st Earl of Orford, and then by descent; Christie's 14 December 1988, lot 249; Spink and Son Ltd; J. Ortiz-Patiño

Exh: *Paul de Lamerie, At the Sign of the Golden Ball: An Exhibition of the Work of England's Master Silversmith, 1688–1751*, Goldsmith's Hall, London, 16 May – 22 June 1990, no. 51

Lit: Banister, 1989

The J. Ortiz-Patiño Collection

The Treasury inkstand illustrated here stands on four anthemian and scroll feet. It has a central hinge with a double lid. The covers are engraved in the centre with, on one side, the arms of Sir Robert Walpole and those of his first wife, Catherine Shorter, and on the other the Walpole crest and motto. Both are flanked by supporters. The arms and edges of the lid have flat-chased decorative borders inside. The inkstand houses a pen tray on one side and on the other a cylindrical inkpot and cover, and a pounce pot with pierced cover. Each has an engraved square frame and two empty rectangular wells.

The inkstand was commissioned by Sir Robert Walpole, and was the first of two of this type that he had made. The second, dating from 1733–4, which now belongs to the Governor and Company of the Bank of England, was commissioned for Peter Burrell (1692–1756) of Langley Park, Beckenham, Kent, whose monogram it bears. He was, as Horace Walpole wrote, 'attached to my father'.

Both inkstands are of a type known as Treasury inkstands. They are thought to have derived from those given by the Treasury in 1686 to the Lords of the Council, but the form can be traced back to an example made in about 1669 by John Ruslen. Stylistically the inkstand is closely related to the Walpole Salver (cat. 60).

Fig. 53 (above) The Little Bed Chamber, 1921. Sir Robert's bedchamber with its mahogany panelling. The marble bath is a later addition. (below) The Little Dressing Room, 1921.

The Little Bed Chamber and Little Dressing Room

[The Marble Dressing Room and The Dowager's Dressing Room]

The first of these two rooms was Sir Robert's own bedchamber, which was reached via the Common Parlour and the Library. As with the latter room, it is entirely lined in mahogany, only here the walls are articulated with Ionic pilasters. A screen of square columns separates the bed alcove, where the damask bed stood, and there are little closets with curved doors on each side. (The alcove now contains an Edwardian marble-lined bath.)

The Earl of Oxford described Sir Robert's bedroom somewhat disdainfully: 'I took notice of Sir Robert's own bedchamber; the bed shut up in a box, a case made of mahogany with glass, as if it was a cabin...'[1] By 1745 a painted taffeta bed stood in place of the 'great damask bed' that was mentioned by Sir Matthew Decker in 1728. This has now gone but was probably similar to one surviving on the bedchamber storey today.

Over the modest, grey-and-white marble chimneypiece, hung Michael Dahl's portrait of Sir Robert's first wife, Catherine Shorter (cat. 23). She does not appear to have shared the bedchamber or indeed the house itself, as the couple led largely separate lives by the late 1720s. By 1743 the three-quarter length portrait of his second wife, Maria Skerrett (cat. 24), was hung opposite, facing her predecessor.

Through another pair of sound-deadening double doors, a servant's ante-room leads to the Little Dressing Room. This formed the closet to the main family apartment on the principal floor, with the Blue Damask Bedchamber in the larger, southwest corner room.

The Dressing Room is more delicately decorated than the Little Bedchamber, with Corinthian pilasters and painted wainscoting. This lightness might indicate that the room was originally designed to form part of Lady Walpole's apartment, although there is no record of it having ever been called by her name. Over the chimney was a Claudian landscape by Walpole's favourite landscape painter, Wootton (cat. 25). By 1745 there was a blue silk 'field-bed' (a demountable four-poster) in the room.

It is interesting to note that in the progression of rooms on this floor, following the order in Horace Walpole's catalogue, no architectural gilding appears until the next room, the Blue Damask Chamber (although the Dressing Room has been altered at a later date). Because this larger bedroom and its adjoining drawing room lead off from the Saloon, Kent and his associates must have decided that these west-facing family rooms were important enough to warrant some gilding, although by no means to the degree used later in the state apartments.

1 Harley, 1732

23 Michael Dahl

Stockholm ?1659 – London 1743

Catherine Shorter (1682–1737), later Lady Walpole, c.1710

Oil on canvas, 99 x 82.5 cm

Prov: Sir Robert Walpole at Houghton Hall; then by descent to present owner

Exh: London, 1959 (43); Norwich, 1992 (37)

Lit: Walpole, 1747, p. 47; Moore and Crawley, 1992, pp. 105–6

The Marquess of Cholmondeley

Sir Robert Walpole's biographer William Coxe describes Catherine Shorter as 'a woman of exquisite beauty and accomplished manners'. Her portrait was evidently dear to Sir Robert, hung as it was over the chimneypiece of his private wainscoted bedchamber, where it is first recorded in 1736. A full-length portrait of Catherine Shorter by Kneller is also recorded in Walpole's house at Chelsea, in the Yellow Damask Bedchamber, 1736.

There appears to have been some haste or secrecy about their marriage at Knightsbridge Chapel on 30 July 1700. Francis Hare, writing to Robert Walpole on the following 8 August, mentions that Walpole's brother Horatio had only just learnt of it the previous day. Catherine brought Robert Walpole a dowry of £20,000, but was known for her extravagance as a woman of fashion. According to Horace Walpole her dowry was 'spent on the wedding and christening... including her jewels'.

Catherine died at Chelsea on 20 August 1737 and was buried in the Henry VII Chapel, Westminster Abbey. She had borne Walpole three sons and two daughters. The sons were Robert, who succeeded as 2nd Earl of Orford, Edward and Horatio (or Horace) Walpole. The daughters were Mary, who married George, 3rd Earl of Cholmondeley, and Catherine, who died aged nineteen.

Horace Walpole, in the *Aedes*, described Dahl's painting as 'an extreme good portrait'. Michael Dahl had settled in London for good in March 1689 and soon became the most popular portrait painter in England after Kneller. Although a Tory by political persuasion, he was patronised by Tories and Whigs alike, in common with most of the leading portraitists of this period.

Catherine was also depicted in a double portrait with Sir Robert in an engraving by George Vertue, dated 1748, which forms a frontispiece to the *Aedes Walpolianae* of 1752. Both portraits are based on miniatures by Christian Friedrich Zinke. Horace Walpole commissioned John Giles Eccardt (with John Wootton) to paint a double portrait in oils based upon the engraving (HW to Bentley, 18 May 1754).[1] In both the engraving and Eccardt's oil, Sir Robert is shown seated at a table on which there is the Chancellor's seal and busts of George I and George II. Catherine stands beside him, with flowers, shells, a palette and pencils to mark her own love of the arts.

1 W.S. Lewis Library, Farmington, Connecticut (Fig. 47)

24 Jean-Baptiste Van Loo

Aix-en-Provence 1684 – Aix-en-Provence 1745

Maria Skerrett, c.1738

Oil on canvas, 131 x 106 cm

Prov: painted for Sir Robert Walpole; at Houghton by 1744; then by descent to present owner

Lit: MS 1744 (as in the bedchamber); Walpole, 1747, p. 47

The Marquess of Cholmondeley

Sir Robert maintained a relationship with Maria Skerrett during the course of much of his marriage to his first wife, Catherine Shorter, who died in August 1737. Maria became identified in the public eye with the character Polly in *The Beggar's Opera* by John Gay. As early as November 1737 there were rumours that Sir Robert had married Maria Skerrett; the marriage was privately celebrated in March 1738 but she died shortly afterwards in June 1738. A measure of Sir Robert's love for his two wives may be seen in the fact that it was their portraits that hung in his bedchamber at Houghton during the last years of his life.

Jean Baptiste Van Loo came to England in December 1737, leaving in October 1742. By 1739 he is recorded by George Vertue as the Prime Minister's favourite painter. He brought a cosmopolitan elegance to society portraiture in England, having worked in the leading European cities, notably Paris. His portrait of Sir Robert in chancellor's robes hung over the chimney in the Blue Bedchamber (MS 1744).[1]

1 SHM 1130

25 John Wootton

Snitterfield, Warwickshire *c.*1682 – London 1764

Classical Landscape, c.1740

Oil on canvas, 124 x 141 cm

Prov: Sir Robert Walpole; ? the Little Dressing Room, Houghton Hall, by 1747; by descent to present owner

Lit: MS 1744, 'Anti chamber – over chimney'; Walpole, 1747, p. 47

The Marquess of Cholmondeley

John Wootton's particular accomplishment was as a painter of landscapes and horses, and it was for this talent that Sir Robert Walpole chiefly employed him. The inventory of Walpole's collection in 1736 records three overdoor landscapes in the Yellow Drawing Room at Houghton, two more overdoor landscapes in the Great Middle Room at Downing Street and a hunting piece in Walpole's Dressing Room at Grosvenor Street. The hunting element was emphasised in his London homes with a further six paintings of horses and hounds, by the same artist.

It is in the Little Dressing Room at Houghton that Horace Walpole records 'a landscape by *Wootton* in the stile of *Claude Lorrain*, over the chimney'. Early in his career Wootton developed a style of landscape painting influenced by Claude and Gaspar Dughet. This painting, in its Kentian frame, is typical of Wootton's Italianate style, designed for decorative overmantels. Although unrecorded as such, this is almost certainly the painting that hung in the Little Dressing Room.

In 1722 George Vertue commented that Wootton had entered into Gaspar Dughet's manner.[1] Both Dughet and Claude appealed to Wootton and his patrons not simply for their compositional formulae but also for their representation of stoic ideas. The Arcadian motifs Wootton employs here suggest the passing of time. His treatment of trees and foliage achieves a delicate texture enlivened by flecks of light pigment and owes much to his study of Claude.

1 Vertue, I, p. 101

The Drawing Room
[The Yellow Drawing Room]

Fig. 54 The Drawing Room, 1921. The seat furniture shown here was listed in the Marble Parlour in 1745.

This is the principal family room on the piano nobile and in Sir Robert's day it was characterised by a group of portraits by Van Dyck, pastel drawings of his surviving children and a suite of yellow upholstered furniture of a rather comfortable type. Because it was a more formal space than the ancestral and family 'gallery' on the ground floor, the Drawing Room's decoration and paintings placed greater emphasis on Walpole's official position rather than his own family history. This is shown in the white stucco ceiling, which is dominated by a large Garter Star at its centre. Horace Walpole noted the ceiling's special significance for his father: 'The Ceiling is exactly taken, except with the Alteration of the Paternal Coat for the Star and Garter, from one that was in the Dining room of the old House, built by Sir Edward Walpole, Grandfather to Sir Robert' (Walpole, 1747). Robert Walpole had revived the Order of the Bath in 1725 and was obviously very gratified to be the first commoner in recent times to receive the Garter: so much so that he became known as 'Sir Blue-String'.[1] The plan for the ceiling, with its deep decorative beams and guilloche decoration, seems to have been inspired by the ceiling of Inigo Jones's Banqueting House, Whitehall. It has more in common with Colen Campbell's designs than Kent's work at Houghton.

The fine set of seventeenth-century portraits was originally hung on yellow caffoy damask, a woollen and silk material of a lesser quality than the silk used in the State Apartment. Though it was replaced on the walls by 1792 with rose-coloured silk, it probably remains on the matching chairs and couch now placed in the Library. There are also traces of a plain green and a yellow, hand-coloured wallpaper beneath the present hangings. These are the remains of two later nineteenth-century decorative schemes.

The Duke of Wharton's collection of family portraits by Van Dyck, together with *Charles I* (SHM 537) and *Henrietta Maria* (SHM 541), were purchased by Sir Robert in 1725, so this room may have been designed to fit them.[2] A portrait of the 3rd Duke's daughters (SHM 533) hung over the fireplace. In Ware's elevation of 1735 he shows a large frame to the left of this, which may have been made for one of the two large, square works by Luca Giordano, *Judgement of Paris* (SHM 9965) and *Bacchanal* (SHM 197), the other probably filling the adjoining end wall. Such a combination of history painting and portraits from the courts of James or Charles I was not uncommon in collections assembled in the early eighteenth century.

Beneath the large oil paintings would have hung Carriera's pastels of three of Walpole's children (cats. 27–9), together with Arthur Pond's pastel of Maria, only daughter of Sir Robert and Maria Skerrett and a sketch of Mary Walpole (later Viscountess Malpas) by Charles Jervas.

The furniture in 1745 comprised a marble-topped, giltwood pier table and glass,[3] the yellow caffoy-upholstered suite of chairs, settees and a couch,[4] a card table, a pair of curtains and chandelier; all furniture suitable for an evening's conversation and diversion.

1 Plumb, 1960, p. 107; blue ribbon featured regularly in Sir Robert's accounts for this period.

2 George Vertue recalled having seen eleven Van Dycks from Lord Wharton's collection bought by Walpole, whilst unframed at Mr Howard's the framer. It is possible that they were reframed as a set for this room. See Vertue, I, p. 109, and above, pp. 51–2

3 Illustrated in Macquoid 1906, fig. 20

4 Christie's, 1994 (lot 128). Probably supplied by Thomas Roberts, 24 Nov. 1728

26 Anthony van Dyck

Antwerp 1599 – London 1641

Philip, Lord Wharton, 1632

Oil on canvas, 133 x 106 cm

Inscribed, lower left, 'P. S[r] Ant: vandike'; and lower right, 'Philip Lord Wharton / 1632 about ye age / of 19'

Prov: Philip, Lord Wharton, Winchendon, near Aylesbury, Buckinghamshire; bought from his heirs by Sir Robert Walpole, 1725; by descent to George Walpole; bought by Catherine II, 1779; the State Hermitage Museum, St Petersburg; bought by Andrew Mellon, 1932, given by him to the National Gallery of Art, (NGA 1937. 1.50), Washington, DC, 1937

Exh: Washington, DC, 1990–1 (63)

Lit: Larsen, 1988, no. 1029; Millar, 1994, pp. 517–30

National Gallery of Art, Washington, DC

Philip, 4th Lord Wharton (1613–96), was the eldest son of Sir Thomas Wharton (1587–1622) and his wife Philadelphia Carey (d. 1654). During the 1630s Philip was a prominent member of the court and King Charles commissioned portraits of himself and Queen Henrietta Maria as gifts for Lord Wharton. Philip became one of Van Dyck's most important patrons in the late 1630s and Lord Wharton constructed a special gallery of portraits in his house at Winchendon, near Aylesbury. Vertue records that this gallery held twelve full-length and six half-length portraits by Van Dyck. This portrait of Lord Wharton was one of Van Dyck's earliest private commissions in England, almost certainly painted to commemorate Philip's marriage to his first wife, Elizabeth Wandesford. The mood of the painting is one of Arcadian youth and refinement.

Lord Wharton's collection of Van Dycks grew by acquisition as well as through commissions. The collection was chiefly of his relations, but also included contemporaries such as Anne Cavendish, Lady Rich and Archbishop Laud. In the time of his son, the 1st Marquess of Wharton (1648–1715), Houbraken 'noted thirty-two portraits, including fourteen full-lengths'.[1] Sir Robert Walpole's purchase of the collection from the 1st Marquess's successor, the Duke of Wharton (1698–1731), in 1725 was arguably his single most important acquisition. The majority were sold by George Walpole to Catherine II in 1779, although nine were included in his sale of 13–14 June 1751 (1st day, lots 46–9; 2nd day, lots 32, 51–4).

1 A. Houbraken, *De Groote Schonburg*, I, Amsterdam [1718], pp. 147–8

27 Rosalba Carriera

Venice 1675 – Venice 1758

Robert Walpole, c.1722–3

Pastel, 61 x 49 cm

Inscribed (by Horace Walpole) on the backboard, 'Robert, Lord Walpole, eldest son to Robert Walpole now Earl of Orford. Painted by Rosalba'

Prov: painted for Sir Robert Walpole; in Lady Walpole's Drawing Room, Downing Street, by 1736; Yellow Drawing Room, Houghton, by 1744; then by descent to present owner

Lit: MS 1736; MS 1744; Walpole, 1747, p. 49; Moore, 1985, pp. 88–9; Sani, 1988, no. 94

Exh: Norwich 1985 (8)

The Marquess of Cholmondeley

The Walpole family was amongst Carriera's most long-standing admirers. Sir Robert's eldest son Robert was the first Walpole to sit to the artist and it was this portrait that was to inspire Sir Robert to seek a set of pastel portraits of his three sons. Rosalba Carriera was much admired for her ability to produce, quite rapidly, a delicate and apparently spontaneous likeness in pastels.

Robert Walpole (1700–51) was the eldest son and heir of Sir Robert. Educated at Eton, in 1723 he was created Baron Walpole of Walpole. He spent much of the period 1722–3 abroad on his Grand Tour and was the first of Walpole's sons who ventured abroad to bring back works of art for their father's growing collection. Before 1720 Sir Robert's collection was already significant, but it was during the following decade, as the house at Houghton grew, that his collecting quickened pace. Robert Walpole's most spectacular purchase on behalf of his father was the life-size bronze version of the *Laocoön* in Rome, made from casts prepared by the Keller brothers under the direction of François Girardon (1628–1715).

Robert Walpole purchased the bronze *Laocoön* in Paris; Rosalba Carriera had herself visited France, including Paris, in 1721–2 and so it is possible that Robert Walpole sat for the artist when she was in Paris. However, he also visited Rome and Venice while on his tour and so could also have sat for her while in Italy. As the first of the Walpole brothers to meet Rosalba he could well have been the purchaser of her 'Apollo, half length in crayons'[1] and its companion 'Diana with a Greyhound, ditto'.[2] Recorded by Horace Walpole as in Downing Street in 1736; by 1744 these paintings had been removed to Houghton where they hung in the Carlo Maratti Room.[3]

1 Engraved, J.B. Michel, 18.7 x 13.9 cm; published Boydell, 1 Sept. 1785

2 Stipple, C. West, 18.6 x 14 cm; published Boydell, 1 Sept. 1785

3 A version of cat. 27 was formerly in the collection of Dorothy Neville, sold Sotheby's, 23 March 1971, lot 80.

28 Rosalba Carriera

Venice 1675 – Venice 1758

Edward Walpole, c.1730

Pastel on paper, 60.5 x 48.5 cm

Inscribed (by Horace Walpole on the backboard), 'Edward Walpole, Clerk of the Pe[?]ls, 2nd son to Robert Walpole, Earl of Orford. Painted by Rosalba'

Prov: painted for Sir Robert Walpole; in Lady Walpole's Drawing Room, Downing Street, by 1736; Yellow Drawing Room, Houghton, by 1744; then by descent to present owner

Lit: MS 1736; MS 1744; Walpole, 1747, p. 49; Moore, 1985, p. 89; Sani, 1988, no. 95

Exh: Norwich 1985 (9)

The Marquess of Cholmondeley

Edward Walpole (1706–84) visited Venice early in 1730. He is referred to in the correspondence of Colonel Elizeus Burges, who at that time was on his second mission as Resident in Venice, and he mentions 'Mr. Walpole, Sir Robert's 2nd son' as in Venice for the carnival, on 20 January 1730. Two months later Burges records the fact that Walpole had joined up with Gustavus Hamilton, 2nd Viscount Boyne (1710–46): 'Lord Boyne & Mr. Walpole chuse to continue here till ye Opera begins at Picenza, rather than go to any other town in Italy' (17 March 1730).[1]

Edward's plans were delayed when he fell 'extremely ill here of a fever and was in so bad a way that nobody expected he would recover...' (Burges, 12 May). He did recover, however, and proceeded on his tour with Lord Boyne, leaving Venice in July 1730. Edward had most probably sat for Rosalba Carriera at carnival time, along with his companion Lord Boyne, whose splendid pastel portrait (private collection) shows him in carnival dress.

George Vertue records seeing '4 portraits of the family – Rose alba' in Sir Robert's collection at Whitehall, almost certainly an error. Horace Walpole himself records his own 'Head in crayons' by George Knapton hanging in Lady Walpole's Drawing Room at Downing Street in 1736 in association with Rosalba's portraits of Robert and Edward. The fourth portrait at this time was almost certainly that of Maria Walpole, commissioned by Sir Robert from Arthur Pond in order to complete a set of pastel portraits of his four children.

1 For Burges correspondence see Public Record Office, SPF 99/63

---

29 Rosalba Carriera

Venice 1675 – Venice 1758

Horace Walpole, 1741

Pastel, 61 x 46.5 cm

Inscribed (by Horace Walpole, in ink on the backboard), 'Horace Walpole / 3rd son to Robert Earl of Orford / Anno Aetatis suae 23 / painted by Rosalba'

Prov: painted for Sir Robert Walpole; in the Yellow Drawing Room, Houghton, by 1744; then by descent to present owner

Exh: Norwich 1985 (77)

Lit: MS 1744; Walpole, 1747, p. 49; Adams and Lewis, 1968–70, pp. 9–10; Moore, 1985, p. 133

The Marquess of Cholmondeley

Sir Robert's third son, Horace Walpole (1717–97), was in Venice between 9 June and 12 July 1741. Either this portrait or an unknown second portrait of Walpole was seen in Rosalba's studio by Madame Suares (1697–1773) and her daughters, Vittorina and Teresina, in March 1742. Madame Suares wrote to Horace Mann of their visit, describing how Vittorina exclaimed, 'Oh, Mr. Walpole, how happy I am to see you here!' Teresina 'for half an hour kept bowing and making compliments to the portrait'. Madame Suares added that, 'Never in my life have I seen a portrait of such perfection and verisimilitude'. Rosalba informed her that it had been sold to the English banker 'Smit'. This suggests that the new Consul in Venice, Joseph Smith, had been acting as Walpole's agent.

According to the anecdotist and grand tourist Joseph Spence (1699–1768), who had one of his 'chit-chats' with Rosalba, she had seen Walpole 'but twice or thrice' while he was in Venice, but she was able to give Spence as good an account of his character as 'I could have done myself'. This was in an effort to convince Spence that she was well able to 'know people's tempers by their faces'.[1]

While in Italy, Horace Walpole acquired the artistic education that was to inform a lifetime of writing and collecting. His father's house at Houghton was Horace Walpole's inspiration throughout his European Grand Tour (29 March 1739 – 13 September 1741). Sir Robert grew to depend upon his opinion: 'I go in three weeks to Norfolk; the only place that could make me wish to live at St. James's. My Lord has pressed me so much, that I could not with decency refuse; he is going to furnish and hang his picture gallery, and wants me. I can't help wishing that I had never known a Guido from a Teniers – but who could ever suspect any connection between painting and the wilds of Norfolk?' (Horace Walpole to Horace Mann, 25 April 1743, Arlington Street. Lewis XVIII, p. 218).

1 Klima, 1975, p.16

Fig. 55 The Great Staircase, 1996

The Great Staircase

Guests at Houghton ascending from the Arcade with its low ceiling are surprised by the height and grandeur of the Great Staircase, rising around a central well reaching from basement to roof. All the joinery is extravagantly made from solid mahogany, crisply carved, and the walls are covered with *trompe l'oeil* architectural decoration painted by William Kent. The roof lights and high key of these paintings make the whole seem flooded with light by day: at night the globe candle lamps on brackets would have flickered light off the walls.

On the second floor, sash windows light the internal bedchamber corridor and there is also a simpler version of this arrangement in the basement for the servants' access. Kent incorporates the upper windows into his painted scheme to give the impression of a courtyard open to the air, as in an Italian palazzo. The inspiration for this was once again Inigo Jones, in this case his design for Whitehall Palace, which Kent was publishing from Lord Burlington's collection of drawings around 1727.[1] The illusion of being in an exterior space was increased by the placing of a bronze cast of the antique Borghese Gladiator on a storey-high, stone tempietto; a giant plinth of the Doric order. Sir Thomas Robinson, visiting in 1731, admired its theatrical effect:

a fine gilt gladiator, given him by Lord Pembroke and which is very prettily placed on four Doric columns with their proper entablature, which stands in the void... the figure stands... and fronts the door which goes into the hall and has a very fine effect when you go out of that room.[2]

By contrast, when the grudging Earl of Oxford visited Houghton the following year his response was very critical. He found it 'a most clumsy pedestal' and the whole 'very ill placed, for you cannot stand anywhere to have a good view of it'.[3]

The bronze figure was the gift of Thomas, 8th Earl of Pembroke (1656–1733), and came from his garden at Wilton in Wiltshire. Horace Walpole attributed it to Giambologna, but it is now given to Hubert Le Sueur (d. 1670).[4] Kent is usually credited with providing the plinth, but might he just have designed the base for the figure while Henry Herbert, the Architect-Earl (1693–1751) (and son of Thomas) provided the design for the architecturally correct lower part? He is known to have designed the Water House at Houghton.[5]

The imagery of the staircase continues the hunting theme from the basement floor: painted busts of Diana, trophies with boars' and foxes' heads herald Kent's two large scenes in their simulated frames: *The killing of the Calydonian Boar* and *Meleager presenting the Boar's Head to Atalanta*. All is a riot of sporting blood lust executed in monochrome.

1 Information kindly supplied by John Cornforth

2 Robinson, 1731

3 Harley, 1732

4 Haskell and Penny, 1981, p. 221. Another cast by Le Sueur stood at the end of the canal in St James's Park, and was removed to Hampton Court for William III, where it may well have been admired by Sir Robert. It is now at Windsor Castle.

5 Another architectural link between Pembroke and Sir Robert may also be found in Sir Andrew Fountaine, who was described by Robert Morris in 1728 as a 'practitioner of architecture' (see Moore, p. 53).

30 Pierre Fourdrinier *fl.* mid-eighteeth-century; after Isaac Ware d. 1766

Cross-sectional elevation of the Staircase looking east, with plate 18 from Thomas Ripley and Isaac Ware's The Plans, Elevations and Sections; Chimney-pieces and Ceilings of Houghton Hall in Norfolk..., *1735, reissued as plate 12 by John and Josiah Boydell in* A Set of Prints... in the collection of Her Imperial Majesty, the Empress of Russia, 1784

Engraving, 45.7 x 28.2 cm (plate size)

Prov: Todd Collection, Norfolk Museums Service, acquired 1954

Lit: Harris and Savage, 1990, p. 476

Norfolk Museums Service (Norwich Castle Museum)

This cross-section and plan give a good impression of the height of the Great Stairs and the effective use of top-lighting on William Kent's grisaille decorative scheme. The sense of being in an exterior space created by the painted decoration and in particular, the arcade of windows and niches, comes across even more strongly on paper.

Kent seems to have enjoyed taking this illusion to greater extremes the higher he worked, so that on the bedchamber landing he painted simulated Arcadian statues standing on consoles, interspersed with trophy reliefs. The details are Roman rather than Palladian, but the whole is in a style that Kent made all his own and was to repeat in several houses. Throughout the plates of the book from which this engraving derives, Ware has omitted features that he and Ripley were not responsible for; in this instance the great plinth for the Gladiator is conveniently overlooked, in spite of the impression it made on early visitors.

Ripley and Ware's volume was the first architectural book devoted to a single building (see John Harris, p. 24) and was also a remarkable piece of self publicity by two aspiring architects looking for new private commissions. The book is dedicated to their influential patron, Sir Robert Walpole, and makes no mention of those who would today be called his architectural consultants, Gibbs and Campbell. In the plates Ripley is invariably given as architect, except for the chimneypieces and ceilings that are ascribed to Kent, whilst Ware is the draughtsman. As the architect and assistant responsible for carrying out the work at Houghton, the two younger men must have seized the opportunity around 1735, with Campbell dead and Gibbs following his own path, to take most of the credit in a book that was a lavish advertisement for the Palladian style.

31 Design attributed to William Kent

Bridlington 1685 – London 1748

Hall settee or bench, c.1730

Mahogany, 112 x 140 x 69 cm

Prov: probably Sir Robert Walpole; then by descent to present owner

Lit: Hussey, 1963, p. 29; Gilbert, 1968, II, pp. 324–5

The Marquess of Cholmondeley

This splendid settee does not obviously match any description in the 1745 and 1792 inventories for Houghton Hall, although it suits its position beneath Kent's simulated frames on the Great Stairs remarkably well. It is possible that it was overlooked or removed after Sir Robert's death or perhaps came from a garden building or London property where Kent also provided furniture.[1] Certainly the carved Venus shell and Vitruvian scroll ornament would make it appropriate for a building associated with water, such as the Earl of Pembroke's Water House at Houghton.

The design shares much in common with a pair of benches by Kent for Sherbourne Lodge, Gloucestershire, which were made by James Moore the Younger in 1731 (Temple Newsam House, Leeds City Art Galleries). This was published in John Vardy's *Some Designs of Mr Inigo Jones and Mr William Kent*, 1744, plate 42. The variations are only in the position of the beautifully carved scallop shell and the apron beneath the seat. Interestingly, in the Houghton example, the back above the dado rail level is moulded and well-finished, suggesting that it might have been intended to sit against a window. Kent also provided similar hall seats, at about the same time as he was working at Houghton, to Sir Robert's mentor and brother-in-law, the 2nd Viscount Townshend, at Raynham.

Like the Stone Hall settees, the quality of carving and careful selection of figuring for the seat backs suggests the work of a major London carver, such as James Richards, Master Carver in Wood to the Office of Works, although any connection with him can only be by association.

1 For a discussion of Kent's possible role in Walpole's London properties see Thornton, 1993

Fig.56 The Stone Hall, 1996

The Stone Hall

[The Hall]

The formal entrance hall to Houghton was originally approached from the external double stone staircase that was removed by the 3rd Earl of Orford. It provides a suitably imperial introduction to what is in effect the palace of Britain's first Prime Minister. The room has a rather cool appearance, with practically no colour, the only light relief coming from the antics of Artari's lifelike *putti*, who clamber around the coving. Lord Hervey, visiting in 1731, was suitably impressed: 'the first room is a hall, a cube of 40 foot finished entirely with stone, a gallery of stone around it and the ceiling of stucco, the best executed of anything I ever saw in stucco in any country.'[1]

Credit for the Hall's design, with its harmonious combination of modern and antique ornament, must surely go to William Kent. Campbell did provide a preliminary design, based on the hall at Inigo Jones's Queen's House, in Greenwich, around 1722 (RIBA, Campbell 7/19). This is carefully thought out but more reticent in its decoration than the original model. Kent, together with his collaborators Artari and the sculptor Michael Rysbrack, transformed Campbell's idea from 1726 onwards, using Sir Robert's newly acquired Garter Star as one of the motifs for the ceiling.

Looking upwards, observers are faced with Walpole's coat of arms, surrounded by quarters with trophies of Diana's mask and foxhounds. On the coving are four portrait roundels: of Sir Robert opposite Catherine Walpole and his son Robert, Lord Walpole, opposite his wife Margaret Rolle. These are almost teased by the gymnastic *putti* who surround them. Moving down the wall, all the decoration beneath the ceiling is carved in fine sandstone, with many of the figures and reliefs carried out by Rysbrack or under his supervision (see cat. 33).

Resting on the pediments to the four smaller doors are pairs of languid *putti* and above these is a set of bas-reliefs by Rysbrack, based on the antique. They include over the northeast door, a *Hunt of the Trajans*, copied from the Arch of Constantine, and a *Sacrifice of a Bull*, after an antique relief in the gardens of the Villa Medici, Rome.[2] John Cornforth discusses above how the sculptor relied on 'paper archaeology' for his sources. Rysbrack's finest work is seen in the chimneypiece and overmantel, with a *Sacrifice to Diana* (cat. 32). Complementing these modern interpretations of the antique was a group of classical busts of Roman emperors and historical figures on console brackets and pedestals (cat. 34) with carved festoons above them. The odd man out amongst these was a self-portrait bust of the Renaissance sculptor Baccio Bandinelli, as Horace Walpole believed it to be.[3] Pride of place opposite the fireplace went to Girardon's full-scale bronze cast of the *Laocoön* on a sculptural plinth designed by Kent.

The furnishing of the room was typical of the spare style considered suitable for a hall of the 1720s. There were six mahogany benches (cat. 36) fitted beneath the busts and the great pair of mahogany side tables, carved with wood-spirit masks, on which were placed pairs of small bronzes after the antique (cat. 35). The only colour and brightness came from the gilt-bronze 'lantern' with its eighteen lights. This was a prodigal purchase of 170 guineas that was famously ridiculed in *The Craftsman* journal and later, rather tellingly, sold to Lord Chesterfield. It was replaced in 1748 with the present giltwood chandelier, bought from the impoverished 3rd Earl of Cholmondeley.

1 Hervey, 1731

2 Webb, 1954, p. 127; Bristol, 1982, pp. 35–41 (81 and 82)

3 This has recently been attributed to the important Venetian sculptor Alessandro Vittoria (1524–1608). (Information kindly supplied by Dr Charles Avery.)

32 William Kent and ?Henry Flitcroft

Bridlington 1685 – London 1748; Twiss Green, Lancs 1697 – London 1769

Preparatory drawing for an engraving of the Stone Hall chimneypiece, Houghton, 1726

Inscribed verso, 'Wm Kent / 1726'

Traces of pencil, pen and grey–black ink, grey wash, 23.9 x 17 cm

Prov: Jacob Isaacs; Sir Robert Witt, bought at Calman's, n.d.; Courtauld Institute of Art, 1952 (3217)

Exh: London, 1961 (30); Kingston-upon-Hull 1985 (51); London, 1995

Lit: Kent, 1727, pl. 64; Ware, 1735, pl. 26; Beard, 1981, pp. 174–5; Bristol, 1982, p. 37; Hull, 1985 (51)

The Courtauld Institute Galleries

This drawing seems to be the final preparatory work for the engraving published by Kent in the *Designs of Inigo Jones*, 1727, although it is not clear why he should require a second drawing for this plate when Henry Flitcroft had already produced one in his characteristically finished style (RIBA, Flitcroft album). The details of the classical relief, showing a *Sacrifice to Diana*, appear much as Rysbrack was to carve them, but the bust has been reversed. (The details are not complete in the drawing in the RIBA, which is surely earlier.) This may be an allowance for the engraver, Pierre Fourdrinier, who did not bother to reverse the rest of the composition.[1] John Cornforth has suggested that the drawing should be reattributed to Flitcroft, cited as draughtsman in the publication.[2] This is quite plausible, although as the RIBA drawing by that artist is incomplete, it is also possible that Kent may have contributed the details for the design for the relief and the term figures to this drawing. These are drawn in a looser style than the rest of the chimneypiece.

The design of the chimneypiece owes much to Inigo Jones, whose work Kent was publishing about this time. However, the detail in the terms is similar to those made by contemporary sculptors such as G.B. Guelfi and Rysbrack himself. Rysbrack's classical relief is based on antique examples, probably copied from engravings. In his workshop sale of 1767 a terracotta relief of the same subject was sold, which may have been the original model: this has since disappeared.[3] The sculptor was pleased with the work as he repeated it at Woburn Abbey, Bedfordshire, some twenty-five years later.

1 To confuse matters further, Isaac Ware redrew the finished chimneypiece for his 1735 publication, managing to turn the relief back the right way but reversing the bust once again in the engraving.

2 Correspondence with Norwich Castle Museum

3 Webb, 1954, p. 127

33 John Michael Rysbrack

Antwerp 1694 – London 1770

Bust of Sir Robert Walpole, c.1726

Marble, height 63.5 cm

Prov: made for Sir Robert Walpole for Houghton Hall; by descent to present owner

Lit: Walpole, 1747, p. 68; Vertue, III, p. 31; Webb, 1954, pp. 128–9; Cooper, 1965, p. 226; Kerslake, 1977, pp.197–8; Bristol, 1982, p. 9

The Marquess of Cholmondeley

George Vertue saw this bust or a clay model for it in Rysbrack's studio in 1726, 'modeld from the life… a large head, broad face', and the finished marble arrived at Houghton in December 1730, when it was reported in the *Norfolk Gazette*.[1] It was commissioned to sit in the Stone Hall on the bracket in front of the same artist's overmantel relief of a *Sacrifice to Diana*, as shown in Kent's design of about 1726 (cat. 32). However, the way Sir Robert stares away from the visitor at the entrance door into space may suggest that Rysbrack's directions were unclear or misunderstood.[2] It might be expected that the portrait should face the entrance, where the sitter could also be seen to be contemplating figures of Peace and Plenty over the door.

The bust is remarkable for being both a good portrait likeness and also an early example of the Roman style of bust, with the sitter wearing a toga without a wig, which was to become popular, particularly with statesmen. Naturally, Sir Robert demanded that the artist compromise his classical prototypes and include his newly acquired Garter Star. (This was a formula later used in a bust of Lord Chesterfield, who interestingly also had a Garter Star ceiling at his London villa.)

Vertue described a terracotta version of the bust on another visit to Rysbrack's studio in 1738/9, which is likely to have been the similar version now in the National Portrait Gallery; this is dated 1738 and may be a later replica of a lost original (NPG 2126).[3]

Somewhat ironically, Horace Walpole kept a prized bust by Rysbrack of James Gibbs, his father's rejected architect, at Strawberry Hill.

1 Kerslake, 1977, n. 8

2 In the Kent/Flitcroft design (cat. 32) the bust does face to its left, towards the entrance; see also cat. 58

3 Another marble version is that now in the Walpole family collection (Private Collection).

34 Roman, 2nd century AD (restored)

*Bust of Faustina the Elder (*d. *AD 140)*

Marble, 81 x 65 cm

Prov: Sir Robert Walpole, Houghton Hall, probably by *c.*1730; by descent to present owner

Lit: Walpole, 1747, p. 69

The Marquess of Cholmondeley

Horace Walpole listed ten busts on console brackets and 'terms' around the Stone Hall, and many of these are indicated in Ware's engravings of 1735. Most are antique, or made up from antique fragments and include emperors and writers, with the exception of one, which Horace described as a self-portrait of the sixteenth-century sculptor Baccio Bandinelli[1], and this single female bust.

William Kent used classical sculpture and copies to lend an instant gravitas to his monumental hall spaces. It was a theme he was to develop some years later in the Sculpture Gallery at nearby Holkham, a room that became a *locus classicus* for younger architects.

Faustina was the aunt of Marcus Valerius and married the future Emperor Antoninus. She died before her husband, who founded a charity for girls, the Puellae Faustinianae, in her memory. This particular bust appears to have been made from a separate head and body and has been restored, the nose in particular. Other Faustina busts formed part of the earlier antique collection of Lord Arundel, and there is also one in the 2nd Earl of Egremont's collection at Petworth House in Sussex.

It is likely that Sir Robert was supplied with antique busts by his agents abroad, including his second son Edward, who wrote to his father while on his Grand Tour in Italy: 'I have seen every statue and piece of that kind of antiquity that is worth seeing at Rome among which there is nothing to be had that could possibly serve your purpose.'[2] He goes on to say how he will try to obtain some pieces and at the best price possible. George Vertue made a point of including a classical bust showing Sir Robert, amongst the other impedimenta included in his frontispiece for *Aedes Walpolianae*. As with his Library, Sir Robert was plainly keen to project an image of classical erudition as well as political power through the choice of contents and decoration for the Stone Hall.

1 See also p. 114, note 3

2 Plumb, 1960, p. 86, no. 2

35 Attributed to an Italian workshop, probably early eighteenth century

Pair of table bronzes after the antique Borghese and Medici vases, ?early 1700s

Bronze: Borghese, 65 x 38 cm; Medici, 65.5 x 38 cm

Prov: Sir Robert Walpole, Houghton Hall, by 1743; by descent to the present owner

Lit: Walpole, 1747, p. 68; Cooper, 1965, p. 232; Haskell and Penny, 1981, pp. 314–16

The Marquess of Cholmondeley

This pair of reductions of two celebrated antique vases is typical of the kind of small bronze that was to become ubiquitous in English houses by the end of the eighteenth century. They are likely to have been sent by Sir Robert's agents or admirers in Italy,[1] or alternatively they may not be of Italian manufacture but French and were perhaps acquired by Sir Robert's brother, Horatio, whilst Ambassador to Paris.[2]

The antique models for the vases come from entirely different sources, but were regularly copied as a pair from the middle of the seventeenth century, in a variety of media. The marble Borghese Vase was discovered in Carlo Muti's garden in Rome around 1569 but had been removed to the Villa Borghese by 1645 (it is now in the Louvre). The frieze scene is a Bacchic procession, thought to include a drunken Silenus. In copies such as these, the shape of the vase has been adapted to that of the Medici Vase, which was displayed in the Villa Medici, Rome, by 1598; it is now in the Uffizi Gallery, Florence. The Medici Vase shows a sacrificial scene, once believed to be the fate of Iphigenia. It was reproduced in an imaginative engraving by Stefano della Bella as early as 1656, which may have encouraged the production of early copies.

The pair at Houghton have fluted lids with pine-cone finials, a detail not found on the original vases or on full-scale copies. Some of the earliest copies are those in marble placed round the Bassin de Latone at Versailles. This is a likely source for the manufacture of French versions in bronze, as all the major founders and sculptors of France (such as François Girardon who cast the Houghton *Laocoön*) were making a living working for Louis XIV at the end of the seventeenth century.[3] There is also a small pair in alabaster at Houghton, although these do not feature in early inventories and may have come from another Walpole house.[4]

1 Lewis, XVII, p. 24 n. 2 & 3. In a letter to Horace Mann in Florence, dated 14 May 1740, Horace Walpole discusses a gift from Mann to Sir Robert. Mann had an export licence for '4 cassette 3 con urne d'alabastro ed una con bronzi; dirette per Londra di regalo al Sig. Cav. Roberto Walpole' (n. 2 – Florence State Archive) which could refer to both alabaster and bronze urns, rather than simply bronze figures. His 'Giambologna' statuette (cat. 44) was sent to Houghton some three years later.

2 Plumb, 1960, p. 87 n. 1

3 Souchal, 1977, I, p. 114

4 These may well have been sent by Mann; see note 1 above. Similar copies, but without lids, are at Osterley House, Middlesex, and Longford Castle, Wiltshire (Macquoid, 1906, Fig. 68).

36 Design attributed to William Kent

Bridlington 1685 – London 1748

Hall settee or bench, c.1728

Mahogany with beech and oak, 100 x 165 x 65 cm

Prov: made for Sir Robert Walpole for Houghton Hall; by descent to present owner

The Marquess of Cholmondeley

This hall settee comes from a set of six, of unique design, made for the Stone Hall. The way the two chair-backs are neatly incorporated allows the settees to fit perfectly under the large console brackets for the marble busts on three sides of the great room. The settees' solid, mahogany finish originally provided the only note of warmth against the stone of the hall, apart from the corresponding side tables and the chandelier. Sir Matthew Decker knew of their imminent arrival in 1728, when the hall must have been reaching completion: 'The seat or benches in the hall, will all be of fine mahogany wood.'

The details of the settees have much in common with one designed by Kent and published by Vardy in 1744 (pl. 42, cf. cat. 31) and makes an attribution to Kent very probable; the scrolled seat-backs, echoed by the ends of the arms, is precisely the subtle detail he enjoyed. The settees also have a practical quality in the way all the exposed carved detail is tucked under the seat and inside the legs, out of harm's way. The quality of carving matches that of the bench now on the Great Stairs (cat. 31) and may be the work of James Richards and his workshop, who are believed to have carried out much work at Houghton.

The use of solid mahogany on such a scale in this and the following rooms must have been intended as a statement of Walpole's wealth as well as one of fashion. The wood was also becoming increasingly easy to obtain in larger quantities at the end of the 1720s[1] although Sir Robert was reputed to have attempted to impose crippling excises on mahogany after he completed Houghton.

1 Wilson, 1984, p. 100

The Saloon

The largest and most splendid reception room at Houghton was still unfinished when Sir Matthew Decker saw it in 1728, but was already hung with some of Walpole's most important paintings. Lord Hervey must have seen the room more-or-less completed by 1731 when he commented, 'Behind the hall is the salon, finished in a different taste, hung, carved and gilt large glasses between the windows, and some of his finest pictures round the three other sides of the room...'[1]

The warmth of this room hung with crimson caffoy (a cut and uncut velvet made of wool and silk) is in marked contrast to the bare Stone Hall. The wall hangings were supplied by Thomas Roberts, the second royal carver of that name, between April 1729 and January 1730, at the then great cost of £118 18*s*.[2] Typically, Sir Robert was slow in paying such large bills.

Kent painted the deeply coved ceiling in his gold 'mosaic' manner, in an attempt to imitate ancient Roman decorative schemes. However, his ideas for the room derive from as early as 1725, and were revised greatly by the time he came to paint it (see cats. 38–9). In the centre compartment of the heavy, beamed ceiling is a grisaille painting of Apollo driving his chariot. Kent's iconography for the Saloon is rather loose but the choice of the Sun God is an appropriate foil to the Moon Goddess, Diana, whose image recurs here in the frieze. The room has attic storey top-lighting on the west side, with corresponding lunettes, which Kent filled with grimacing male and female masks. Interspersed with these are medallions of Neptune and Cybele (the earth mother) and the Four Seasons. Once more the Garter Star is incorporated, this time on the chimneypiece.

The arrangement of paintings is discussed below (cats. 38–9) but it is worth noting here that Kent intended even large paintings to be hung so that they almost touched, despite the use of such costly material on the walls. Paintings were to be framed to suit the room and complement one another. The list of works given in *Aedes* includes mostly New Testament subjects and two large mythological paintings, Luca Giordano's *Cyclops at their Forge* (SHM 188) and *Daedalus and Icarus* by Charles Le Brun (SHM 40). Given that Sir Robert later chose to complete his picture gallery rather than his chapel, his preference for religious subjects in the state rooms appears to be more an act of admiration for Italian art than one of religious piety.

From the Saloon onwards all the mahogany joinery is part-gilded, as is the magnificent seat furniture made for this room (cats. 40–3). This colouring is subtly picked up in the use of black-and-gold marble for the chimneypiece and table slabs. In 1745 this great room was still quite sparsely furnished with chairs and sofas and there were giltwood wall-lights and torchères to bring all the gold to life at night. There are no floor coverings mentioned in the first inventory, but one of the great oriental carpets still in the house is likely to have complemented the richly coloured walls and ceiling.

1 Hervey 1731
2 Tipping, 22 Jan. 1921, p. 106

Fig.57 The Saloon, 1996. The portrait given by Catherine the Great hangs over the fireplace.

37 **John C. Murphy, after Luca Giordano**

Ireland *c*.1748 – London 1820

The Cyclops at their Forge, 1 January 1788

Mezzotint, 50.6 x 35.3 cm

Inscribed [Arms in centre], 'Luca Giordano pinxit. John Murphy Scupsit./THE CYCLOPS AT THEIR FORGE. /In the Salon at Houghton. /Size of the Picture 4.F II[I] by 6.[FI]¼ in height. /Published Jan.[y] 1.st 1788 by John and Jofiah Boydell. N° 90 Cheapside London.'

Lit: Boydell, II, 66; Le Blanc, 1970 13 (the title in closed letters)

The Hon. Charles Lennox Boyd

The original oil upon which this mezzotint is based formerly belonged to Grinling Gibbons.[1] It was one of a number of particularly glorious paintings of grand scale that hung in the Saloon against a 'crimson flower'd Velvet'. These included Van Dyck's *Holy Family*, Le Sueur's *Stoning of Saint Stephen* and *Daedalus and Icarus* by Le Brun.[2]

Giordano (1632–1705) was particularly productive as a painter and decorator, influenced by José de Ribera during his early years. The dramatic effects of light and shadow offered by Giordano's treatment of *The Cyclops at their Forge* are well rendered by Murphy in this engraved translation. The exaggerated effects of chiaroscuro and foreshortening that could be achieved with this subject attracted Giordano more than once,[3] sometimes as a background to scenes of *Mars and Venus*.[4]

Sir Robert's collection featured seven works by or attributed to Luca Giordano, all of which had entered his collection by 1736. *The Cyclops at their Forge* (also known as *The Forge of Vulcan*) dates from the artist's early period, when his manner was close to that of Ribera. The subject is from Virgil's *Aeneid*. The second two most important compositions were both hung in the Yellow Drawing Room, *Sleeping Bacchus with nymphs, boys and animals*[5] and *The Judgement of Paris*.[6]

1 Gibbons's sale, 1722, lot 87: '*The Cyclops at Work*, large.' Horace Walpole notes 'there is a copy of this at St. James's by Walton' (Walpole, 1747, p. 53)

2 SHM 188, 539, 1170, 40, respectively

3 For a similar composition, Sanct Lucas Sale, Vienna, 11–12 May 1921, lot 65, 194 x 142 cm

4 For example London, 1960 (361), Denis Mahon Collection

5 SHM 197

6 SHM 9965

38 William Kent

Bridlington 1685 – London 1748

Proposed design for the elevation with picture hang of the north wall of the Saloon, 1725

Pen and black ink with grey and brown washes, 25.7 x 25.7 cm

Inscribed verso, 'Wm Kent delint.', and in another hand 'Drawn by Mr Kent'

Prov: sale of William Kent, 1749; 'H.R.'; Dukes of Newcastle until 1938; sold Sotheby's, 7 July 1983 (lot 100); Sotheby's, 19 Nov. 1992 (lot 31)

Exh: London, Wiggins, 1987 (7)

Lit: Harris, 1985, pp. 211–14; Russell, 1989, p. 136; Sotheby's, 1992 (lot 31)

Private Collection

One of a pair that provide some of the earliest examples of designs for a total architectural scheme for a collection in England, and certainly the earliest dated drawings by Kent for Houghton. The Saloon was not completed until 1731 and so these are very much Kent's first thoughts for Sir Robert's collection, perhaps neatly finished as presentation drawings to woo his great patron. Kent would have been familiar with similar, earlier drawings by his friend, the architect, John Talman.[1] The importance placed on such drawings is known, for Kent was paid £50 for a draft of the picture hang of the Drawing Room at Kensington Palace in 1727.[2]

This proposal shows two of Frans Snyders's great market scenes, the *Fish Market* and *Game Market* (SHM 604, 602) jammed up above the door pediments, and also a painting that Sir Robert never managed to buy, Van Dyck's portrait of Snyders's family, in the overmantel. The wall was completed by smaller works by Van Dyck and probably Gaspard Dughet. All were to be framed to match the Roman decor of the room.

Kent proposes a chimneypiece and great overmantel frame in the style used by Rysbrack elsewhere in the house and above this a baroque ceiling scheme with the Loves of Jupiter. At this end of the room were to be Io's and Leda's fates in the lunettes, with Venus rising from the Sea between them. This was all abandoned in favour of a less provocative series of Seasons and Gods, whilst the great overmantel was dropped, perhaps because the Van Dyck portrait never arrived at Houghton. Only the foxhounds on the room's frieze survived to the building stage, but this was completely remodelled to accommodate the omnipresent Star and Garter.

1 Harris, 1985, p. 213

2 London, Wiggins, 1987 (7, 8)

39 William Kent

Bridlington 1685 – London 1748

Proposed design for the elevation with picture hang of the south wall of the Saloon, 1725

Pen and black ink with grey and brown washes, 25.7 x 25.7 cm

Inscribed verso, 'Wm Kent 1725' and in another hand 'Bought at the Auction of Mr Kent's Collection. Ano. 1749 by / H.R.' and 'Saloon at Houghton with the companion / designed and drawn by Mr Kent'

Prov: sale of William Kent, 1749; 'H.R.'; Dukes of Newcastle until 1938; sold Sotheby's, 7 July 1983 (lot 100); Sotheby's, 19 Nov. 1992 (lot 31)

Exh: London, Wiggins, 1987 (7)

Lit: Harris, 1985, pp. 211–14; Russell, 1989, p. 136; Sotheby's, 1992 (lot 31)

Private Collection

The companion to cat. 38 gives a greater impression of how the Saloon was designed to show off Sir Robert's largest paintings, many of which were to be moved to the Picture Gallery as the collection outgrew the main house.

In this design Snyders's *Flower Stall* and *Vegetable Stall* face the pair on the north wall and in between them, in a more elaborate

frame, was to be Jacob Jordaens's self-portrait with his family (SHM 484). This was intended to complement the Snyders family portrait opposite. The lower tier comprised a pair of Jacopo Bassano scenes of the seasons. When the room actually came to be hung, the canvases by Snyders were hung vertically, creating an effect that Edward Harley disapproved of:

> but I think they are very oddly put up, one is above the other and joined in the middle with a thin piece of wood gilt. It is certainly wrong because as these pictures of the markets were painted to one point of view, and to be even with the eye, they certainly ought not to be put one above the another, besides the narrow gilt ledge that is between the two pictures takes the eye and has a very ill effect.[1]

Facing Venus on the ceiling is Neptune, the only part of the ceiling design to survive as far as execution, although they were placed in a simpler, medallion-relief format. The pair of lunettes at this end contain scenes of *Danaë and the Shower of Gold* and *Leda and the Swan*. Kent also shows a side table, designed to fit the architecture of the room exactly. In the event, his great table was far more ambitious and sculptural (see cat. 43).

1 Harley, 1732

---

40 Design attributed to William Kent

Bridlington 1685 – London 1748

Armchair, c.1731

Part-gilt mahogany frame with beech and oak secondary timbers; upholstered in the original crimson wool-and-silk caffoy, with silk braid and gilt decorative nails, 115.5 x 72 x 66 cm

Prov: made for Sir Robert Walpole, Houghton Hall; by descent to present owner

Exh: Twickenham, 1966; (1 chair from set) Washington, 1985–6 (153)

Lit: Macquoid, 1906, p. 71 fig. 65; Tipping, 1921, p. 70 fig. 11; Jourdain, 1948, fig. 139; Macquoid and Edwards 1954, I, p. 267 fig. 129; Hussey, 1955, pp. 80–1 figs. 105, 107; Jackson-Stops and Pipkin, 1984, p. 90; Wilson, 1984, p. 109 fig. 30; Washington, DC, 1985–6 (153); Beard, 1986, p. 1282 pl. II; Cornforth, 1987, p. 106

The Marquess of Cholmondeley

This armchair, together with cats. 41 and 42, comes from a set of twelve armchairs, four stools and two settees designed for the Saloon around 1731. They are a superb example of the use of parcel-gilding on hardwood, made to be seen against the carved and gilded joinery of the room.

Their design is almost certainly by Kent, for they demonstrate his particular familiarity with Italian Baroque furniture, tempered by his own sense of architectural form. The upholstery was provided, with the matching wall hangings, between 1729 and 1730 by the royal chair maker, Thomas Roberts. The cost of the rich caffoy material was 14*s*. 6*d*. a yard and this probably came from Utrecht. John Cornforth has noted the way in which the lengthy pattern repeat fits the carved detail of the seat-backs so well, suggesting that the frames were likely to have been made with the velvet to hand. This makes it more than likely that the carving was done on site by someone from Roberts' workshop, or by James Richards (d. 1767), a regular partner to Kent, who had been working at Houghton.[1]

Kent carries the Venus theme from the ceiling on to this furniture, with Venus's mask, fish scales and a double scallop shell. Several details in the construction are worth noting. The backs of the chairs are covered with stamped moreen, a cheaper wool fabric, that echoes the pattern of the caffoy; this very rare survivor shows that this sort of chair was brought out into the centre of the room on occasion. Underneath, there is evidence that the caffoy upholstery may origi-

nally have been made up as close-fitting, case covers. These appear to have been nailed back when the under-upholstery was replaced sometime in the past. There are also thin metal plates supporting all the legs at the point of greatest stress, that could well be original, where the carver has left the wood very thin, in order to achieve the desired curving outline.

1 Beard and Gilbert, 1986, pp. 742, 752–3

---

41 Design attributed to William Kent

Bridlington 1685 – London 1748

Settee, c.1731

Part-gilt mahogany frame with beech and oak secondary timbers; upholstered in the original crimson wool-and-silk caffoy, with silk braid and gilt decorative nails, 125.5 x 133 x 66 cm

Prov: made for Sir Robert Walpole, Houghton Hall; by descent to present owner

Lit: Macquoid, 1906, p. 71 fig. 64; Macquoid and Edwards, 1954, III, p. 267 fig. 39; Hussey, 1955, pp. 80–1 figs. 105, 107; *Apollo*, July 1957, pp. 53–6; Jackson-Stops and Pipkin, 1984, p. 91; Wilson, 1984, p. 109; Washington, DC, 1985–6 (153); Beard, 1986, p. 1282; Cornforth, 1987, p. 106

The Marquess of Cholmondeley

The pair of settees from the Saloon suite (see Fig. 57) demonstrates how the carver has skilfully stretched the design of the chairs, without distorting the ornament or over-exaggerating any one part. The larger area of material on the settee shows off the upholsterer's skill in fitting the pattern perfectly to the settee. When these seats are seen in their original setting, the way in which the pattern runs down from the wall on to their backs can also be appreciated.

In the Saloon the pair of settees was probably intended to sit either side of the great door to the Stone Hall, flanked by pairs of armchairs.

---

42 Design attributed to William Kent

Bridlington 1685 – London 1748

Stool, c.1731

Part-gilt mahogany frame with beech and oak secondary timbers; upholstered in the original crimson wool-and-silk caffoy, with silk braid and gilt decorative nails, 53 x 69 x 66 cm

Prov: made for Sir Robert Walpole, Houghton Hall; by descent to present owner

Exh: Twickenham 1966

Lit.: Macquoid, 1906, p. 71 fig. 66; Macquoid and Edwards, 1954, III, p. 267; Hussey, 1955, pp. 80–1; Jackson-Stops and Pipkin, 1984, p. 91; Wilson, 1945, p. 109; Washington, DC, 1985–6 (153); Beard, 1986, p. 1282; Cornforth, 1987, p. 106

The Marquess of Cholmondeley

These stools, suitable for sitting on, were the only items of centre furniture in the Saloon in 1745. Their provision emphasises that such grand furniture was designed to be moved out into the room when necessary, with the help of footmen (see Fig. 57).

The redundancy of this sort of state furniture at the beginning of this century is brought home in a *Country Life* photograph taken in 1907 where one can be seen in use as a piano stool in the Stone Hall.

---

43 Design attributed to William Kent

Bridlington 1685 – London 1748

Pier table, c.1731

Oil-gilded pine; black-and-gold marble, 88 x 156 x 81 cm (inc. top)

Prov: made for Sir Robert Walpole, Houghton Hall; by descent to present owner

Lit: Macquoid; 1906, pp. 21–2 fig. 19; Tipping, 1921, p. 71; Jourdain, 1948, fig. 143; Macquoid and Edwards, 1954, III, p. 283 fig. 30; Cooper, 1965, p. 222; Wilson, 1984, pp. 97–9

The Marquess of Cholmondeley

This table, together with its companion, the great pier glasses (plate mirrors) and a third larger table supported on sphinxes, form a set, all of which is solid-gilt, in contrast to the part-gilt mahogany of the Saloon itself. That they were not, however, an afterthought is demonstrated by the way the pier tables fit perfectly between the dado plinth of the windows and garden door frames.

Kent developed the design for a side table included in his draft for the room of 1725 (cat. 39) into a much more sculptural piece of furniture, perhaps with the assistance of the carver. The usual Kent arrangement, where he uses figures to support the corners is here transformed, so that a *putto* becomes the centrepiece, sitting in a large scallop shell. In order to make this substantial piece of carving secure it has been made into a fifth leg, complete with rather incongruous bun feet. Equally massive furniture of this type was provided by Kent at Wilton and Chiswick Houses at about the same time as at Houghton.

No maker can be identified for certain, but the quality of the figure carving and the solid construction do suggest the work of James Richards once more.

The choice of slab in black-and-gold, or *porto venere* marble, is particularly successful when seen against the dark mahogany and gilding of the room. Tables such as this were not intended for practical use and for most of the time they were kept protected by leather covers, which are listed in the inventory of 1792. By 1745 there was an alabaster vase on each of the pier tables, with the bronze *Sabine Woman* (cat. 44) on the larger table.

---

44 Florentine workshop, after Giovanni Bologna (Giambologna)

Douai 1529 – Florence 1608

Rape of the Sabine Woman, probably early seventeenth century

Bronze, height 98 cm

Prov: given by Horace Mann to Sir Robert Walpole, August 1743; by descent to present owner

Lit: Walpole, 1747, pp. 50–1; Lewis, 1937–83, XVIII, pp. 298–9, 312–13; Cooper, 1965, p. 232; London, 1978, (56, 57); Avery, 1987, pp. 69, 78–80, 109–14, 143, 254

The Marquess of Cholmondeley

Horace Walpole makes special mention in the *Aedes* of this bronze, which he considered to be by Giambologna:

> On the great Table is an exceeding fine Bronze of a Man and a Woman by John of Boulogne. When he had made the fine Marble Groupe of the Rape of the Sabines in the Loggia of the Piazza del Gran Duca at Florence, he was found Fault with, for not having exprest enough of the Softness of the Woman's flesh, on which he modell'd this, which differs in it's Attitudes...

In fact he was only half correct, for Giambologna began working on a bronze two-figure group for the Duke of Parma in 1579, which he later developed into the full-scale, three-figure marble group of the *Sabine Woman* (placed in the Loggia de' Lazzi, Florence).[1]

This bronze appears to be an early copy after the principal versions, which all display minor variations. Giambologna's assistant Antonio Susini developed an extensive reproduction workshop in Florence, that set high standards for replica bronzes at this time. This tradition was continued into the seventeenth century by Ferdinando Tacca. The chasing and finishing on Sir Robert's bronze is consistent with a workshop of the late sixteenth or early seventeenth century. It is closest in detail to the bronze in the Kunsthistorisches Museum, Vienna.[2]

Horace (later Sir Horace) Mann, the King's Resident at Florence, sent the bronze as a gift, which arrived on Sir Robert's birthday, 26 August 1743. It was obviously greatly appreciated by the son as well as the father, for in his letter written to Mann three days later Horace Walpole describes it placed at the far end of the Picture Gallery,

with the room lit by sixty-four candles: 'There is not the least question of its being original', he claimed. In his reply of 1 October, Mann revealed more than a diplomatic interest in the gift, as he stated that it might be placed on a kind of turntable so as to appreciate it as Giambologna intended.

1 There is a wax model showing the sculpture's development in the Victoria and Albert Museum (Sculpture 4125–1854).

2 (*cf.* London, 1978, no. 57). The other two prime versions are Museo e Gallerie di Capodimonte, Naples, and the Metropolitan Museum of Art, New York.

Fig. 58 The ceiling of the Carlo Maratti Room, 1996. The room is now hung with the English silk panels that give the room its present name, the White Drawing Room.

The Carlo Maratti Room

[The White Drawing Room]

Although this room was known as the Velvet Drawing Room (after its green velvet upholstery) in inventories made after Sir Robert's death, Horace Walpole knew it as a gallery devoted to the works of Carlo Maratti (1625–1713) and his followers. Maratti was a skilled artist whose late-Baroque classicism suited the taste of connoisseurs across Europe at the end of the seventeenth century. Walpole and his agents' choice of works was the usual mix of religious and mythological subjects. A large *Judgement of Paris* and *Acis and Galatea* filled the end walls, while Maratti's striking portrait of Pope Clement IX presided over the room from the overmantel (cat. 45). It is interesting to speculate whether these works were framed as a group in early, English examples of Maratta frames, which became so popular later in the eighteenth century.

Kent's decoration for the room seems to have been planned before its dedication to this artist, although several of the mythological subjects do relate to the paintings. The room acts as the ante-room to the State Bedchamber in the northwest corner of the house and its imagery introduces the theme of love, which is carried on through the rest of the apartment. The ceiling is divided into polygonal compartments with decorative beams, a *putto* head appearing at each angle. Around the borders the principal pagan deities offer their attributes towards Venus, seated in her shell above the chandelier. As with other decorative schemes by Kent at this period, he is revealed as an inventive designer but a poor painter and he must have been seen to greater disadvantage surrounded by Maratti's suavely executed canvases. Giles Worsley has pointed out that Kent drew his inspiration for such ceiling designs from sixteenth- and seventeenth-century drawings taken from ancient Roman houses. These he would have seen in the collections of friends such as Thomas Coke (for whom he designed neighbouring Holkham) and his chief patron, Lord Burlington.[1]

Lord Hervey recounted the appearance of the state apartment in progress: 'The furniture is to be green velvet and tapestry, Kent designs of chimneys, the marble gilded and modern ornaments. Titian and Guido supply those that are borrowed from antiquity.'[2]

The choice of sumptuous, plain green velvet has been remarked on as unexpected by John Cornforth (see p. 31), for the usual progression towards the State Bedchamber is one of increasingly costly materials and more refined pattern. However, it is in keeping with the theme of love, as green is the colour associated with Venus, goddess of the sea. This reaches its peak with the celebrated green velvet bed in the following room, which Kent designed almost as a temple to Venus.

Twelve giltwood chairs and a pair each of stools and settees in the same plain velvet with gold braid would have stood formally against the walls of the drawing room. These too feature Venus's scallop shell along with bacchic lions or panthers (cat. 46). Horace Walpole made special mention of the pier table of lapis lazuli for which a drawing survives (cat. 47) and four 'Sconces of massive silver'. These last have since disappeared and it is not known if they were solid silver or silvered wood.

Today the room retains a rare set of English woven silk panels, given by George, Prince of Wales, to the 4th Earl, later 1st Marquess of Cholmondeley, in the late eighteenth century.

1 Worsley, 1993
2 Hervey, 1731

45 Carlo Maratti

Camerino 1625 – Rome 1713

Pope Clement IX, 1669

Oil on canvas, 158 x 118.5 cm

Inscribed on sheet of paper on the table, 'Alla Santite / di N. Sig. re Clemente IX / Per / Carlo Maratti'

Prov: Pallavacini Collection (Palazzo Rospigliosi), Rome; Palazzo Arnaldi, Florence; brought to England by Charles Jervas, *c.*1739; by whom sold to Sir Robert Walpole for 200 guineas (Vertue); by descent to George Walpole, 3rd Earl of Orford; by whom sold to Catherine II of Russia, 1779 (SHM 42)

Lit: Bellori, 1695; Vertue, III, pp. 96, 112, 114; Vertue, p. 14; MS 1744 'Green Velvet Drawing Room Ov. ch.'; Walpole, 1747, p. 54; Kustodieva et al, 1989, no. 40, pp. 334–5

The State Hermitage Museum, St Petersburg

Giulio Rospigliosi (1600–69) was a highly cultured servant of the Church. Having studied philosophy and theology at the University of Pisa, he also showed considerable literary talent, writing a number of libretti, notably for the opera *S.Alessio*, performed at the opening of the theatre of the Barberini Palace in 1634. Alexander VII, after naming him governor of Rome, created Rospigliosi a cardinal in 1657. In 1667 he succeeded Alexander, taking the name Clement IX. It was for Clement IX that Bernini conceived the *Angels carrying the Instruments of the Passion* that adorn the Ponte Sant'Angelo.

According to Bellori in 1695, Maratti painted this portrait in the Palazzo di Santa Sabina in Rome, shortly before the Pope's death. Two other versions are known: in the Vatican (signed and dated 1669) and in the collection of the Duke of Devonshire (formerly belonging to Lord Burlington).[1] Until recently it was assumed that the Vatican painting was the prime version. However, the cleaning of Sir Robert Walpole's canvas has revealed the inscription, which corresponds to that Bellori originally recorded. According to George Vertue, Charles Jervas sold this portrait to Walpole shortly before his death in November 1739, having himself brought it back from Rome in May that year.

This canvas reveals Maratti's powers as a portraitist and fully deserved its place of honour over the chimneypiece in the room that came to be named after the painter. Walpole owned a total of thirteen paintings

by Maratti and the majority are now in St Petersburg.[2] Of *Pope Clement IX*, Vertue observed: ''tis a fine picture and in great preservation – a small fraction has happend in the face – the complexion rather pale than florid the cloke red velvet his cap red – the chair richly adornd. gold carv'd...'

1 A replica is in the Staatliche Kunstsammlung, Kassel.

2 Maratti's *Judgement of Paris* now forms the centrepiece of the restored ceiling in the Grand Hall of Rastrelli's Catherine Palace in Tsarskoye Selo. His *Venus and Cupid*, however, has been lost.

46 Anonymous English craftsman, second quarter of the eighteenth century

Side chair, c.1731

Oil-gilded and sanded walnut frame with beech and pine secondary timbers, original plain green silk velvet upholstery with serge back and silver-gilt braid (tarnished)
100 x 66 x 74 cm

Prov: made for Sir Robert Walpole, Houghton Hall; by descent to present owner

Lit: Macquoid, 1906, p. 46 fig. 37; Tipping, 1921, p. 72; Macquoid and Edwards, 1954, I, p. 268 fig. 131; Cooper, 1965, p. 223; Cornforth, 1987A, p. 107, fig. 9; Christie's, 1994, lots 131–2

The Marquess of Cholmondeley

The State Apartment, consisting of the Maratti or Drawing Room, Bedchamber and Dressing Room was upholstered en suite in green velvet, with the same pattern of chairs used throughout. In the Maratti Room in 1792 there were listed: 'Twelve Chairs Stuffed & covered with green / velvet gilt frames & serge cases / Two Sophas finished to correspond / Four Stools en suite.' In all, there were thirty-nine matching seats between the rooms, including armchairs with lion head arms and an 'easy chair'.

The velvet is likely to have been provided by Richard or the younger Thomas Roberts[1] and it is possible that they also provided the frames of the seats. As Messrs Turner, Hill and Pitter had made the great quantity of passementerie for the Green Velvet Bed and curtains, they almost certainly supplied the two kinds of diaper-pattern gold 'lace' for the chairs.

The chair frames themselves continue the themes of both Bacchus and Venus found elsewhere in the apartment. At the centre of the chair's apron is a satyr's mask, representing the followers of Bacchus, and there are leopard (or lion) masks on each leg. Venus is alluded to by her shell at the sides of the chairs and fish scales on the armchairs from the set. Although it is unlikely that the chair maker had a deliberate iconographic programme in mind, he would have undoubtedly come across works of art where Venus and Bacchus were shown together. In seventeenth-century art in particular, they were linked in a popular saying by the Roman playwright Terence, which declared that without wine (and food too, brought by Ceres) love would grow cold.

The chair's design pays a debt to Kent, but differs from furniture he is known to have provided designs for at this period. As well as Roberts, another possible maker is William Bradshaw (d. 1775) who did make very similar chairs for Chevening, in Kent (see Cornforth above). There are some interesting details in the set's upholstery. The colour and trimming of the velvet varies between the Dressing Room and two other rooms, indicating that they may have been made in two lots.[2] Several of the side chairs' covers are removable case-, or 'false' covers, as they were sometimes referred to, attached underneath on short pins.

1 Beard and Gilbert, 1986, p. 754
2 Christie's, 1994 (lots 131–2)

47 William Kent

Bridlington 1685 – London 1748

Design for a pier table, 1731

Pencil, pen and ink with brown wash, 24 x 37 cm

Inscribed verso, 'For Sr Rt Walpole at Houghton. Novr. 1731'

Prov: bought by the South Kensington Museum from E. Parsons, 1877 (Prints and Drawings 8156)

Exh: London V&A, 1984/B (B8); Kingston-upon-Hull, 1985 (52)

Lit: Vardy, 1744, pl. 41; Jourdain, 1948, fig. 134; Ward–Jackson, 1958, p. 18; Beard, 1975, p. 870; London, 1984/B, (B8); V&A leaflet, 1984, p. 11; Kingston-upon-Hull, 1985 (52); Wilson, 1984, fig. 35

Trustees of the Victoria and Albert Museum

This is one of a handful of drawings by Kent that can be directly associated with a surviving piece of furniture. The design is remarkably close in detail to the 'Table of Lapis Lazuli' that Horace Walpole describes first of all in the Carlo Maratti Room. Indeed, if it were not for Kent's doodle of cardinals (recalling his time in Rome) it would be tempting to see this finished drawing not as a design, but as a copy made for the engraver, John Vardy, who later published the design in his book of Inigo Jones and Kent designs of 1744. There is, however, no reason to doubt the date given in the inscription, which ties in with the completion of the Maratti Room.

The table in question is a gilded pier table with a very unusual veneered top of blue and yellow lapis lazuli. Kent's design uses classical ornament along the top rails of the table, overlaid with more sculptural elements that give it a Baroque feeling; cornucopiae of fruit, ribbon-tied swags and a lion's mask in the centre. He builds up the extraordinary legs from a number of components: a fish-scale pattern scroll at the top is placed on to a fluted, square-section baluster and the whole leg ends with a bun foot. However, the way in which each ornament relates to the others ensures that the result, both in the drawing and in the table, is entirely convincing.

Kent appears to have reused the design with variations for the table in the Marble Parlour, which is likely to have been made a year or so later (cat. 59).

Fig. 59 The Tapestry Dressing Room, 1996; showing the set of Mortlake tapestries of the house of Stuart

The Dressing Room
[The Tapestry Dressing Room]

This room formed the private closet, a sitting-room to the state Green Velvet Bedchamber and, as with that room, the walls are still hung today with tapestries. Here there is a set of English tapestries, woven by a worker from the Mortlake workshop, Francis Poyntz, in 1672, who based his designs on full-length portraits of the Stuart dynasty: Charles I and Henrietta Maria after Van Dyck; James I, Anne and her brother Christian IV of Denmark after Paul van Somer. The tapestries have bold, grotesque borders incorporating portrait roundels of the royal children and a frieze of playful *putti*. Poyntz wove his signature and the date into the background of the portrait of James I. They may well have been made for the old house in Sir Robert's father's day and reused in this room.[1] Of the three paintings hanging in the Dressing Room in 1743, the most significant was the overmantel, Jean Le Maire's *Consultation of the Sibyllic Oracles*. None of the images seems to relate to Kent's painted ceiling representing Spring (or Flora) – the niceties between decoration and art did not always fall into place.

As in the Green Velvet Bedchamber, the windows were hung with 'Two rich green Velvet hang down Window Curtains lined with green silk and trimmed with gold lace Valens, fringed', according to the 1792 inventory, which elaborates on the earlier one. Against the walls would have been another ten from the set of giltwood and green velvet 'chamber chairs' found in the preceding two rooms.

Two more unusual and prized items of furniture were the glass-topped, gilt-gesso table (cat. 49) and a 'Glass case filled with a large Quantity of Silver Philegree, which belonged to *Catherine* Lady Walpole' (Walpole, 1747). There is a bill for such a display cabinet from a Christopher Cock in 1734 for £113 16*s*. 5*d*., a very costly item.[2] As in the other bedchambers and dressing rooms, the only practical piece of furniture for storing clothes and possessions was a lacquer or japanned cabinet.

1 Plumb, 1956, p. 93
2 Beard, 1981, p. 175; John Cornforth has recently identified this cabinet in the private rooms.

48 Peter-Charles Canot, after Charles Jervas

France 1710 – Kentish Town 1777

Dogs and Still Life, 2 March 1778

Line engraving, 22.9 x 26.8 cm, trimmed to plate mark

Inscribed, 'J'ervase Pinxit/ Jos.[h] Farington delin[t]/ DOG AND STILL LIFE/ P.C. Canot sculpsit/ In the Dressing Room at Houghton/ size of the Picture 3[F] 1½[I] by 4[F] 1½[I] in length / published March 12 1778 by John Boydell Engraver in Cheapside London', with Walpole Arms: 'FARI QUE SENTIAT'

Lit: Boydell, I, 37

The Trustees of the British Museum

This is one of two engravings by Canot of overdoors by Charles Jervas, based on drawings undertaken by Joseph Farington (1747–1821) on behalf of John Boydell. Farington visited Houghton in 1773 to make his copies of a number of paintings for subsequent engraving.

Jervas's two canvases are themselves most likely to be copies. A fashionable portrait painter, Jervas was also employed by Sir Robert (and others) as a copyist. His studio sale shortly after his death in November 1739 included numerous replicas, among them copies after paintings by Van Dyck, Carlo Maratti, Frans Snyders and Andrea Sacchi (all Sir Robert's collection).[1] Sir Robert almost certainly commissioned Jervas to produce two Flemish school-type overdoors to complement the fine series of Mortlake tapestries after portraits by Van Dyck and Van Somer.[2]

1 One such copy, day 2, lot 206, was a *Wild Boar's Head and Dog* bought by 'Lord Walpole' for £14 3*s*. 6*d*. (NAL, Houlditch MSS 86.00.18/19).

2 The second overdoor is published in Boydell I, 38 (on the same sheet). Both were *in situ* by 1736.

49 Anonymous English craftsman, first quarter of the eighteenth century

Side table with mirrored top, c.1725

Water-gilded gesso on pine with beech secondary timbers, silvered *verre églomisé* top, 70.5 x 75 x 46 cm

Prov: at Houghton Hall by *c.*1743; by descent to present owner

Lit: Macquoid, 1906, p. 30, fig. 24; Macquoid and Edwards, 1954, III, p. 282; Cooper, 1965, fig. 224

The Marquess of Cholmondeley

Houghton has many pieces of fine quality furniture dating from Sir Robert's lifetime that do not owe a debt to the influence to William Kent and his associates, such as this elegant little side table. Unlike much of the furniture designed for the house, it is the product of a gilder who has used gesso rather than carved wood for its decoration.

The extravagant inclusion of a mirrored top with Sir Robert's monogram could suggest that the table was made by a specialist mirror manufacturer from London, such as John Belchier (d. 1753). At this period such manufacturers would have mostly worked with gesso. In 1726 he supplied a similar, though more elaborate, table to Erddig, now in Clwyd.[1] This has the arms of Meller in its mirrored top.

The monogram can be read as 'RWK', perhaps standing for Robert Walpole Knight and therefore providing a date of around 1725, when he received the Order of the Bath. This means that it might have been specially ordered or given to commemorate his knighthood. The slender lines of the table are typical of the earlier part of the 1720s and not in keeping with the heavier gilded furniture of Houghton. This could suggest that the table was brought from another home, perhaps Sir Robert's town house in Arlington Street or Orford House in Chelsea.

1 National Trust guide, 1988 edn, p. 23

The Embroidered Bed Chamber

Fig. 60 The Embroidered Bed Chamber, 1996; Sir Robert Walpole's arms are embroidered on the great bed

The second state bedchamber may not have been completed until after 1731, for several guests recount the visit of the Duke of Lorraine, future Holy Roman Emperor, that year when he used the 'wrought bed' (i.e. the embroidered bed) whilst in the Green Velvet Bedchamber. Lord Oxford recounted, 'They showed us with ceremony, this the room [the Green Velvet Bedchamber] the Duke of Lorraine lay in, a very indifferent room. I suppose, it is always to go after his name.'[1]

Kent provided another indifferently painted ceiling, with a rather unusual choice of subject, which may indicate that this room was intended to be the second state bedchamber for the Queen, or the wife of the guest of honour. In the central, round panel is the story of Luna, moon goddess, with the shepherd Endymion: she may also be identified as Diana, chaste goddess of hunting; a suitable choice for a lady's chamber. The whole of the ceiling is painted as a canopy of night, and features owls and bats against a dark-blue ground. Owls are of course also a symbol of Minerva (who is often found in the imagery of women's quarters), and they too feature in the simulated cameos on the coving where they are attended by *putti*.

The great bed of *c*.1726–31 is described by Horace Walpole as made of 'Indian' needlework, which was the common term given to any embroidered textile that was either imported or copied from the Far East. In this instance the bed hangings are of Indian manufacture, with the Walpole arms and Garter Star, together with the decidedly western motifs on the valences, and were made to order in India. The shape of the bed is rather old-fashioned in comparison to Kent's *tour-de-force* in the Green Velvet Bedchamber. This may explain the demotion of this particular bed.

Green silk window curtains matched those put up around the bed to protect it, all adding to the much lighter feeling of this room, in contrast to the State Bedchamber. The walls still have their set of Brussels tapestries showing the story of *Bacchus taken from Naxos*, the *Marriage of Bacchus and Ariadne* and a *Bacchanal* obscured by the bed. Horace Walpole singled out the overmantel, which in 1736 was Nicolas Poussin's large *Holy Family* (cat. 51).

The seat furniture comprised eight part-gilt, walnut chairs, again covered in green velvet. These would have been formally arranged around the bed for the reception of visitors in the mornings. Also used in the Cabinet next door, their design is probably older than the rest. They may well therefore have been supplied before the new Hall was complete.[2]

1 Harley, 1732 2 Illustrated in Christie's, 1994, lots 126, 127

50 Peter-Charles Canot, after Rosa da Tivoli

France 1710 – Kentish Town 1777

The Goats-Herd, 1 December 1778

Line engraving, 44.6 x 31.8 cm, trimmed to the platemark

Inscribed, 'Rosa da Tivoli Pinxit Joseph Farrington delint. The GOATS-HERD In the Embroidered Bed Chamber at Houghton. Size of the Picture F3 I1½ by F4.4¾ in length Published Sept. 30th 1776 by John Boydell Engraver in Cheapside London'

Lit: Boydell, I, 29

The Trustees of the British Museum

Canot's engravings of the overdoors in the Embroidered Bedchamber serve as a reminder of the integrity of Sir Robert's decorative schemes. The Brussels tapestries that furnished the walls of this room remain *in situ* today. They represent, on one wall, the taking of Dionysius from Naxos and, on the opposite wall, his marriage to Ariadne. The pastoral settings are echoed in the furnishing pictures which Sir Robert selected as overdoors.

Philip Roos (1657–1706), known as Rosa da Tivoli, specialised in pastoral landscapes and had studied in Rome before settling in Tivoli. His landscapes were invariably populated with animals, sometimes set against classical ruins. *The Goats-Herd* and its pair *The Shepherd* are named simply in the *Aedes* as 'two pieces of cattle'. Sir Robert's pictures by Rosa da Tivoli were recorded by Vertue in 1730.[1]

1 Vertue, III, p. 44

51 Nicolas Poussin

Les Andelys 1594 – Rome 1665

The Holy Family with Sts John and Elizabeth, 1655

Oil on canvas, 172 x 133.5 cm

Prov: painted by Nicolas Poussin for his friend and patron Paul Fréart de Chantelou; ?Comte de Fraula collection, Brussels, by 1720; probably acquired by Sir Robert Walpole through Lord Waldegrave, 1735; first recorded at Houghton, 'in the work'd Bed Chamber', 1736; then by descent to George Walpole, 3rd Earl of Orford; by whom sold to Catherine II of Russia, 1779 (SHM 1213)

Exh: Chicago and New York 1990 (4)

Lit: Houghton, MS 1736 and MS 1744; Walpole, 1747, pp. 60–1; Boydell, II, 18

The State Hermitage Museum, St Petersburg

Poussin's composition, inspired by Raphael's late images of the Holy Family, achieves an extraordinary monumentality, imbued with an austere grandeur. Horace Walpole in the *Aedes* described this painting as 'one of the most capital Pictures in this Collection'. The painting hung as an overmantel in the Embroidered Bed Chamber and provided a calm centre of gravity to the richly decorated room.

Sir Robert almost certainly acquired the painting in Paris through the agency of James, 1st Earl Waldegrave in 1735. A group of Waldegrave manuscripts survives which demonstrate that Sir Robert was purchasing a work through Waldegrave in 1734/5. Although the correspondence does not mention the title of the Poussin in question, it is evidently a major work for which Sir Robert was prepared to pay £400 in the belief that this was 'the highest price that was ever given for a Picture of Poussin' (see also p. 53). Waldegrave wrote to Sir Robert on 16 August 1735: 'I hope that before this time you have received yr Poussin, now it is gone the People that were about it, would give more than you gave for it. I am heartily glad it is yours'.[1] Sir Robert finally paid £320.[2]

The 1736 inventory records eight examples of the work of Poussin in Sir Robert's collection at that time. These included *Moses striking the Rock* (SHM 1177) and *The Continence of Scipio* (see cat. 67).

He was also offered one of the series of Poussin's *Seven Sacraments,* in the knowledge that the artist was to his taste (see cat. 16). In addition, he acquired *The Nurture of Jupiter* (National Gallery of Art, Washington, DC, no. 1104), which hung in Downing Street.

1 Houghton archive, File Lib 45

2 This precludes the provenance suggested by Blunt 1966, no. 56, (which he gives as: '...Possibly Comte de Fraula collection, Brussels, by 1720 (Richardson, Account, p. 6); sold de Vos, Brussels, 21ff. vii. 1738, lot 20 (size given as 85½ x 60 inches, which might correspond if the frame were included...)'. This is not possible as the painting is recorded at Houghton in 1736 (see Lit. above).

Fig. 61 The Cabinet Room, 1996, with the overmantel painting replaced by a mirror and the late eighteenth-century Chinese wallpaper

The Cabinet

In the early plan attributed to Gibbs (Fig. 9) for Houghton this room was intended as a bedchamber, as were the other tower rooms and the Library. The splendid giltwood overmantel, with Venus mask and shell, and the continuation of green velvet on the walls certainly fitted in with this early scheme. However, Kent's painted ceiling featuring Minerva, with the Walpole arms on her shield, crushing Envy, is not a subject to contemplate from the bedside.[1] At an early stage there must have been a change in function and the room became Sir Robert's Cabinet; a picture closet where his fine, smaller works could be admired in private.

An early design for the elevations and frieze for the room is now in the Ashmolean Museum, Oxford (Anonymous British architectural drawings – now given to Kent). This shows the ceiling outline as intended, but instead of windows shows a curious niche opposite the chimneypiece that is suitable for a statue. Only one work of art is shown; Rubens's large cartoon for *Meleager and Atalanta* (see cat. 66), filling an entire wall. This was the painting Lord Burlington had failed to fit into his design for General Wade's new town house.[2]

The Cabinet underwent several rehangs as Sir Robert increased the size and quality of his collection at Houghton: these are discussed with the drawing of the room of about 1742 (cat. 56). This hanging plan, made before the influx of cabinet pictures from Downing Street, shows a very architectural approach to the placing and framing of paintings, which are subordinate to the overall appearance of each wall. Symmetry and balance were certainly more important than subject matter or artistic school.

By the time Horace Walpole came to write his *Aedes* there were more than fifty-one, mostly small, works in the room, including what he believed to be Van Dyck's (now given to Rubens) *Hélène Fourment* (Lisbon, Gulbenkian Collection), given pride of place in the overmantel. When not pressing their noses to the small pictures, guests sat on more of the walnut suite of velvet chairs, of which there were no less than fifteen, with a pair of settees. On the darkest, window wall were 'two Glass oval Sconces with three branches each' (1745); these accord with those shown in the elevation of this wall, suggesting that it is fairly reliable in its detail and not merely a sketch design.

After the sale of paintings to Russia the green velvet would have been very worn and pock-marked with nail holes, so by 1792 it had been replaced with the enchanting blue Chinese wallpaper found on the walls of the Cabinet today. This change in taste and colour was cheaply reconciled with the heavy, older furniture by providing blue tammy covers to the green velvet seats: a fortuitous measure that helps to explain their good condition today.

1 Worsley, 1993, fig. 7
2 London, Wiggins, 1987 (9)

---

52 Ascribed to Diego Velázquez

Seville 1599 – Madrid 1660

Pope Innocent X, c.1650

Oil on canvas, 49.2 x 41.3 cm

Prov: Sir Robert Walpole by 1747; by descent to George Walpole, 3rd Earl of Orford; by whom sold to Catherine II of Russia, 1779; bought from the Soviet Union, 1931, by M. Knoedler & Co for Andrew Mellon; given by him to the National Gallery of Art Washington, DC, 1937 (1937.1.80 (80))

Lit: Walpole, 1747, p. 63; Brown and Mann, 1990 , pp. 123–7

Engr: Valentine Green after George Farington, mezzotint, 1 Oct. 1774

National Gallery of Art, Washington, DC

This portrait head was ideal for Sir Robert's cabinet of 'very small' pictures. Hung against green velvet, it was one of those which Horace Walpole appreciated enough to recount the story of the original commission: '[Velázquez] was sent by the King of Spain to draw this Pope's Picture; when the Pope sent his Chamberlain to pay him, he would not receive the Money, saying the King his Master always paid him with his own Hand: The Pope humoured him. This Pope was one of the Pamphilii Family, was reckoned the ugliest Man of his Time, and was raised to the Papacy by the intrigues of his Sister-in-law *Donna Olimpia*, a most beautiful woman and his Mistress'. Horace added an extensive footnote to the 1767 edition of *Aedes Walpolianae*, increasing the panoply of anecdote surrounding this picture.

The quality of the painting is now recognised as distinctly inferior to the original portrait (Galleria Doria-Pamphili, Rome) painted by Velázquez either in 1649 or 1650, during his second trip to Italy. A letter from the Nuncio at Madrid, Giulio Rospigliosi, to Cardinal Pamphili in Rome, dated 8 July 1651, states that Velázquez had returned from Italy bringing with him 'a portrait closely resembling His Holiness which has greatly pleased his Majesty'. While this could refer to the version that is now in the Wellington Museum, London, Walpole's version, also in a reduced format, shows pentimenti and is of good contemporary quality.[1]

1 Sir Robert owned a second painting attributed to Velázquez, the *Death of Joseph*. In Lady Walpole's Drawing Room, Downing Street, in 1736, this also later hung in the Cabinet at Houghton by 1744. This too was sold to Catherine II of Russia in 1779.

53 Richard Earlom, after Sebastien Bourdon

London 1743 – London 1822

Jacob burying Laban's Images, 1 June 1785

Etching with mezzotint, 41.3 x 49.8 cm

Inscribed '[Arms in centre], 'John Boydell, excudit. 1785. / Seb. Bourdon Pinxit R. Earlom Fecit. / JACOB BURYING LABANS IMAGES / In the Cabinet at Houghton. / Size of the picture 3.[F] 1[I] ¾ by 4.[F] 4[I] ½ long. / publish'd June 1.st 1785 by John Boydell, Engraver, in Cheapside, London.'

Lit: Boydell, II, 42; Wessely, 1886, 3 ii/ii

The Hon. Charles Lennox Boyd

Richard Earlom originally published this mezzotint in 1766, as part of John Boydell's earlier project, *A Collection of Prints Engraved after the Most Capital Paintings in England*. As such, it was one of Earlom's earliest prints and does not exploit the full richness of tone that is evident in his later oeuvre.

By 1736 Sir Robert owned four paintings by or attributed to Sebastien Bourdon (1616–71). Three hung in Grosvenor Street, London, until two were sent up to Houghton around 1742. The fourth, *Samson and the Lion*, hung in the closet, Downing Street.

Laban searching for his Images was in fact one of the larger paintings to be hung in the Cabinet (excluding Rubens's magnificent overmantel, *Hélène Fourment*). The composition is a somewhat languid interpretation of the subject of Laban's search for his idols stolen by his daughter Rachel (Genesis 31).[1] The second painting by Bourdon to be moved to Norfolk was also hung in the Cabinet, his *Murder of the Innocents*.[2]

1 The oil is now SHM 3682.

2 SHM 1223

54 Jean-Baptiste Michel, after David Teniers II

Paris 1748 – 1804

Boors at cards, 1 December 1778

Line engraving, 36.6 x 25.9 cm, trimmed to platemark

Inscribed, 'David Teniers Pinxit J.B. Michel sculpsit/ Josiah Boydell delin^{t} / Boors at cards/ In the cabinet at Houghton / Picture the same size as the print / Published Dec 1st 1778 by Jno Boydell / Engraver in Cheapside London'

Lit: Boydell, I, 53

The Trustees of the British Museum

Eighteenth-century collectors in Britain were pleased to hang their small Dutch and Flemish works in a setting such as a Cabinet Room. Horace Walpole, in his introduction to the *Aedes Walpolianae*, had little that was good to say of Dutch painting (his judgement was coloured by the fact that he had not visited Holland and Flanders on his grand tour). However, he recognised their popularity and himself asked the question: 'as for the Dutch Painters, those drudging Mimics of Nature's most uncomely coarseness, don't their earthen pots and brass kettles carry away prices only due to the sweetness of Albano, and to the attractive delicacy of Carlo Maratti?'

Despite his son's lack of enthusiasm for Dutch and Flemish works of this type, Sir Robert owned four works by David Teniers II (1610–90) at Houghton. Teniers was strongly influenced by Adriaen Brouwer, but his depiction of peasants and boors are invariably more genteel, lending a fashionable refinement to his tavern scenes. Two paintings entitled *Boors at cards* (SHM 569, 577) hung in the Cabinet.[1] In addition, 'Cows and Sheep, by *Teniers*, in his best Manner' hung in the Picture Gallery. The most splendid was *A Cook's Shop* (SHM 586) which hung in the Common Parlour in the company of a similar subject by Martin de Vos (SHM 610).

J.-B. Michel specialised in engravings after Old Masters and engraved nineteen of the Houghton pictures for Boydell.

1 These had both hung in Lady Walpole's Drawing Room at Downing Street.

55 Richard Earlom, after Jan van Huysum

London 1743 – London 1822

A Flower Piece, 25 June 1778

Mezzotint, 55.7 x 41.9 cm

Inscribed [Arms in centre], 'John Boydell excudit 1778 / Van Huysom Pinxit. Richd Earlom Sculpsit. / Joseph Farington delin.^{t} / A FLOWER PIECE. / In the Cabinet at Houghton. / Size of the picture 2^{F}. 2^{I} by 2^{F}. 7^{I} high. / Published June 25th 1778 by John Boydell Engraver in Cheapside London.'

Lit: Boydell, I, 59; Wessely, 1886, 144 iii/iii

The Hon. Charles Lennox Boyd

Earlom's prints after Sir Robert's two paintings by Jan van Huysum (1682–1749) have long been recognised as two of the finest mezzotints ever produced. John Boydell's introduction in *The Houghton Gallery* comments, 'N.B. The two prints from these pictures are particularly admired by all lovers of the arts, and are allowed to surpass, in point of execution, every print before engraved in this manner!'

The esteem in which Van Huysum's flower pieces, in particular, were held lay in his facility in painting flowers from nature. This realism combined with a symbolism associated with the plant world: the butterfly is seen as the personification of the soul, while insects and full-blown roses are emblems of the transitory nature of earthly life. In the background of *A Flower Piece* can be seen a sculptural group modelled on Bernini's *Apollo and Daphne* which carries a similar message.

The original painting (SHM 1051) is dated 1722, but it is not certain when this and its companion *Fruit Piece* (SHM 1049) were acquired by Sir Robert. They were both hanging in the Green Velvet Drawing Room at Houghton in 1736. He may have acquired them through van Huysum's brother Michiel van Huysum (1704–*c*.60) who was patronised by Sir Robert. The 1736 inventory records: 'All the pictures over the chimneys & Doors in the Attic Story are drawn by a Brother of Van Huysum's, who liv'd in Sr Robert's House [i.e. Houghton Hall].' The inventory also records two more flower pieces by van Huysum in Lady Walpole's Drawing Room at Chelsea.[1]

1 Sold Lord Orford, 1748, day 1, lots 65, 66 Pictures &c at Houghton, 1744 (Houlditch MSS)

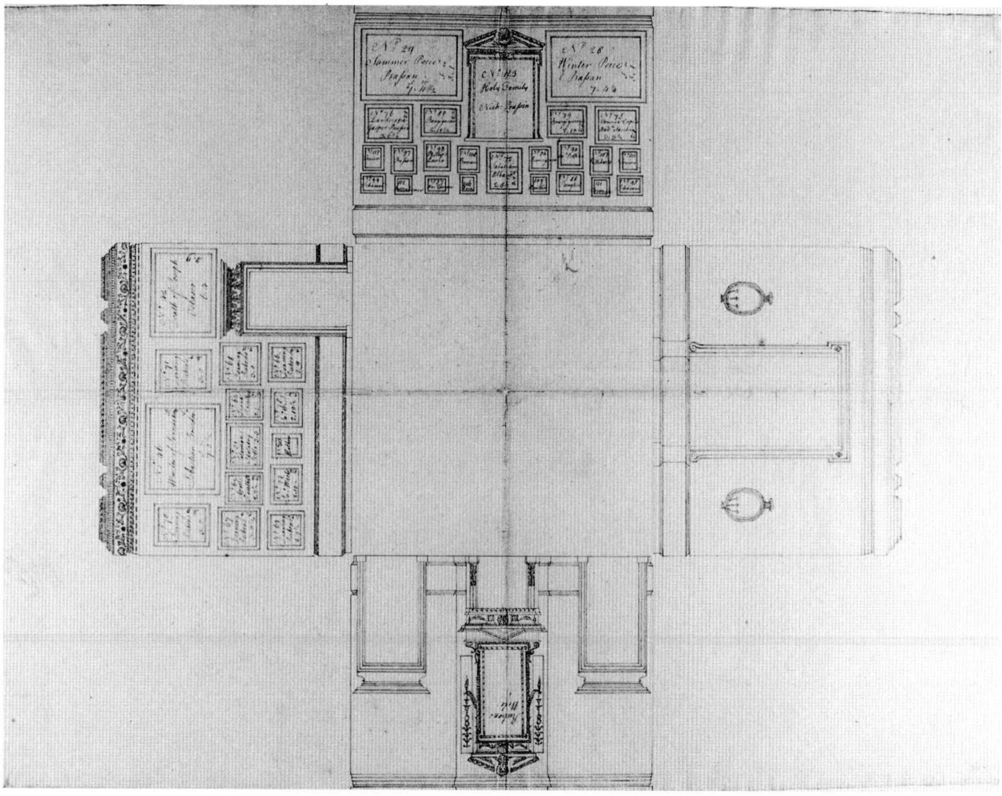

56 Anonymous draughtsman

A plan of the picture hang in the Cabinet, c.1742

Sepia and black ink on laid paper, 75.5 x 54.2 cm

Prov: Houghton Hall archive; by descent to present owner (Houghton MSS A84)

The Marquess of Cholmondeley

This is one of a series of planned picture arrangements which was made before Sir Robert's paintings from London were hung at Houghton, in about 1742–3 (see cat. 14). In 1736 'the Corner Drawing Room' simply housed two full lengths and three half lengths from the Wharton Collection, the huge cartoon of *Meleager and Atalanta* by Rubens and the full-length of *Hélène Fourment*, at that time believed to be by Van Dyck.[1]

The decision to transform the room into a cabinet room to house a massed display of mainly small-scale easel paintings in common with contemporary fashion was possible once the Picture Gallery was built. The full lengths and the cartoon of *Meleager and Atalanta* were moved out. In their stead a host of fifty-one pictures were hung on, effectively, just two walls. The preliminary plan shows a hang of just thirty-eight pictures in a carefully worked out scheme based upon frame sizes. In the event, more paintings had to be hung. The *Family of Rubens* by Jordaens (SHM 484), which had belonged to the Duke of Portland, hung here in place of the *Holy Family* by Poussin, which remained instead in the adjacent Embroidered Bed Chamber (see cat. 51).

The two canvases by Jacopo Bassano were placed as planned.[2] This was also where Sir Robert arranged his six oil sketches for triumphal arches by Rubens. These were all *modelli* by Rubens for the decorations to celebrate the triumphal Entry of the Infant Ferdinand of Austria into Antwerp, and of high quality. One other Rubens hung in the Cabinet, the original design for the central compartment of the ceiling for the Banqueting House in Whitehall, representing the apotheosis of King James I (SHM 507).

The effect of so many fine works hung against the green velvet must have created exactly the effect of richness required. Sir Robert no doubt found his new Cabinet more to his taste than that from which he had been summarily dismissed in Downing Street.

1 Now recognised as by Rubens (Gulbenkian Collection, Lisbon). (See Fig. 36)

2 Larger paintings were hung in the uppermost register, where small paintings would be difficult to distinguish.

Fig. 62 The Marble Parlour, 1996

The Marble Parlour

The Marble Parlour, or Great Dining Room, as it is given in the 1745 inventory, was the final room in the main house to be completed. This should come as no surprise, for there were several other eating rooms at Houghton, not least the great Stone Hall itself. The extensive use of statuary and fine coloured marbles for the room cannot have expedited work, or Sir Robert's payments to the craftsmen and work continued well into the 1730s. Sir Thomas Robinson remarked upon its state in 1731: 'There is only one dining room to be finished and which is to be lined with marble, and will be a noble work.'[1]

Rooms dedicated to dining were still a novelty in country houses at this time, and the double buffet alcoves, set behind the central fireplace, show how the architect of the room enjoyed a certain amount of freedom from conventions. If the anonymous early floor plan in the RIBA (Fig. 9) is by Gibbs, then it is to him that credit is due for this concept.[2]

The design for the interior of the Marble Parlour was developed between 1728 and 1732 and is shown in another early drawing for an interior at Houghton (cat. 58). Kent's completed solution was for an arched screen along the buffet wall, executed entirely in different coloured variegated marbles. The great buffets themselves are also made of marble and are plumbed-in, with silver taps to fill the granite wine coolers, one of which survives in the room. This scheme is similar to Kent's more modest dining room and buffet at nearby Raynham, remodelled at about the same time as Houghton.

In the centre of the buffet wall is the splendid sculpted chimneypiece featuring Rysbrack's overmantel relief of a *Roman Sacrifice* (see cat. 57).

The remainder of the room is totally given over to bacchic ornament: every ceiling field painted with gorging *putti*, every beam and cornice, pier glass and table covered in gilded grape vines. Lord Hervey has left a vivid description of how Sir Robert's guests were entertained to dinner at Houghton, perhaps in this very room.

> Our company at Houghton swelled at last in so numerous a body that we used to sit down to dinner a little snug party of about thirty odd, up to the chin in beef, venison, geese, turkeys, etc., and generally over the chin in claret, strong beer and punch... In public we drank loyal healths, talked of the times and cultivated popularity; in private we drew plans, and cultivated the country.[3]

The early furnishing of the room included twelve armchairs and a settee which were giltwood, with eagle arms and covered in green silk damask. It is odd that they do not continue the theme of Bacchus, and this, together with the absence of any permanent dining tables in the room in 1745, might suggest a change in use from a regular dining room to a parlour for receiving guests and conversation later in Sir Robert's life.

1 Robinson, 1731
2 Harris, 1985, p. 6; Harris, 1989, p. 93
3 21 July 1731; quoted in Plumb, 1960, p. 88 no. 1

57 **John Michael Rysbrack**
Antwerp 1694 – London 1770
A Roman Sacrifice: cartoon for the overmantel relief in the Marble Parlour, c.1732

Black chalk, heightened with white, on twelve sheets of buff paper; contemporary giltwood frame, 117 x 158.5 cm (sight size)

Prov: Sir Robert Walpole; by descent to George Horatio, 5th Earl of Cholmondeley; presented to the British Museum, 1952 (1952-10-11-1)

Lit: Webb, 1954, pp. 128, 228; Bristol, 1982, p. 40; E. Croft-Murray, Unpublished catalogue of British Drawings, Department of Prints and Drawings, British Museum, London, Rysbrack (no. 2)

The Trustees of the British Museum

Edward Harley mentioned the relief for which this cartoon was made on his second visit to Houghton in 1737: 'The fine marble room is finished, and a most beautiful chimneypiece made by Rysbrack as can be seen'.[1] It had certainly not been hinted at in Kent's earlier design for the buffet wall of the Marble Parlour (cat. 58) and was in place by 1733 when there is a voucher for masons taking down and re-erecting the Dining Room (i.e. Marble Parlour) chimneypiece to insert the 'barsrelieve'.[2] The subject of the overmantel relief is very likely to be based on Roman examples, taken from engravings, as Rysbrack is known to have done with the reliefs in the Stone Hall.[3] A very similar relief was also made for the hall at Clandon Park, Surrey, around 1731–5.

It is very rare for a drawing of this type to survive from an artist working in the eighteenth century in England and even more unusual for it to be made by a sculptor. Quite how Rysbrack used such a drawing is not yet clear. It is not pricked through to transfer the image and there are a number of variations from the relief in the positions of the figures and their individual poses. As the cartoon does not give any fine detail for the figures' faces or anatomy, it seems likely to have been used as a life-size guide for the overall design, with the sculptor adding detail as he carved.

The chimneypiece into which it is set is very well executed and could also be Rysbrack's work. However, the London carver Abraham Swan had a hand in it as well (see Geoffrey Beard, p. 27), though he may have been working under Rysbrack's supervision. The chimneypiece itself is very naturalistically carved, right down to the inclusion of slugs and snails on the vine leaves with which it is garlanded. This is in marked contrast to the detached, Neo-classical manner of the relief.

1 Harley, 1737
2 Tipping, 1921, p. 98; 22 Sept. – 6 Oct. 1733
3 Bristol, 1982, p. 37

58 William Kent

Bridlington 1685 – London 1748

Design for the west wall of the Marble Parlour, 1728

Pen and grey and brown ink, with brown wash on paper, 38 x 10.25 cm

Inscribed verso, 'for your great dining room at Houghton WK 1728'

Prov: sold Sotheby's, London, 1 April 1993, lot 37

Lit: Ware, 1731; Sotheby's, 1993, lot 37; Cornforth, 1996

Private Collection

A good understanding of how William Kent developed and revised his ideas for a room interior can be gained from this recently discovered drawing of 1728, made some four years before the completion of the Marble Parlour.

In it Kent has fleshed out the bones of Gibbs's plan, with its two buffet alcoves either side of the fireplace. At this early stage in the design, he is toying with the idea of using Serlian arches for the buffet openings; a motif he would have seen his patron Lord Burlington employing extensively at Chiswick House about this time. However, it is clear from the drawing that these would have not only obscured some of the plate, sketched in on one side of the buffet, but also hindered the silent ingress of servants during dinner, from a door hidden behind the chimneypiece. The inclusion of a variety of plate and a great wine cooler is relatively unusual in a drawing for an interior of this date.[1]

In the design the chimneypiece itself is much plainer than the great sculptural one, dedicated to Bacchus, that was eventually installed here, and Kent does not hint at Rysbrack's superb classical relief in the overmantel as built. Instead, he includes the bust of Sir Robert Walpole that he went on to use in the Stone Hall chimneypiece (see cat. 32). This may well explain the fact that the bust shows Sir Robert facing to his right, which would have been towards the Marble Parlour entrance.

Kent must still have kept an interest in the rejected ideas from this design as it was published by Ware in his *Designs of Inigo Jones*, 1731.

There exists at Houghton a later design for the buffet side of the room (Houghton MSS A6) showing the more conventional arched screen that was finally built. This is marked up with indications for the types of marbles to be used, including white statuary, purple-and-white 'Plimoth' marble and black-and-gold marble. Even at this much later stage the idea of making the buffet tables themselves out of solid marble had not been considered. Instead, the Houghton drawing shows a table with lion monopods, deriving from the carved lion table shown on the right of Kent's 1728 design.

1 Cornforth, 1996

---

59 Design attributed to William Kent

Bridlington 1685 – London 1748

Pier table, c.1732

Oil-gilded pine, black-and-gold marble, 88 x 146 x 73 cm (with top)

Prov: made for Sir Robert Walpole, Houghton Hall; by descent to present owner

Lit: Tipping, 1921, p. 100 fig. 3; Jackson-Stops and Pipkin, 1984, p. 120 (illus.)

The Marquess of Cholmondeley

The Bacchic decoration of the Marble Parlour almost flows from the ceiling, on to the pier glass and over this table, on which vine-stuffed cornucopiae link the legs and hang, rather comically, from a lion's mouth. The table has much in common with the slightly earlier one in the Maratti Room. Yet this table appears rather less weighty, an effect created by the double volutes that make up the legs and cause them to look as if they are about to spring. With such designs for state furniture Kent is constantly looking for new inspiration and here he cleverly adapts the somewhat old-fashioned fielded-baluster shape of the legs to something entirely novel.

James Richards is once more the most likely maker for the table, which like others at Houghton is well-constructed, in addition to being carved with great vitality.

In 1745 there was only one marble table in the room, besides the great buffets behind the screen, and this table may have been used to display plate as well. The accompanying pier glass still retains its pair of giltwood sconces, which would have helped to bring the carving to life in the evening.

The pupose behind such a piece of furniture, along with the rest of the decoration of the Marble Parlour, was the celebration of the convivial effects of food and wine. It should come as no surprise to learn that Sir Robert spent £1,118.12*s*.10*d*. with his wine merchant and returned 522 empty bottles in 1733 alone.[1]

1 Cornforth, 1996; this bill covered the cost of wine at all Walpole's properties.

60 **Paul de Lamerie**

's Hertogenbosch 1688 – London 1751

The Walpole Salver, London 1728

Britannia standard silver, 49.3 x 49.2 cm, weight 134 oz

Prov: supplied to Sir Robert Walpole, 1st Earl of Orford; Horace Walpole, 4th Earl of Orford; Strawberry Hill sale 1842, bought in for family; sold Christie's, 7 December 1955, lot 147; purchased by the Victoria and Albert Museum (M 9–1956)

Exh: London 1990 (50)

Lit: S. Hare (ed.), Catalogue for *Paul de Lamerie At the Sign of the Golden Ball. An Exhibition of the work of England's Master Silversmith (1688–1751)*, London 1990, p. 94; R. Paulson, *Hogarth*, 3 vols., New Haven and London 1992–3, I, pp. 171–2; T. Schroder, 'Paul de Lamerie: Businessman or Craftsman', *Silver Society Journal*, No. 6 Winter 1994, pp. 267–75 pl. 3

Trustees of the Victoria and Albert Museum

Paul de Lamerie was one of the most celebrated silversmiths working in England in the first half of the eighteenth century. He became a freeman of the Goldsmith's Company in 1712 and then four years later was appointed Goldsmith to the King. He adopted the unadorned Queen Anne style at the beginning of his career, but by the 1730s and 1740s he was working in the Rococo manner.

The Walpole Salver is one of the most important pieces of English eighteenth-century silver. It is engraved with two roundels depicting the obverse and reverse of the Second Exchequer Seal of George I, which was in use from 1724–7. They are supported by a figure of Hercules representing Heroic Virtue. On either side are the allegorical figures of Calumny and Envy with Wisdom and Virtue above. In the background is a view of the City of London. The border includes cartouches surrounding faces representing the four seasons alternating with the cypher RW, and the Walpole arms and crest appear at the corners. The arms are Robert Walpole's quartered with those belonging to Catherine Shorter, his first wife. The salver stands on four cast feet and the rim has been cast and applied.

By 1728 it was a tradition for the holders of Crown Office to have their term of office commemorated with a piece of silver, either a salver or a cup bearing an engraving of the designs from the seals associated with that position. The weight of the piece was frequently close to that of the seals that were a prerequisite of the post. Sir Robert Walpole was Chancellor of the Exchequer for two periods during the reign of George I and each term of office was celebrated with a silver salver. Both salvers were sold in the 1842 Strawberry Hill sale. The second is marked by William Lukin and is engraved and signed by Joseph Sympson.[1]

There is much evidence for the engraving to be attributed to Hogarth (see Lit.), who engraved silver for a variety of clients until his career as a painter became much more securely established in the late 1720s. It has been suggested that Walpole himself requested that Hogarth should be the engraver, but it is much more likely that the commission came via Hogarth's original master, the goldsmith Ellis Gamble, who was a business partner of de Lamerie. Stylistically the allegorical figures are very similar to work known to be by Hogarth, the trade card for Ellis Gamble and the engraving *The Lottery* (1724), which were based on Sir James Thornhill's depictions of the Protestant Succession in the Great Hall at Greenwich.

In addition to the documented silver produced by de Lamerie for Sir Robert Walpole, a red chalk drawing of a chandelier, now attributed to de Lamerie, survives in a private collection. This design bears the Walpole crest and a second chalk design, also for a chandelier, survives at Houghton. In addition, there is a surviving bill of 1730 in the archives at Houghton which is addressed to Sir Robert by G. Hubert. It is for a selection of branches, some for sconces, and a 'fine french lustre neatly repaired composed of french mettle and cristal cutt' (see cat. 16).

1 C. Oman 'English Engravers on Plate III Joseph Sympson and William Hogarth', *Apollo* Vol LXV, no. 389, July 1957, p. 286 fig. 1

61 William Lukin

fl. 1704–*c.*1750

Pair of wine coolers, London 1716

Britannia standard silver, height 21 cm; weight: (a) 124 ounces 2 penny weight, (b) 122 ounces 12 penny weight; marks: (a) inside lip engraved no 1, (b) inside lip engraved no 2

Prov: Sir Robert Walpole, 1st Earl of Orford; Horace Walpole, 4th Earl of Orford; sold Strawberry Hill Sale, 6 May 1842, lot 127 p. 122; Bertram, 5th Earl of Ashburnham, Christie's, 29 March 1919, lot 59; Marchioness of Cholmondeley, Sotheby's, 2 November 1950, lot 150; Metropolitan Museum of Art, New York (68.141.128, 129)

Exh: London, 1929 (760) pl. 55; London, 1938 (141); London, 1950 (85)

Lit: *Highlights of the Untermeyer Collection, Metropolitan Museum of Art*, 1977, no. 80

The Metropolitan Museum of Art, New York

These wine coolers were made for Sir Robert Walpole, 1st Earl of Orford, and were inherited by his younger son Horace. In 1842 they were included in the Strawberry Hill sale where they were described as, 'A pair of splendid octagon WINE COOLERS, chased rose flower tablets, arabesque borders and scroll handles'.

Stylistically the coolers show the influence of French silver of the period, but their design is essentially classical without any indication of the asymmetry of the Rococo, which was gaining popularity at this date. This would indicate that Lukin either employed French silversmiths or sold their work under his own name. It is known that Lukin took eleven apprentices in the period 1704–32.

The coolers that are closest to these in design are a gilt metal pair previously in the Puiforcat collection.[1] A comparable pair of attenuated octagonal shape coolers, one bearing the mark of Pierre Platel 1703 and the other the mark of Paul de Lamerie, London 1716, are in the collection of the Philadelphia Museum of Art. Platel was a pupil of de Lamerie. Another similar cooler by David Willaume, London 1718, was exhibited in London in 1929 in *Queen Charlotte's Loan Exhibition of the Old Silver at Seaford House, London* (no. 461, pl. 69).

1 Gallérie Charpentier, Paris, Dec. 1955, lot 98 pl. XXI, now in the Louvre (*Catalogue de l'orfèvrerie du XVII*e, *XVIII*e *et du XIX*e, Paris 1958, no. 24, pl. VIII where they are described as 'Paris end of the seventeenth century'.

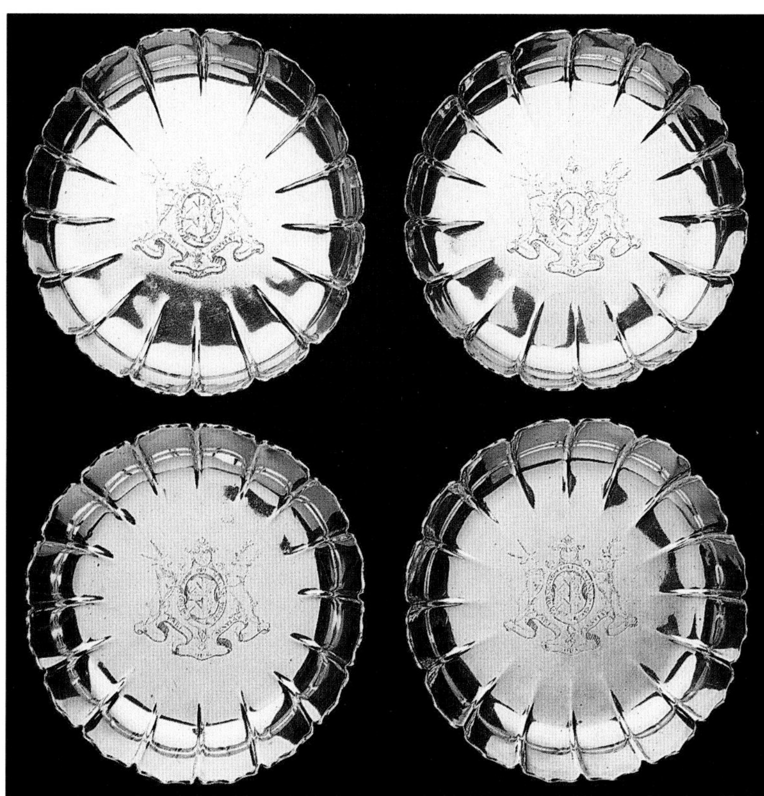

62 Paul de Lamerie and David Willaume

's Hertogenbosch 1688 – London 1751; Metz or Mer-en-Blaisois 1658 – 1741

Four Silver Strawberry Dishes

Diameter 19 cm, weight 52 oz

Prov: Sir Robert Walpole, 1st Earl of Orford; Horace Walpole, 4th Earl of Orford; Strawberry Hill Sale 1842, lot 134; purchased by an English family and thence by descent to Lady Freyborg; sold 1992, acquired by the J. Ortiz-Patiño Collection

The J. Ortiz-Patiño Collection

The dishes are engraved with the arms of Sir Robert Walpole and those of his wife Catherine Shorter. The supporters are those seen flanking the royal arms on the exchequer seal. The dishes were described as, 'Four handsome 7½" circular ribbed preserve dishes' in the 1842 catalogue.[1]

1 In the Cholmondeley archive at Cambridge University an account book (no. 22) lists a bill paid to David Willaume on 5 August 1726 (£123 18s.).

63 Unknown designer

Group of five armorial plates, Chinese c.1730

Two plates, 34 cm diameter; two plates, 31 cm diameter; one plate, 22.3 cm diameter

Porcelain, painted in underglaze blue with overglaze enamel colours and gilding

The centre of each plate bears the Walpole coat of arms painted in gold and sepia with gold mantling. The borders are decorated in red and blue with gilding, the underside with prunus sprays and an auspicious emblem

Prov: the Walpole family at Houghton, and then by descent to the present owner

Exh: two plates are currently on display at 12 Downing Street, London, on loan from the present owner

The Marquess of Cholmondeley

These Chinese decorated porcelain plates were made in China for the European export market. Blue and white porcelain was first produced specifically for the European market as early as the fifteenth century. However, it was not until about 1700 that polychrome armorial dinner services were first made. They were extremely popular throughout Europe but particularly in England. The best known factories were in Jingdezhen. Families would send drawings or prints of their coats of arms to the factories in China so that they could be included in the design. The Chinese painters occasionally misinterpreted these with amusing results. Similar examples of porcelain survive in the ownership of the descendants of Sir Robert's brother Horatio, 1st Baron Walpole of Wolterton (Private Collection).

64 Unknown designer

Goblet, c.1735

Round funnel bowl wheel engraved 'Fari quae Sentio Prosperity to Houghton', with floral and twig decoration around the rim and scalloped facet cutting on the lower part; the stem has a cushion knop with air bubbles above a facet cut inverted baluster. Plain conical foot. Height 11.2 cm

Prov: Museum of London (Acc no. 34.139/110: Garton collection; Sir Richard Garton collection; Hamilton Clements collection (Sotheby, 16 July 1930, lot no. 131); Cecil Davis, 1920; Sir Henry Bedingfeld, at Oxburgh Hall, 1907

Lit: Charles Jerningham, (ed.), 'The Oxburgh Glasses', *The Connoisseur*, XXI, May 1908, pp. 17–18; Cecil Davis advertisement 'at his newly opened premises at 6, St Mary Abbott's Terrace, W14', *The Connoisseur*, LVII, June 1920, xxii; Daisy Wilmer, *Early English Glass*, London 1910, pp. 160–2; Francis Buckley, *Old English Glass*, London 1925, xix, 95, pl. xxiv; R.J. Charleston, *English Glass*, London 1984, 153, pl. 50a

Museum of London

The first reference to this glass appears in Jerningham's article in the *Connoisseur* of 1908, in which he describes and illustrates a group of glasses discovered in a 'mixed collection of modern glass' in the 'china closets' at Oxburgh Hall, the ancient family seat of the Bedingfield family. It was found with ten other glasses which appear to have 'Jacobite' sentiments or connections. Jerningham notes that the glass bears 'a hitherto unknown motto: "Fari quae Sentio. Prosperity to Houghton".'

The present supposition is that Sir Robert Walpole – the celebrated statesman – had glasses made of this pattern at the time he was building Houghton, the palatial residence in Norfolk that has been somewhat of an encumbrance to the less prosperous of his descendants. The 'Fari quae Sentio' inscription provides a puzzle. There appear to be three methods in the Walpole family of using the family motto; one branch gives it as Lord Orford does, *feri quae sentiat* – 'to speak what he feels', another *feri quae sentias* – 'to speak what you think', and another still, *feri quae sentient* – 'to speak what they shall feel'. The wording on the Houghton glass is, besides, not grammatically accurate.

The motto on the glass would seem to be a rather charming variation on the original quotation from Horace *Epistles*, I.4.9: 'qui sapere et fari possit quae sentiat'. Thus the Latin phase might be translated as 'To prophesy (*or* say, *or* speak) what I think (*or* feel): Prosperity to Houghton'. This would have been a fitting sentiment for a gift to the owner of Houghton at any period.

The form of the goblet is rather unusual for an English lead glass, the lower part of the bowl and the baluster stem being cut over in the manner of mid-eighteenth century Silesian glass or the stem of a cut sweetmeat dish. The nearest example to it is perhaps the goblet shown as No. 841 in Bickerton's *Eighteenth Century English Drinking Glasses* (1986) from the Hartshorne Collection. That glass is described as having a Dutch royal coat of arms and being signed on the foot by Jacob Sang. It also has a cut foot, unlike the Houghton Goblet, and Sang's engraving is vastly superior to the thinner decorative border and inscription of the latter. Five other Sang goblets with comparable cut stems are listed by F.G.A.M. Smit in his 1992 catalogue of wheel engraved glasses by Jacob Sang. They are all signed and dated from 1761 to 1776.[1] The goblet should now be regarded as associated with the struggle to preserve Houghton which culminated in the eventual sale of the old master paintings to Catherine the Great in 1779.

1 Peter Lole kindly pointed this out.

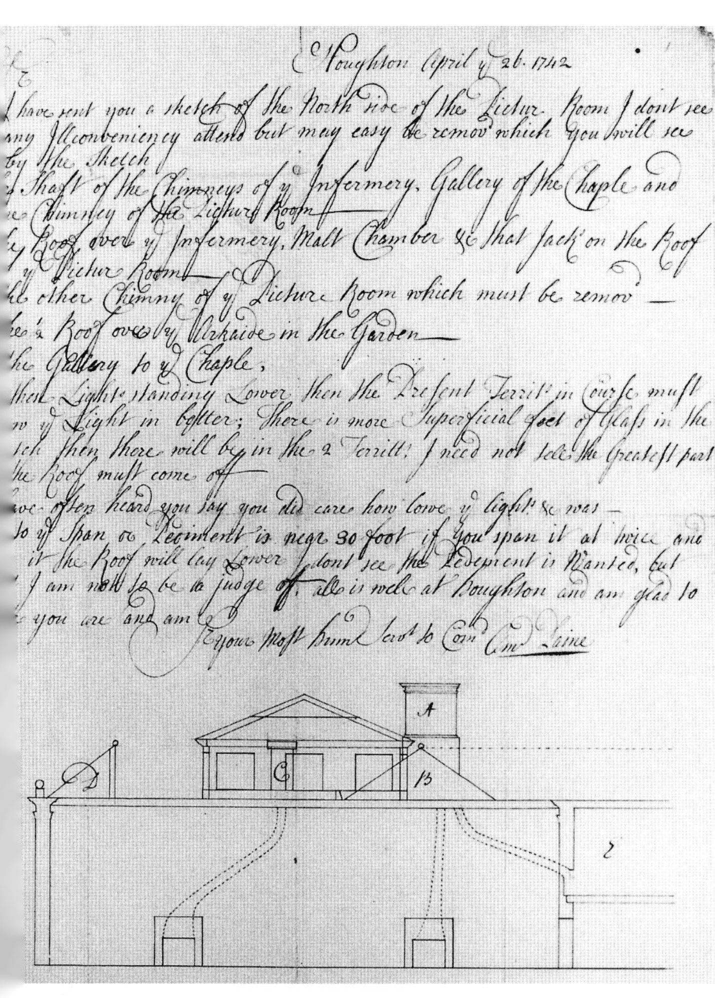

Houghton April ye 26. 1742

I have sent you a sketch of the North side of the Pictur Room I dont see
any Illconveniency attend but may easy be remov which you will see
by the Sketch
Shaft of the Chimneys of ye Infermery, Gallery of the Chaple and
Chimney of the Pictur Room
Roof over ye Infermery, Malt Chamber &c that Jack on the Roof
ye Pictur Room
other Chimny of ye Pictur Room which must be remov —
Roof over ye Arkaide in the Garden —
the Gallery to ye Chaple,
Lights standing Lower then the Present Territ in Course must
ye Light in better; There is more Superficial foot of Glass in the
then there will be in the 2 Territt; I need not tell the Greatest part
the Roof must come off
often heard you say you did care how lowe ye light &c was —
ye Span or Pediment is near 30 foot if you span it at twice and
it the Roof will lay Lower I dont see the Pediment is Wanted, but
I am not to be a judge of. all is well at Houghton and am glad to
you are and am
Your Most humb Servt to Comd Amb Paine

Fig. 63 In this letter to Sir Horace Walpole, his Houghton agent, Ambrose Paine, discusses a proposal to alter the 'Picture Room' roof to accommodate a large roof-light.

The Gallery

If Houghton's initial building history remains complicated, then the history of the Gallery in the northwest wing provides an architectural conundrum all of its own. By the 1730s the country-house long gallery had fallen completely out of fashion, yet there was still a need for long rooms in which to exercise in bad weather and also a greater desire than ever to display paintings. So, when Sir Robert proposed a purpose-built picture gallery as early as 1731 his advisers were on unfamiliar territory. Kent and later Horace Walpole would have seen great continental picture cabinets or early clerestoried galleries such as the Tribuna of the Uffizi and they or other well-travelled advisers to Sir Robert are likely to have sown the seed of this idea.

It was always to be in a separate part of the house, with its formal approach through the Saloon and down the garden steps to the outdoor colonnade, the route described by Horace Walpole in his *Aedes*. Sir Thomas Robinson mentioned proposals in 1731 for 'a large room which looks on the parterre, designed for a gallery, there being the same in the opposite wing for a green house.'[1]

Isaac Ware shows a large, side-lit gallery in his plan published in 1735, when work should have been completed. However, no pictures hung here in the paintings inventory of 1736 (cat. 17) and it does not seem to have been fitted up as a gallery until the late 1730s. As Horace Walpole recounts in 1742, when his father retired from politics and consolidated his collection at Houghton, proposals to refurbish the Gallery had developed to using all four walls of the seventy-three foot room and installing what was a very early example of clerestory top-lighting. A group of unsigned drawings from the early 1740s survives at Houghton (see cats. 69, 70) and the vagaries of actually designing and hanging the room with Sir Robert's expanding collection have been discussed by David Yaxley in some detail.[2]

The hang of some fifty or so works was dominated by the large Flemish works that had proved awkward to hang early on in the Saloon and Cabinet: Snyders's four great market scenes (see cat. 65) and the Rubens cartoon (see cat. 66). These were arranged in a balanced and symmetrical pattern typical of the period at the ends of the long walls, with the Rubens in the centre of the fireplace wall. By 1745 the paintings were arranged in two and three tiers with the largest at the top. The effect on entering from the single door in the east end must have been stunning, especially when it is remembered that nothing on this scale had been seen in an English country house before. Furthermore, the list of sixteenth- and seventeenth-century artists' works given in *Aedes* reads as a 'Who's Who' of Old Masters.

Horace Walpole describes the paintings being hung on Norwich (i.e. wool) damask, an economic choice for this size of room. There were five tables, twenty-four armchairs and twelve India chairs; perhaps the 'twelve walnut wood chairs with India backs and seats, veneer'd, at 13/– each' supplied by P. Bodham in 1724. A couch and lacquer screens completed what was, in effect, a great drawing room.

It is small wonder that Horace Walpole lamented the sale of his father's collection after he had seen it assembled and finally brought together in such a splendid setting. As a final injustice, the Gallery was burnt out in 1789 and later remodelled by the 4th Earl of Orford as a rather plain, conventionally lit long-room.

1 Robinson, 1731; this description may be somewhat confused, as the writer is suggesting that there was a greenhouse in the north-facing wing, where the sculleries were, and a large and empty room facing south opposite. Sir Thomas's details might well have been second-hand as the house was still only partially habitable.

2 Yaxley, 1995

65 Richard Earlom, after Frans Snyders

London 1743 – London 1822

The Fruit Market, 25 March 1775

Mezzotint, 41.6 x 57.3 cm

Inscribed, [Arms in centre] 'Snyders & Long John. Pinxit Rich.[d] Earlom Sculpsit. / Published March.25th 1775 by John Boydell Engraver in Cheapside London'

Lit: Boydell, I, 12; Wessely, 1886, 3 ii/ii

The Hon. Charles Lennox Boyd

The four great market pieces by Frans Snyders were among the earliest acquisitions by Sir Robert. George Vertue records in 1723 'lately bought for Mr Walpole in flanders, four great pictures of F. Snyders. 7 foot by a 11 foot. for which he paid. 428 pounds these are Capital pictures of this Masters painting...'[1] Each one of this magnificent series depicts stalls of various kinds of food – game, fish, fruit and vegetables. The series represents allegories of the four elements, the five senses and the four seasons and was originally commissioned as a decorative scheme in its own right.

Sir Robert placed the group in the Saloon at Houghton, although not initially in the arrangement proposed by Kent in his designs of about 1725.[2] The series was later removed to the much larger picture gallery during the refitting of Houghton with those pictures that had been hanging in London.

The Fruit Market was the first of the series to be published by Boydell (25 March 1775). Earlom followed a copy drawing by Joseph Farington for both this and *A Herb Market* (published 13 Nov. 1779). *The Fish Market* followed, based on a drawing by George Farington (published 1 June 1782). The last of the series appears not to have been copied. In order to complete the set, Earlom engraved a nearly identical version of *A Game Market* in the collection of the Duke of Newcastle (published 2 June 1783). The statement, recorded in the engraved inscriptions, that the paintings were the joint production of Snyders and Jan Boeckhorst ('Long John') stems from a comment by Horace Walpole concerning the similar series owned by the Duke of Newcastle (*Aedes*, 2nd edn 1767).[3]

1 Vertue, III, p. 18

2 Moore, 1988, pp. 13–15

3 A fine version of *The Fruit Market* is now at Glamis Castle, the property of Strathmore Estates (approx. 200 x 350 cm, inv. no. H 5846).

66 Richard Earlom, after Peter Paul Rubens

London 1743 – London 1822

Meleager and Atalanta, 1 January 1781

Mezzotint, 52.1 x 88.9 cm

Inscribed, [Arms in centre] 'P.P. Rubens pinx.[t] R. Earlom sculpsit. / London. 1780. / John Boydell Excudit. Published January 1.st 1781'

Lit: Boydell, II, 51; Wessely, 1886, 81 i/ii (with the artists' names and publication line in scratched letters)

The Hon. Charles Lennox Boyd

Richard Earlom's mezzotint of *Meleager and Atalanta* is the most magnificent plate in Boydell's *Houghton Gallery* by virtue of its scale. The largest print in the collection, it is a magnificent translation of a large-scale version related to Rubens's canvas now in the Prado, Madrid: *Landscape with Atalanta and Meleager pursuing the Calydonian Boar*.

Sir Robert's version of this composition was an enormous cartoon, probably intended as the model for a tapestry. The cartoon was hanging in the 'Corner Drawing Room' at Houghton in 1736 before that room was refurbished as the Cabinet and hung with small-scale paintings. By 1744 the cartoon was hanging in the centre of the northern wall of the Picture Gallery at Houghton. Horace Walpole records that the cartoon, 'larger than life', was brought out of Flanders by General George Wade (1673–1748). If this is the case, the cartoon could have reached England around 1702–4 when Wade was serving in Flanders.

George Wade's house in Cork Street, London, was designed by Lord Burlington and built in 1723. In a letter to George Montagu on 18 May 1748, Horace Walpole wrote of how Sir Robert came to acquire Wade's large cartoon: 'It is literally true, that all the direction he gave my Lord Burlington was to have a place for a large cartoon of Rubens that he had bought in Flanders: but my Lord found it necessary to have so many correspondent doors, that there was no room at last for the picture; and the Marshal was forced to sell the picture to my father: it is now at Houghton.' (Lewis, 1937–83, IX, p. 56)

Earlom has achieved considerable richness and density of effect in his translation of the subject, and his design is itself based on a drawing copy by George Farington, a fact recorded on other impressions of this plate.

---

67 John Murphy, after Rembrandt

Ireland *c.*1748 – London 1820

Abraham's Sacrifice, 1 September 1781

Mezzotint, 50 x 35.2 cm

Inscribed, [Arms in centre] 'John Boydell excudit 1781. / Rembrandt Pinxit. J. Murphy Sculpsit. / ABRAHAM'S SACRIFICE. / In the Gallery at Houghton. / Size of the picture 4.F 3.I¾ by 6.F 3I high. / Publish'd Sep.r 1.st 1781 by John Boydell Engraver in Cheapside London'

Lit: Boydell, II, 33; Le Blanc, 1970, I (with the title in closed letters)

The Hon. Charles Lennox Boyd

Sir Robert Walpole owned four paintings attributed to Rembrandt, of which *Abraham's Sacrifice* was the finest. Although the authorship of Rembrandt (1601–69) has not been seriously questioned, comparisons between the original canvas and a second version now in the Alte Pinakothek, Munich, fully confirms the status of Walpole's version as by Rembrandt's own hand.

Murphy's mezzotint amply demonstrates the power of Rembrandt's composition. The spatial quality is enhanced by the drama of the hand gestures at the moment that Abraham drops his knife. According to Jewish legend, Abraham's hair turned white at the prospect of having to sacrifice his son. Murphy faithfully reproduces both the drama and the poignancy of Rembrandt's chiaroscuro.

Sir Robert Walpole acquired *Abraham sacrifices Isaac* (SHM 727) at some point shortly after the 1736 inventory was made.[1] The painting was hung next to a painting of another episode in the life of Abraham, Pietro da Cortona's *Abraham, Sarah and Hagar*, on the west side of the Picture Gallery at Houghton. A second Rembrandt at Houghton was *Rembrandt's Wife*, which hung in the Common Dining Parlour.[2] Two other portrait heads are recorded in Walpole's collection in 1736 as attributed to Rembrandt, but these are now untraced.

1 The picture is listed among 'pictures bought since the catalogue was made', 1736 MS Pierpont Morgan Library.

2 Charles Jervas sale, 11–20 March 1740, lot 279, bought by Walpole, now Pushkin Museum, Moscow

---

68 Francis Legat, after Nicolas Poussin

Edinburgh 1755 – London 1809

The Continence of Scipio, 1 January 1784

Line engraving, 47.3 x 60.7 cm, trimmed to the platemark

Inscribed, 'Nichs. Poussin pinxit J Boydell excudit 1784 Francis Legat Sculpsit Published Jan.y 1st 1784 by John Boydell Engraver in Cheapside London'

Prov: British Museum (1982-u-1714)

Lit: Boydell, II, 52

The Trustees of the British Museum

Legat's engraving lends a curiously eighteenth-century mien to the features of the protagonists in the story told by Plutarch (*Moralia*, 196B) and most fully in Livy (XXVI, 50). The composition shows the young Allucius paying homage to the Roman general Scipio Africanus the Elder. Between them stands Scipio's captive, the fiancée of Allucius. Scipio, in an act of clemency, reunites the couple.

Before entering Sir Robert's collection, the original painting (dated *c.*1640) was in the collection of C.-J.-B. Fleuriau, Comte de Morville, who died in 1732. The precise date the painting entered Sir Robert's collection is not known: it was hanging in Sir Robert's dressing room at Downing Street in 1736, when it was identified as *Scipio's Abstinence.*[1] It was copied by the copyist Ranelagh Barrett in 1742.[2] The subject of Scipio's judicious generosity eminently suited Sir Robert's view of himself, as reflected in his collection. The painting was hung at Houghton on the lower register of the west wall of the Picture Gallery, paired with *Moses striking the Rock*, also by Poussin.[3]

1 It is likely to have come to Sir Robert through the Earl of Waldegrave. The painting was transferred from St Petersburg to the Pushkin Museum of Fine Arts, Moscow, in 1927.

2 Vertue, III, p. 112; and also engraved by C. Duborc, 1741

3 SHM 1177 (Fig. 33)

69 Unidentified draughtsman

East and west elevations of the Gallery, showing a proposed picture hang, c.1742

Pencil, black and brown ink on paper, 75.5 x 54 cm

Prov: Sir Robert Walpole, Houghton Hall, by descent to present owner (Houghton MSS A66)

Lit: Yaxley, 1995

The Marquess of Cholmondeley

This is the most worked-up drawing in the series of proposals for the Gallery. It probably gives the best impression of its interior decoration as well as the manner in which the paintings were hung. Unfortunately the accompanying elevations for the long walls have not survived, although an earlier hang for the southern wall exists. When this is considered in conjunction with *Aedes*, the 1745 inventory and the grangerised volume with its complete hang (cat. 20), a good idea of the arrangement of the room's walls around 1742–5 can be gained.[1]

In this design the Gallery is enriched with a modillioned cornice and Ionic door architrave at the eastern end, which is on scale with that of the Saloon. Horace Walpole mentions that the actual frieze was derived from the Sybil's Temple at Tivoli (the Temple of Vesta) and that the ceiling was copied from Serlio's design for the Inner Library at St Mark's, Venice.

All of the paintings shown on the west wall are listed in the first edition of Horace's catalogue. Only the Le Sueur, Carracci and the pair of Palma Vecchios from the east or entrance wall remained in the room according to the *Aedes*. What comes across is the importance of symmetry to the hang and the way the paintings are arranged in tiers, with the largest at the top.[2] Sadly, the types of frames are not detailed, but the drawing does give a good idea of the proportion of frames in relation to the canvases and how they were fairly evenly spaced. It is known that paintings were reframed specially for Sir Robert.[3]

1 Yaxley, 1996,

2 For a discussion on early English picture hanging arrangements see Russell, 1989.

3 See above, Andrew Moore, p. 49

---

70 Ambrose Paine

fl. 1742

Letter to Sir Robert Walpole with a cross-section of proposed alterations to the Gallery, 26 April 1742

Pencil and brown ink on paper, 38 x 32 cm

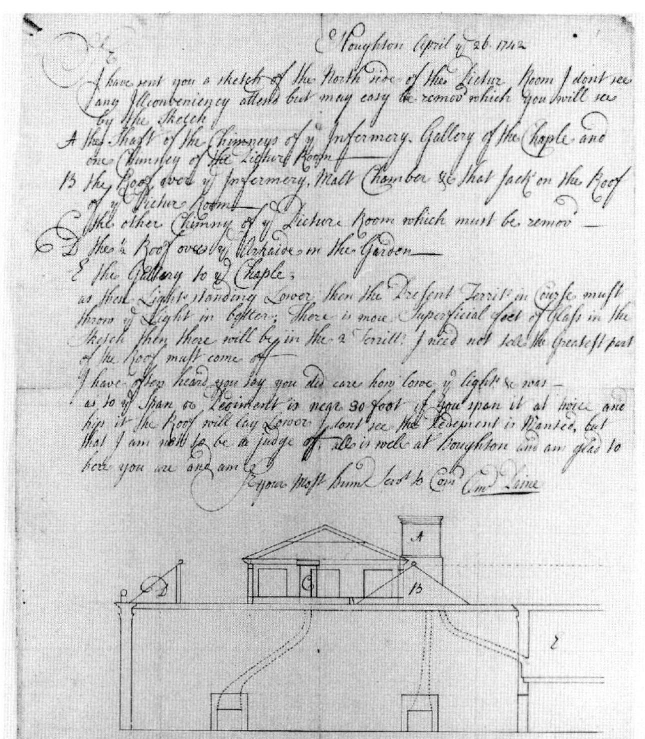

Houghton April ye 26. 1742

Sr
I have sent you a sketch of the North side of the Pictur Room I dont see any Illconveniency attend but may easy be remov which you will see by the Sketch
A the Shaft of the Chimneys of ye Infermery. Gallery of the Chaple and one Chimney of the Pictur Room
B the Roof over ye Infermery, Malt Chamber &c that lack on the Roof of ye Pictur Room
C the other Chimny of ye Pictur Room which must be remov —
D the 2 Roof over ye [illegible] in the Garden —
E the Gallery to ye Chaple;
as their Lights standing Lower then the Present Territ in Course must throw ye Light in better; there is more Superficial foot of Glass in the Sketch then there will be in the 2 Territt. I need not tell the Greatest part of the Roof must come off
I have often heard you say you did care how lowe ye light &c was —
as to ye Span or Pediment it is near 30 foot if you span it at twice and hip it the Roof will lay Lower I dont see the Pediment is Wanted, but that I am not to be a judge of. all is well at Houghton and am glad to here you are and am
Sr
Your Most humble Servt to Com. Amb Paine

Prov: sent by Ambrose Paine to Sir Robert Walpole, 26 April 1742; by descent to present owner (Houghton MSS A64)

Lit: Yaxley, 1995

The Marquess of Cholmondeley

In this letter to Sir Robert, his Houghton agent, Ambrose Paine, discusses a proposal to alter the 'Picture Room' roof to accommodate a large roof-light. The implications of this were that several existing structures would have to be removed and most importantly, the 'greatest part of the roof must come off' together with the '2 Territts' (i.e. turrets, some kind of roof-lights or lanterns). Paine writes: 'I have often heard you say you did care how lowe ye light &c was.' This may reveal that the gallery was already in use for paintings before this date, but that its lighting was inadequate.

Paine's proposal was to place an almost thirty-foot long roof-light, or monitor, with eight windows, which Horace Walpole mentions were 'eight feet higher' (*Aedes*), along the axis of the gallery. This meant moving chimney-stacks with their flues and two of the roofs, presumably because they kept out the light. Two similar sections (Houghton MSS A70, A77) provide more detail on the new arrangement of chimneys and roofs. They also show the decorative ceiling beams indicated by Horace Walpole.

Walpole's agent comments how his master has complained of the low lighting levels in the Gallery and says that he intends greatly to increase the amount of glazing. However, he is also anxious that the new roof should be as low as possible to avoid its being visible from the ground.

Judging by Horace's description this is more or less what was built. If this is the case then Paine's modest design is probably the earliest top-lit picture gallery in Britain – and by many years, for they did not become common until the end of the century.[1]

1 The development of early gallery day-lighting has been discussed by Michael Compton; Dulwich 1991, pp. 37–47.

The 1779 Sale to Catherine the Great

Fig. 64 Richard Earlom, *John Wilkes*, MP *c.*1778; pencil 34.3 x 23.5 cm; National Portrait Gallery

There was a certain inevitability about the sale of the Houghton paintings. On Sir Robert Walpole's death his son Horace commented to Horace Mann: 'It is very certain, he is dead very poor... in short, his fondness for Houghton, has endangered Houghton... another such debt must expose it to sale' (15 April 1745). With the death of Sir Robert's son and heir in 1751, the family incurred more debts. By 1761 Horace commented to Lord Montagu: 'Houghton, I know not what to call it, a monument of grandeur or ruin!' (25–30 March 1761).

A matter of family concern became one of national importance when John Wilkes, MP for Middlesex, raised the matter in the House of Commons. On 28 April 1777 he proposed that the Houghton pictures be purchased by the nation as the basis for a National Gallery, to be housed in a purpose-built gallery within the grounds of the British Museum:

> The *British Museum*, [Mr. Speaker], possesses few valuable *paintings*, yet we are anxious to have an *English School* of painters. If we expect to rival the Italian, the Flemish, or even the French school, our artists must have before their eyes the finished works of the greatest masters. Such an opportunity, if I am rightly informed, will soon present itself. I understand that an application is intended to parliament, that one of the first collections in Europe, that at *Houghton*, made by Sir Robert Walpole, of acknowledged superiority to most in Italy and scarcely inferior even to the Duke of Orleans's in the Palais Royal at Paris, may be sold by the family. I hope it will not be dispersed, but purchased by parliament, and added to the *British Museum*. I wish, Sir, the eye of painting as fully gratified, as the ear of music is in this island, which at last bids fair to become a favourite abode of the polite arts. A noble gallery ought to be built in the spacious garden of the *British Museum* for the reception of that invaluable treasure...[1]

At that stage the Empress of Russia's interest in the collection may not have reached Wilkes's ears. A deal was struck with Empress Catherine's representative in London, Count Musin-Pushkin, by July 1779. The price paid was based upon the valuation provided by James Christie on the advice of Benjamin West and G.B. Cipriani.

Four years later, the dust had still not entirely settled on the affair. The letter which 'C.D.' wrote to the editors of *The European Magazine* in February 1782, employed arguments which remain in force over issues of cultural heritage today:

> The removal of the Houghton Collection of Pictures to Russia is, perhaps, one of the most striking instances that can be produced of the decline of the empire of Great Britain, and the advancement of our powerful ally in the North. The riches of a nation have generally been estimated according as it abounds in works of art, and so careful of these treasures have some states been, that, knowing their value and importance, they have prohibited the sending them out of their dominions.

In 1824 the dealer William Buchanan believed the loss to the nation's artistic heritage was surpassed only by the dispersal of the collections of Charles I through the Commonwealth sales.

1 *The Speeches of Mr Wilkes in the House of Commons*, London 1786, pp. 142–3

71 Fedot Ivanovitch Shubin

Archangel Province 1740 – St Petersburg 1805

Bust of Catherine II, 1771

Marble, height 65.1 cm

Signed and dated

Prov: early history uncertain; according to one account it was commissioned by Count Andrew Shuvalov and according to another it was given to Catherine II by Shuvalov; it passed to the Galitzine collection at Petrovskoye; after the Russian Revolution it was owned by Voldemar Wehrlin (who believed the bust was presented by Shubin to Catherine II, who subsequently gave it to Shuvalov); purchased from Wehrlin by the Victoria and Albert Museum with contributions from the friends of the late Mrs Syrie Maugham, 1964 (A32–1964)

Trustees of the Victoria and Albert Museum

Fedot Shubin was born in a region known for its tradition of skilled bone-carving. Shubin moved to St Petersburg where he developed his carving skills at the Academy of Arts, between 1761 and 1766, under the guidance of Nicolas-François Gillet. He won an Academy scholarship which gave him the opportunity to visit Italy, France and England in 1767–3. On his return to Russia his busts in marble gained him the reputation of a leading portraitist. His most celebrated portrait of Catherine was a statue of the *Empress Catherine as Lawgiver.*[1]

Shubin's bust of Catherine is his earliest known work. One of his most sensitive portraits, it was presumably derived from a painting. The sculptor appears in sympathy with an empress, who was herself inspired by the philosophers of the Enlightenment in Western Europe, notably Voltaire, with whom she maintained a long correspondence. It is a markedly more acutely observed portrait than the enormous state canvas given to George Walpole by the Empress by February 1780 to mark her acquisition of his grandfather's collection. That portrait, by G. Roesslin (1710–98),[2] hangs today in the Saloon at Houghton, resplendent in a frame surmounted by the Empress's crown, sword and sceptre.

Catherine II (1729–96) reigned for thirty-four years, continuing the tradition of absolutism established by Peter the Great (1672–1725). The Austrian diplomat, the Prince de Ligne, described how she operated: 'How much talk there is of the St. Petersburg cabinet! I know none smaller. It is only a few inches wide. It stretches from temple to temple and from nose to nose.'

1 Now in the Academy, St Petersburg. Another bust of Catherine II by Shubin (1792) is in the Winter Palace.

2 W.S. Ovchinkova records that this is a replica, by the artist, of Roesslin's signed portrait, at Peterhof in 1962. See also D.A. Rovinsky, *Russian Engraved Portraits*, II, p. 798. (Richard Hare to Lady Cholmondeley, 27 May 1962, Houghton archive.)

72 Robert Dighton

?London *c.*1752 – London 1814

The Specious Orator, 1794

Engraving on paper, platemark 20 x 15 cm

Inscribed, bottom left: 'R. Dighton 1794' and 'THE SPECIOUS ORATOR / WILL YOUR LADYSHIP DO ME THE HONOR TO SAY £50–00 / – A MERE TRIFLE – A BRILLIANT OF THE FIRST WATER / an unheard of price for such a lot, surely'

Christie's, London

James Christie (1770 – 1803), the founder of the well-known firm of auctioneers, was conducting sales at Little Castle Street (now Eastcastle Street), London, from at least June 1764. He held his first sale in new premises in Pall Mall on 5–10 December 1766. Two years later he moved again, this time to 83–4 Pall Mall. On 14 April 1768 he received the freedom of the City of London by redemption in the Worshipful Company of Spectacle Makers, a good indication of his growing status in London.

Christie's standing as an auctioneer was confirmed when, in 1778, he became actively involved in promoting one of the major deals of the century. Rumours that Lord Orford was prepared to dispose of the celebrated collection of his grandfather were enough to strengthen Christie's resolve. It is almost certain that it was Christie who suggested quite how to dispose of the collection. In 1778 Lord Orford asked Christie in the 'most profound secrecy' to value the collection.

It is not altogether clear how much Christie himself knew about pictures; he was particularly respected for his knowledge of gems.[1] He entrusted the task of valuing the Walpole Collection to the artists Benjamin West (1738–1820), G.B. Cipriani (1727–85) and the painter-dealer of Flemish origin, Philip Tassaert (1732–1803). Their valuation of 178 pictures was £40,455.

1 See Marrillier, 1926, and Sutton, 1966, for James Christie's biography

73 James Christie to Carlos Cony

Manuscript letters 23, 29 November 1778

Folio, 23 x 36.5 cm, folded

Prov: Stanley Edwards MSS collection; to Bradfer Lawrence Collection via Ralph Rye, 4 November 1954; bequeathed to Norfolk Record Office by Harry Bradfer Lawrence, 1967

Norfolk and Norwich Record Office

Negotiations concerning the sale of the Houghton paintings were conducted between George Walpole, 3rd Lord Orford, and James Christie with the help of Lord Orford's attorney at law and agent based at King's Lynn, Carlos Cony. The delicacy of these negotiations can be seen in these letters.

On 23 November 1778 Christie wrote:

Sometime ago I receiv'd a letter from Lord Orford desiring I would go to Houghton Hall and form a valuation on The Collection saying it must be completed in a fortnight and also that I was to get two catalogues elegantly Bound and that I was to write to his Lordship in Suffolk. Accordingly I set off on the Wednesday following with a proper assistant and finish'd the business, wrote, and directed my letter agreeable to his Lordship's desire, but not hearing from his Lordship I begin to fear my letter has not met with him. Supposing that should have been the case I beg to repeat the substance matter of it – that I had with a competent viewed and valued the collection and marked against each picture or pr. of pictures our opinion in the margin of a catalogue and that those several sums amounted to 40555£ exclusive of the family pictures and some few Furniture Pictures also four or five Pictures my reason for which I woud communicate when I had the honor of waiting on his Lordship...

Christie finishes his letter by commenting that Cony 'will best judge what part of this letter is proper to communicate to' Lord Orford. Cony evidently passed the entire letter on, replying by return of post on 26 November.

James Christie's subsequent reply to Cony on 29 November implies that only then did Lord Orford receive the formal valuation: 'I send with this the catalogue on which I made the valuation... I am exceedingly at a loss to account for my two letters not reaching his Lordship.' It is at this point that Christie offers to provide more than simply a valuation:

I am sorry to hear there is likely to be a negative put on the expected treaty with the Empress. The collection is truly worthy of her. With respect to myself I consider it a matter of too much consequence to attempt, but I think if I had the pleasure of some conversation with you I coud form a plan that might facilitate the sale of them in one lot which I cannot communicate by letter.

Christie ends his letter of 29 November by expressing an opinion based upon the views expressed in Parliament by John Wilkes the previous year (28 April 1777):

If the Minister had a mind to immortalize himself I coud put him in the way to do it effectually by causing this collection to be purchas'd at the expense of the publick and Building a Room at the British Museum for their reception. I would undertake that it woud be the means of bringing all the Foreigners of Taste from different parts of the World to see them and it would most undoubtedly correct the Taste and qualify the Judgements of our Modern Artists.

This argument continued to be invoked long after the Houghton sale and into the nineteenth century, in the debate surrounding the foundation of a National Gallery of Art.

TO
Her most Sacred Majesty
CATHARINE the SECOND
Empress of all the Russias.
Whose transcendent Wisdom, admirable Policy and parental Affection, extended to every part of Her vast Dominions, have completed the immense Work begun by the
Immortal Peter.
As a just Tribute to this August Princess, the avowed Patroness of Genius, and
UNIVERSAL PROTECTRESS
OF
Art, Science and Literature,
These Volumes
Are with the profoundest Respect and Gratitude Dedicated
By Her Imperial Majesty's
Most obedient and most devoted Servant
John Boydell.

74 *A Set of Prints Engraved after the Most Capital Paintings in the Collection of Her Imperial Majesty the Empress of Russia, Lately in the Possession of the Earl of Orford at Houghton Hall in Norfolk*

Two volumes, 69.5 x 53 x 3.5 cm

Published by John Boydell, 1774–88

Prov: George Walpole, 3rd Earl of Orford; then by descent to present owner

Lit: Rubinstein, 1991

The Marquess of Cholmondeley

John Boydell (1719–1804), himself an engraver, set up as a printseller and publisher of engravings around 1751. He became a leading citizen, being Sheriff of London, 1785 and Lord Mayor, 1790. Particularly well known for his nationalistic programme of art projects (notably *The Shakespeare Gallery*, 1786), his project known as *The Houghton Gallery* was very much in this vein of jingoistic art patronage. The ultimate success of his concept may be judged from the fact that it is only in these two volumes that the scale and magnificence of the art collection amassed by Britain's first Prime Minister may be seen in Britain today.

The 162 prints that represent the most splendid works in the collection (excluding family portraits) were published, usually ten at a time, between 1774 and 1788. In 1788 they were gathered into two folio volumes, each prefaced by a text catalogue based on Horace Walpole's *Aedes Walpolianae* (1747). A total of forty-five engravers contributed plates to *The Houghton Gallery*, most notably Richard Earlom (1743–1822), J.-B. Michel (1748–1804) and Valentine Green (1739–1813).

Volume I consists of an engraved frontispiece, title-page and dedication page, followed by twenty-eight 'plans, elevations, perspective views, chimney pieces, ceilings &c' of Houghton Hall (first published by Isaac Ware) and sixty (numbered) prints after paintings in the collection. Volume II contains an engraved frontispiece and title-page and sixty-nine prints after paintings. The prints of the paintings consist of sixty-one mezzotints, fifty-five line engravings, seventeen stipple engravings and one aquatint.

Boydell published a Prospectus, dated 25 March 1775, in which he promised that 'the subscribers shall have the First Impressions' and that 'no more than Four Hundred complete sets shall be printed'.

---

75 **John Sell Cotman**

Norwich 1782 – London 1842

Lee Shore, with the wreck of the Houghton pictures, books &c., sold to the Empress Catherine of Russia, 1838

Pencil and watercolour with bodycolour and gum arabic, 68 x 90.2 cm

Prov: the artist's sale, Christie's, 17–18 May 1843, lot 160; bought by Leggatt; presented by Joseph Prior to the Fitzwilliam Museum, Cambridge, March 1919

Exh: London, 1838 (223); London, 1982 (108)

Lit: Kitson, 1937, pp. 343–4; Rajnai, 1982, p. 140

The Syndics of the Fitzwilliam Museum, Cambridge

On 14–16 December 1779 the *Whitehall Evening Post* reported, 'The celebrated Houghton collection of pictures, late the property of Lord Orford... are totally lost at sea; the *Natalia*, the ship in which they were carrying to Russia, having foundered'. When William Cole heard this news he wrote to Horace Walpole, 'I hope and wish that the news we had in all our papers, that the Houghton Collection of pictures are at the bottom of the sea, is false. Good God! what a destruction! I am shocked when I think of it'. The rumour had also been reported in the *London Chronicle*, 11–14 December 1779.

Sir Horace Mann gave a more measured response in his letter to Horace Walpole of 3 January 1780: 'In the last newspaper I read an article that the ship with the Houghton pictures was cast away. This I believe I can contradict by the authority of a Russian officer who told me a fortnight ago that they were arrived safe at Petersbergh.' The rumour had, only days previously, been denied in the *Whitehall Evening Post*, 25–6 December, where it was stated that 'the master of the ship... saw them safely unpacked in the Empress's palace'.

John Sell Cotman's watercolour is an inventive resurrection of this rumour. In a letter of 14 April 1838 he describes how he set about transforming a composition begun by his eldest son, Miles Edmund: 'What I done to Miles' Sea View, in words, will tell against me. He will not know his picture... "The sea shore", if I can get the catalogue altered will be christened "The Wreck of the Houghton pictures, consigned to the Empress Catherine of Russia, including the gorgeous landscape of Rubens of the Wagoneer" – for such I have made it, by introducing pictures & things... in the foreground.'

Houghton Today

Fig. 65 View of the estate from Houghton

As with all great houses that are still occupied by a family, Houghton has had to change with the vicissitudes of time and ownership. What is remarkable is that since the doors re-opened to visitors in the spring of 1996 following its most recent 'refit', little appears to have changed to the fabric of the house itself.

The care and attention spent on Houghton during the late Dowager Marchioness of Cholmondeley's long period of residence has been continued by the present Lord Cholmondeley, who has been faced with the problem of maintaining a country house plagued with ageing building fabric and services, together with the needs of the estate in which it is set.

In the middle of this century the interiors of Houghton were characterised by the tastes of two politicians and great collectors, Sir Robert Walpole and Sir Philip Sassoon, together with that of his sister Sybil Cholmondeley. Elegant French Sassoon pieces were carefully mingled with Sir Robert's great furniture of state.

Sadly, the financial demands on the present owner, combined with a desire to preserve the majority of the Walpole possessions, led to the sale in 1994 of a significant portion of the Sassoon collection. However, this was only the culmination of a gradual process: the Dowager Marchioness, like the Earls of Orford in the eighteenth century, came to realise that the size and splendour of Sir Robert's house would always bear too heavily on its owner's purse. The parallels with Horace Walpole's concerns for the future of his father's collection cannot be ignored.

Today the presentation of the interiors encourages a greater understanding of Sir Robert's home than ever before, though of his paintings only the family portraits remain. The sets of both the state and simple family furniture can now be fully appreciated, often in their original positions.

Another outcome of recent changes and research is that the contributions of the 3rd Earl of Orford and 1st Marquess of Cholmondeley, made at the end of the eighteenth century, can now be better understood. Their sympathetic (but period) redecoration and patronage of fashionable portrait painters such as John Opie and John Hoppner are no longer overshadowed by the works chosen with undoubted flair by Philip Sassoon.

The present Lord Cholmondeley has continued this enthusiasm for collecting, although without the benefit of the seemingly bottomless resources of his great ancestor. Interestingly, Lord Cholmondeley's taste is very much in accord both with that of his forebears and with efforts to preserve eighteenth-century Houghton today.

76 William Hogarth

London 1697 – London 1764

The Cholmondeley Family, 1732

Oil on canvas, 71 x 90.8 cm

Inscribed, 'W. Hogarth Pinx[t] 1732', signed on base of column lower right

Prov: painted for Viscount Malpas, later 3rd Earl of Cholmondeley, then by descent to present owner

Exh: London, 1959 (15); London, 1971/A (42); Washington, DC, 1985–6 (163); London, 1987–8 (67); Norwich, 1992 (43)

Lit: Millar, 1963, p. 183, no 555; Paulson, 1971, I, pp. 305–6; Moore and Crawley, 1992, p. 110

The Marquess of Cholmondeley

Successive members of the Cholmondeley family have sought to replace the gaps at Houghton caused by the loss of Sir Robert's picture collection, and those to the interior decoration of the parade rooms in particular. Paintings were brought from both London and

Cholmondeley Castle in Cheshire and each generation has initiated change. Hogarth's painting of the Cholmondeley family is a particularly appropriate addition to Houghton and was at Houghton at least by 1852, in the Marchioness's dressing room.

This painting was commissioned by George Cholmondeley, Viscount Malpas, later 3rd Earl of Cholmondeley (1703–70), who is shown seated, wearing the ribbon of the Order of the Bath. He turns towards his wife Mary (*c.*1705–31), daughter of Sir Robert Walpole and his first wife, Catherine Shorter. Mary holds their youngest son Frederick, who was to die in 1734. Behind George Cholmondeley stands his brother James (1708–75), Colonel of the 34th Regiment of Foot, who later rose to the rank of General. George Cholmondeley's two other sons are George (1724–64), who later became Viscount Malpas, but died before his father, and Robert (1727–1804), who entered the church and became Rector of St Andrew's, Hertford.

The painting almost certainly commemorates Lady Malpas, who died of consumption in France late in 1731. Her body was lost in a shipwreck while being brought home in April 1732. The stiff pose suggests that Hogarth was copying her likeness from another picture, quite possibly the unfinished 'Head of Crayons' by Charles Jervas that was recorded in Lady Walpole's drawing room at Houghton in 1736.[1] The *putti* hovering overhead mark her spiritual existence. The family coat-of-arms high above the bookcase emphasises the commemorative spirit of the commission. The setting is presumably based upon Cholmondeley's library and picture collection at his house at Arlington Street.

1 1736 MS, 'Lady Walpole's Drawing Room. Lady Malpas, ditto [i.e. 'A Head of Crayons']. Jervase'; 1744 MS, 'Yellow Drawing Room, Houghton. R H Lady Cholmondeley not finish'd. Jervais'; Walpole, 1747, 'The Drawing Room. A Profile Sketch, by Jervase'.

77 **Thomas Gainsborough**

Sudbury 1727 – London 1788

Mr and Mrs Browne of Tunstall, c.1754–55

Oil on canvas, 83.8 x 141 cm

Prov: John and Elizabeth Browne; by descent to their daughter Anna Maria Browne, who in 1780 married the Revd Nicholas Bacon, Vicar of Coddenham; passed to Mrs Bacon's half sister, Charlotte, who married the Revd John Longe, also vicar of Coddenham; by descent through the Longe family of Spixworth Park; Francis B. Longe, Christie's, London, 27 July 1917, lot 141; bought Agnew; Viscount d'Abernon; from whom bought by Sir Philip Sassoon, Bt, 1929; inherited 1939 by Mrs David Gubbay; from whom acquired by Sybil, Marchioness of Cholmondeley, *c.*1947

Lit: Singh, 1927, II, p. 306; Waterhouse, 1958, no. 85

Exh: London, 1959 (19); Washington, DC, 1985–6 (328)

The Marquess of Cholmondeley

This is one of the most charming compositions by the young Gainsborough, readily comparable to *Mr and Mrs Robert Andrew* now in the National Gallery, London. Gainsborough became a master of the small-scale portrait in a landscape setting that is neither simple topography nor a mere backdrop. John Browne is thought to have been a wool merchant at Ipswich. He owned property at Tunstall, near Wickham Market, in Suffolk. He is seen here with his wife Elizabeth, sister of Gainsborough's lifelong friend Samuel Kilderbee (1725–1813). The little girl is their elder daughter Anne Maria (1753–95).

The provenance of the picture reveals just how this painting has returned to East Anglia. Entering the Sassoon collection in 1927, the painting was not, in fact, bequeathed by Philip Sassoon to Sybil Cholmondeley, who acquired it for Houghton only in 1947.

78 Thomas Patch

Exeter 1725 – Florence 1782

View of Florence from the Cascine Gardens, 1771

Oil on canvas, 76.2 x 115.5 cm

Signed, 'T. Patch fecit. Flor. 1771'

Prov: Horace Walpole (through Horace Mann), December 1771; by whom given to Houghton Hall, 1797; then by descent to present owner

Lit: Watson, 1940, p. 39

The Marquess of Cholmondeley

Thomas Patch worked in Joseph Vernet's studio in Rome, 1747–53, where he painted landscapes in emulation of his teacher. Forced to leave Rome in 1755 (on grounds of 'moral turpitude') he moved to Florence where he spent the rest of his life. He specialised in crisply painted views of Florence for the Grand Tourist, but also in caricature groups of Anglo-Florentine society.

Patch was patronised by Sir Horace Mann (1701–86), British envoy at Florence and long-time correspondent with Horace Walpole. It was through Mann that Horace acquired a pair of views of Florence by Patch. This view looks west along the River Arno with the Ponte alla Carità in the distance and the Ponte Vecchio beyond it.[1] The two paintings were delivered to Horace Walpole in December 1771 and probably hung in his house at Berkeley Square. When Walpole received the two views his comment to Mann was that he found them 'a little hard', adding 'I speak plainly that he may correct' (28 December 1771).

Horace Walpole was deeply upset by the experience of witnessing at first hand the deterioration of Houghton in the 1770s and the sale of the paintings in 1779. Although he became resigned to the sale, at one point Horace wrote to Lady Ossory (1 February 1779) 'It is the most signal mortification to my idolatry for my father's memory, that it could receive. It is stripping the temple of his glory and of his affection...' Horace attempted to make some reparation by passing a group of paintings from Berkeley Square to Houghton. The 'inventory & valuation of Pictures late the Property of the Earl of Orford deceased left to go to Houghton' lists thirty-two paintings, including 'two views of Florence by Patch', valued at six guineas.

1 The second view, painted in the same year, depicts a view of Florence looking along the River Arno from near the Torre della Zecca Vecchia. This too remains at Houghton today.

79 Abraham Danielsz. Hondius

Rotterdam *c.*1625–30 – London after 1695

A Crowd watching Bear-baiting in a Town Square

Signed, 'Hondius fecit' on the reverse of canvas

Oil on canvas, 77.5 x 87.3 cm

Prov: purchased 1995

The Marquess of Cholmondeley

The present Lord Cholmondeley has been collecting for Houghton over the last ten years and plans to refurbish the original picture gallery in a manner that would have won the approval of Sir Robert Walpole. This example of the work of Abraham Hondius is characteristic of the taste of the early eighteenth-century British collector, with its crisp treatment of a favourite sport of the period. The artist had moved to Amsterdam about 1660 and then to England some six years later.

Lord Cholmondeley's purchases on behalf of Houghton include major works of large scale, as befits their intended site. The seventeenth-century decorative school is well represented with two fine canvases by Rosa da Tivoli (1682–1706), formerly in the collection of the Bathurst family, Cirencester. Perhaps the most potent image is *Samson and Delilah* by the Neapolitan painter Artemisia Gentileschi (1597– after 1651). The taste for earlier Italian altarpieces is beautifully represented by a *Mystic Marriage of St Catherine*, 1537, by Marco Palmezzano (*c.*1458–1539). This large panel was formerly in the Northampton family collection at Compton Wynyates, Warwickshire.

80 John Singer Sargent

Florence 1856 – London 1925

Sybil, Countess Rocksavage, 1913

Oil on canvas, 92 x 71.5 cm

Inscribed and signed, 'To Sybil from her friend / John S. Sargent / 1913'

Prov: gift to the Cholmondeley family and then by descent to present owner

Exh: London, 1914; London, 1925, Royal Academy, London, 1926 (46 ill. RA III p. 7)

Lit: C.M. Mount, *John Singer Sargent*, New York, 1969 edn, pp. 383–4, 434 (132); R. Ormond, *John Singer Sargent: Paintings, Drawings, Watercolours*, London, 1970, pp. 66, 256–7, pl. 112 C. Ratcliff, *John Singer Sargent*, New York, 1982, p. 194; S. Olson, *John Singer Sargent: His Portrait*, London, 1986, p. 259

The Marquess of Cholmondeley

The American artist John Singer Sargent was one of the most prolific, successful and respected portraitists of British high society during the Edwardian period and until his death in 1923. He continued the bravura tradition of Lawrence but was strongly influenced by the work of Manet and Velázquez. His work perhaps owes most to Van Dyck, whose influence was very clearly seen by a number of contemporary reviewers. C.M. Mount suggests that the pose in this portrait was based on one of the figures in *Two Ladies of the Lake Family* by Peter Lely in the collection of the Tate Gallery, London.[1] At the time this painting was in the collection of Sir John Smyth at Ashton Court in Somerset but there is no evidence to suggest that Sargent knew the picture or its owner. In his biography of Sargent, Mount states that the artist came out of retirement to paint this striking portrait, which was painted as a wedding present for Sybil Sassoon on her marriage to the Earl of Rocksavage (later 5th Marquess of Cholmondeley) in 1913. The Countess of Rocksavage had known Sargent since her childhood in Paris, and he became a close friend to her and her brother, Sir Philip Sassoon.

Sargent had already painted Lady Rocksavage's mother, Aline Sassoon, in 1907, and had made charcoal sketches of Sybil Sassoon, as she then was, in 1911 and 1912. Lady Cholmondeley later recalled the enjoyment of sitting for Sargent for this portrait, which involved them playing piano duets. She also described the costume she wore as being a Persian silk shawl produced by the artist from a chest in his studio. The shawl was a popular motif in a number of Sargent's portraits of this period and he gave Lady Cholmondeley one of the shawls worn by his nieces Reine and Rose-Marie in figure studies of about 1907–11.

In 1922 Sargent painted a full-length portrait of Sybil Rocksavage in a Spanish-inspired dress by Worth. The following year he painted her brother Philip Sassoon. Lady Cholmondeley also owned drawings of herself and her two eldest children (1925) by Sargent, while a family autograph-book contains two further drawings. This portrait was taken by the Cholmondeleys to Houghton, where it is still displayed on an easel.

1 C.M. Mount, 'Carolus-Duran and the Development of Sargent', *Art Quarterly*, XXVI, 1963, p. 410

Sir Robert Walpole
A Chronology of his Life

1676 26 August, born Houghton, Norfolk, the son of Robert Walpole (1650–1700), an influential Whig leader in Norfolk, and Mary Burwell (d. 1711).

1690 4 September, admitted to Eton College.

1695 22 April, admitted to King's College, Cambridge.

1698 25 May, resigns his scholarship, and leaves Cambridge, having become heir to the Houghton Estate on his brother's death.

1700 30 July, marries Catherine Shorter, daughter of John Shorter of Bybrook, Kent.

18 November, suceeds to his father's estates (nine manors in Norfolk and one in Suffolk), with a rent-roll of £2,169 a year.

1701 11 January, returned as MP for the borough of Castle Rising, a seat he later transfers to his uncle Horatio.

1702 23 July, returned as MP for the borough of King's Lynn, for which he sat during the rest of his career in Parliament.

1705 28 June, appointed to the council to Prince George of Denmark, Lord High Admiral of England, husband of Queen Anne.

1708 25 February, appointed Secretary at War.

1710 21 January, appointed Treasurer of the Navy.

7 October, general election; returned for King's Lynn, although the Whigs were defeated.

1711 becomes Leader of the Opposition in the House of Commons.

1712 January, accused of corruption over the issue of two forage contracts, and committed to the Tower of London until 8 July; regarded by some as a political martyr.

1714 1 October, sworn a privy councillor.

1715 17 March, leader of the House of Commons in the new Parliament, although his brother-in-law Lord Townshend nominally head of government.

11 October, appointed First Lord of the Treasury and Chancellor of the Exchequer, resigned in 1717.

1717 10 April, introduces a bill to establish the first Sinking Fund to reduce the national debt.

1720 The South Sea Company offers to assist the Government in managing the national debt; despite opposing the scheme Walpole buys considerable South Sea Stock, sells out before the market peaks and then buys shares, losing heavily.

1721 8 April, appointed Chancellor of the Exchequer and First Lord of the Treasury.

1723 10 May, introduces an Act for raising taxes on the estates of Roman Catholics and also non-jurors, (probably his least judicious act).

10 June, the King creates Walpole's eldest son, Robert, a peer, Lord Walpole of Walpole.

1725 Walpole invested with the Order of the Bath.

1726 he resigns the Order of the Bath in order to receive (on 26 June) the Order of the Garter, for which he gained the nickname 'Sir Bluestring'. A rift grew between Walpole and Townshend over foreign affairs.

December, the first edition of *The Craftsman*, an opposition journal.

1727 12 June, death of George I.

24 June, Walpole reappointed First Lord of the Treasury and Chancellor of the Exchequer by the new King, George II.

1729 9 November, the Treaty of Seville deprives the Jacobites of hope of foreign aid from Spain.

1730 15 May, Townshend resigns, Walpole's hold on foreign affairs strengthened.

7 November, *The Craftsman* claims that the housekeeping bills at Houghton amount to £1,500 per week.

1733 attempts unsuccessfully to introduce full tax on wine and tobacco imports; dubbed by the opposition, the Excise Bill.

1737 20 November, Queen Caroline dies, and Walpole's influence with the King wanes.

20 August, Walpole's first wife Catherine dies at Chelsea; buried in King Henry VII's chapel, Westminster Abbey.

1738 early March, privately marries Maria Skerrett; she dies of a miscarriage, 4 June.

Walpole, suffering from gout and stones, gradually loses his hold on Parliament.

1742 3 February, Walpole announces his retirement; 9 February, created Earl of Orford; 11 February, resigns, receiving a promise of a £4,000 annual pension.

1745 18 March, dies of exhaustion from the pain of his disease, aged 68; 25 March, buried at Houghton.

The Walpole and Cholmondeley Families

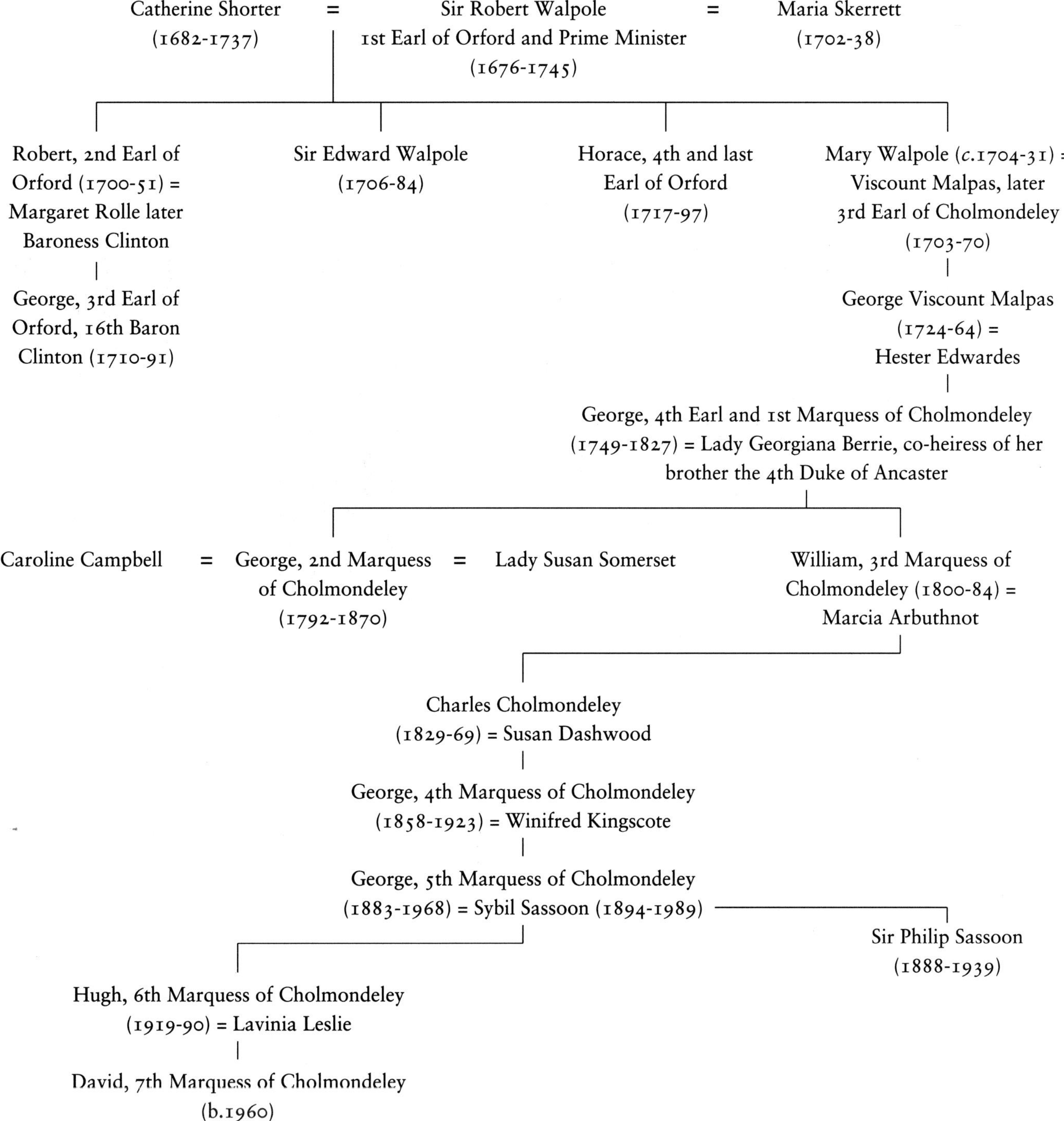

Walpole Family Houses and Residences 1676–1745

All these buildings survive either complete or in part, unless stated otherwise. The list excludes country estates and other land-holdings where Sir Robert and members of the family did not reside, and also offices relating to minor public appointments held. The information is primarily gathered from the various accounts and manuscript sources mentioned in the bibliography, volumes of the *Survey of London*, the *History of the King's Works*, V, 1660–1782, and the Yale edition of Horace Walpole's correspondence. In addition J.H. Plumb's biographies of Walpole, *No 10 Downing Street* by R.J. Minney (1963), *The Royal Hospital Chelsea*, by C.G.T. Dean (1950), and Michael Port's *The Houses of Parliament* (1976) have been referred to.

Norfolk

Crostwight Hall

Sir Robert's son, Robert, 1st Baron Walpole and his wife are recorded living in the sixteenth-century manor house at Crostwight near the north-east Norfolk coast.

Houghton Old Hall

Built in sixteenth century and earlier. Edward Walpole (Sir Robert's grandfather) rebuilt or added to it. The Hall was improved by Robert Walpole, first in early 1701 and again in 1716 and 1719. It was demolished in the early 1720s.

Houghton Hall

The new house was built on a site just to the east of the old mansion. The foundation stone is dated 1722. Building works on the main house continued into the early 1730s.

Stanhoe Manor House

About six miles north of Houghton, this was a seven-bay manor house of 1702, provided for Robert, Lord Walpole, and his mistress, Hannah Norsa. Some Downing Street paintings went to Stanhoe around 1743.

Wolterton Hall

This was built 1726–40 to the designs of Thomas Ripley for Sir Robert's brother Horatio, later Baron Walpole of Wolterton (known as 'Old Horace'). Horatio Walpole also owned Mannington Hall nearby, but members of the family did not live in the Hall until the nineteenth century.

London

Arlington Street, off Piccadilly

Sir Robert leased two houses in 'la rue des ministres', as his son Horace called it. Between 1715 and 1732 he lived in a house on the site later numbered 17, where Horace Walpole was born. The house was often used for ministerial meetings before moving to 10 Downing Street. Sir Henry Pelham commissioned William Kent to rebuild his much larger house, 1741–50, on part of the site. On Sir Robert's resignation in 1742 he returned to the street and joined two houses leased for himself and Horace (later number 5). Sir Robert died here in 1745. The house was left to Horace, who remained in Arlington Street until 1781.

Dover Street, Mayfair

After their removal from Lady Phillips's house in Berkeley Street, Robert and Catherine Walpole leased a house from 1705–15 on the east side of Dover Street. The number is not known. His brother Horatio lived here after Robert moved to Arlington Street.

10 Downing Street, Whitehall

The two houses that make up 'No. 10' were offered to Sir Robert as the King's First Minister, but he preferred to attach the house to his post of First Lord of the Treasury. Kent and Flitcroft substantially remodelled the older house of about 1677 before Walpole's installation in 1735. (Interior drawings in Metropolitan Museum, New York.) Maria Skerrett died here in 1738. Horace Walpole lived with his father at No. 10 until they left on Sir Robert's resignation in early 1742.

Exchequer Offices, Palace of Westminster

As Auditor of the Exchequer, Robert, Lord Walpole had offices in the old Palace, 1739–51. Some portraits by Van Dyck from Lord Wharton's collection were moved from these offices to Houghton on the creation of the new Gallery there. Demolished.

16 Grosvenor Street, Mayfair

Built by Thomas Ripley about 1724 and occupied 1725–38 by Robert, Lord Walpole. A large, five-bay terrace house with first floor great room. A list of paintings hung here is given in the picture list of 1736 (Pierpont Morgan MS.). Altered nineteenth and twentieth centuries.

Orford House, grounds of the Royal Hospital, Chelsea

Walpole's residence as Paymaster General of the Hospital from 1714 until his death, and the former home of his friend Edward Russell, Earl of Orford (from whom he took his title). The small seventeenth-century house, set in a stable yard, was enlarged by Vanbrugh about 1721–3 and the riverside garden increased to 23.5 hectares. This was in the latest fashion and included a river embankment, terrace, orangery, garden house, aviary and two summer houses. Queen Caroline and the Knights of Bath were entertained here in 1729. Part of the house was incorporated into Soane's new Infirmary, which was destroyed in 1941 (replaced nearby).

71 Pall Mall, St James's

Sir Robert reportedly antagonised the Duchess of Marlborough when he refused to give up the lease of this house so that she could make a way to her great house off Pall Mall, in 1725. Thomas Ripley took the lease around 1726 and may have designed the new house built after 1737, and occupied by Sir Robert's son, Sir Edward Walpole, from 1740 to 1778. Demolished after 1830 to build the Oxford and Cambridge Universities Club.

Ranger's Lodge, Spanker's Hill, Richmond New Park

Sir Robert's son Lord Walpole was made Ranger of Richmond Park in 1726, but it was his father, as deputy, who made regular use of this hunting and banqueting lodge. Some £14,000 was spent improving the original Caroline building. Walpole maintained his relationship with Maria Skerrett at the lodge. King George I so enjoyed his visits that he commissioned his own lodge from Lord Pembroke (White Lodge – still extant). Ranger's Lodge was demolished 1839–41. Sir Edward Walpole also had a villa in Richmond Park.

32 St James's Square

Sir Robert leased a house on the east side of the square, the late-seventeenth-century home of the Earl of Ashburnham. According to Horace Walpole, the family lived here, on leaving Arlington Street in 1732, until 1735. However, there are references in Walpole's accounts to a house in the square as early as 1725. Demolished about 1819.

Treasury, Whitehall

Rebuilt by Flitcroft to Kent's designs, 1733–5 and later, to house the only purpose-built government office of the day. Walpole's political power-base, 1735–42. Horatio Walpole, who was Auditor and Surveyor General of American Revenue, lived in a large house across the courtyard (demolished), fronting Whitehall.

Twickenham

Sir Robert's accounts include payments for items at a house in Twickenham. This may have been Lady Mary Wortley Montagu's house in Heath Road, where he wooed Maria Skerrett, 1725–6. Demolished about 1912.

Select Manuscript Sources

Manuscripts referred to in abbreviated form, given in alphabetical order of location

CAMBRIDGE, FITZWILLIAM MUSEUM
Horace Walpole's *Aedes Walpolianae*, 2nd edn, 1775, with MSS notes, values and diagrams
Bequeathed by Sir Robert Hyde Greg, 1953
[cat. 20]

CAMBRIDGE, UNIVERSITY LIBRARY
Cholmondeley MSS
[For a summary of this collection see Chinnery, 1953]

FARMINGTON, CONNECTICUT
W.S. Lewis Library, Yale University
Walpole family papers (some references in the *Yale edition of Horace Walpole's correspondence*, W.S. Lewis, (ed.), 1937–83)

HERTFORDSHIRE, RECORD OFFICE
Pictures at Houghton 1744
7 folios
The Cobbold family, on deposit to Hertfordshire Record Office
[cat. 18]

LONDON, BRITISH MUSEUM
Musgrove MSS, Additional MS 6391, British Museum, 1797
Brief listing of collection

LONDON, NATIONAL ART LIBRARY
(Victoria & Albert Museum)
Houlditch MSS 86.00.18/19
Two volumes of sale catalogues of the principal collections of pictures (170 in total), sold by auction in England 1711–59, the majority with MS additions giving prices and names of purchasers. The source of information concerning acquisitions by Sir Robert Walpole for his picture collection

NEW YORK, PIERPONT MORGAN LIBRARY
A catalogue of Sir Robert Walpole's collection of pictures, 1736
38 folios bound into the author's copy of *Aedes Walpolianae*... 2nd edn, London, 1752 (PML 7586)
[cat. 17]

NORFOLK, HOUGHTON HALL
Houghton Archive
Miscellaneous private papers retained at Houghton Hall.
[see cat. 16]

NORWICH, NORFOLK, AND NORWICH RECORD OFFICE
Harry Bradford Lawrence bequest, 1967, including letters about valuing the Houghton pictures, 1778 (BL VIb (vi))
[see cat. 73]

WILTSHIRE, WILTON HOUSE ARCHIVES
Sir Mathew Decker, 1728, *An account of a journey done into Hartford, Cambridgeshire, Suffolk, Norfolk and Essex, from the 21st June to the 12th July, being 22 days.*

Select Bibliography

Works include those referred to in abbreviated form

ADAMS, C.K., and LEWIS, W.S., 1970
'The Portraits of Horace Walpole', *Walpole Society*, XLII, 1968–70

AVERY, Charles, 1987
Giambologna, Oxford

BAKER, C., and OXFORD, M., 1949
The Life and Circumstances of James Brydges, First Duke of Chandos; Patron of the Liberal Arts, Clarendon

BALDINUCCI, F., 1974–5
Notizie de' professori del disegno da Cimabue in qua, 1691–1728, Florence

BANISTER, J., 1989
'The Walpole Inkstand', *Octagon*, XXV, no.3, pp. 36–9

BARNES, P., 1993
Norfolk Landowners since 1880, Norwich

BEARD, Geoffrey, 1975
Decorative Plasterwork in Great Britain, London

BEARD, Geoffrey, 1981
Craftsmen and Interior Decoration in England, 1660–1820, London

BEARD, Geoffrey, 1986
'William Kent', *Antiques*, June, p. 1282

BEARD, G., and GILBERT, C. (eds), 1986
Dictionary of English Furniture Makers, 1660–1840, Leeds

BEATNIFFE, R., 1795
The Norfolk Tour: or, the traveler's pocket companion..., 5th edn, Norwich

BELLORI, G.P., 1942
Vite di Guido Reni, Andrea Sacchi e Carlo Maratti, ed. M. Piacenti, Rome (MS 1695)

BOWDEN-SMITH, Rosemary, 1987
The Water House, Houghton Hall, Woodbridge

BOYDELL, John
A set of Prints Engraved After the Most Capital Paintings in the Collection of Her Imperial Majesty The Empress of Russia, Lately in the Possession of the Earl of Orford at Houghton Hall in Norfolk, 2 vols., previously published in portfolios, 1774–88

BROOME, Revd J. H., 1865
Houghton and the Walpoles, London and King's Lynn

BROWN, Christopher, 1982
Van Dyck, Oxford

BROWN, Jonathan, and MANN, Richard G., 1990
Spanish Paintings of the Fifteenth Through Nineteenth Centuries, National Gallery of Art, Washington, Cambridge

BRUNTJEN, Sven H.A., 1985
John Boydell, 1719–1804. A Study of Art Patronage and Publishing in Georgian London, Garland

BUCHANAN, William, 1824
Memoirs of Painting, 2 vols., London

CAMPBELL, Colen, 1725
Vitruvius Britannicus III, London

CHAMBERS, John, 1829
A General History of the County of Norfolk intended to convey all the information of a Norfolk Tour, 2 vols., Norwich and London

CHINNERY, G.A., 1953
A handlist of the Cholmondeley (Houghton) MSS. Sir Robert Walpole's archive, Cambridge

CHRISTIE'S, 1994
Works of Art from Collections of the Cholmondeley family and the late Sir Philip Sassoon, Bt, from Houghton, Christie's sale catalogue, 8 December, London

COOPER, D. (ed.), 1965
Great Family Collections, includes J.F.B. Watson, 'Houghton Hall', London

CORNFORTH, John, 1974
Country Houses in Britain – Can They Survive?, London

CORNFORTH, John, 1987/A
'Houghton Hall, Norfolk', *Country Life*, 30 April, pp. 124–9; 7 May, pp. 104–8

CORNFORTH, John, 1987/B
'The Growth of an Idea', *Country Life*, 14 May, pp. 162–8

CORNFORTH, John, 1988
The Search for a Style, Country Life and Architecture 1897–1935, London

CORNFORTH, John, 1996
Houghton Hall: Guide Book, Norwich (forthcoming)

COXE, William, 1798
Memoirs of the Life and Administration of Sir Robert Walpole, 3 vols. 1798 (another ed. 1800)

DAVISON, Alan (ed.), 1988
Six Deserted Villages in Norfolk, East Anglian Archaeology, 44

DESCARGUES, P., 1961
The Hermitage, transl. K. Delavenay, London

FENNER, George and Alayne, 1988
Houghton: The Church', in Davison 1988, pp. 95–9

FINER, Ann, and SAVAGE, George, 1965
The Selected Letters of Josiah Wedgwood, London

GARLICK, K., and MACINTYRE, A. (eds.), 1978
The Diary of Joseph Farington Volume II, January 1795–August 1796, New Haven and London

GILBERT, Christopher (ed.) 1968
Furniture at Temple Newsam and Lotherton Hall, Leeds

GILBERT, Christopher, 1978
The Life and Work of Thomas Chippendale, 2 vols., Bradford and London

GILPIN, William, 1802
Gilpin, An Essay on Prints, London

GIROUARD, M., 1978
Life in the English County House: A Social and Architectural History, New Haven and London

GRIGOR, J., 1847
The Eastern Arboretum, London and Norwich

HARLEY, Edward (2nd Earl of Oxford), 1732
Historic Manuscripts Commission, Portland, VI, p. 160 et seq.

HARLEY, Edward (2nd Earl of Oxford), 1737/8
Historic Manuscripts Commission, Portland, VI, p. 171 et seq.

HARRIS, Eileen, and SAVAGE, Nicholas, 1990
British Architectural Books and Writers, 1556–1785, Bath

HARRIS, John, 1964
'The Prideaux Collection of Topographical Drawings', *Architectural History*, 7, pp. 17–39

HARRIS, John, 1973
'Colen Campbell', *Catalogue of the Drawings Collection, Royal Institute of British Architects*, London

HARRIS, John, 1985
'John Talman's Design for his Wunderkammern', *Furniture History*, London, pp. 211–14

HARRIS, John, 1988
'James Gibbs, Eminence Grise at Houghton', *Georgian Group Annual Symposium*, London pp. 5–9

HARRIS, John, 1989
'Who designed Houghton?', *Country Life*, 183, 2 March, pp. 92–4

HASKELL, Francis, and PENNY, Nicholas, 1981
Taste and the Antique, New Haven and London

HERKOMER, Hubert von, 1892
Etching and Mezzotint Engraving, London

HERVEY, John (Lord Hervey), 1731
Letter to Frederick, Prince of Wales, July 14, quoted in *Memoirs of the Reign of George II*, 1848

HILL, Brian, 1989
Sir Robert Walpole, London

HUSSEY, Christopher, 1955
English Country Houses: Early Georgian, 1715–1760, London

HUSSEY, Christopher, 1963
'Houghton Hall, Norfolk', *Country Life Album*, p. 28 et seq.

JACKSON-STOPS, G. (ed.), 1985
The Treasure Houses of Britain: Five Hundred Years of Private Patronage and Art Collecting, New Haven and London

JACKSON-STOPS, G. (ed.), 1989
'The Fashioning and Function of the British Country House', *Studies in the History of Art*, Washington, 25

JACKSON-STOPS, Gervase, and PIPKIN, James, 1984
The English Country House: A Grand Tour, London

JOURDAIN, Margaret, 1948
The Work of William Kent, London

KENT, William, 1727
The Designs of Inigo Jones..., 2 vols., London

KERSLAKE, John, 1977
Catalogue of the Eighteenth-Century Portraits in the National Portrait Gallery, London

KETTON-CREMER, R.W., 1948
A Norfolk Gallery, London

KITSON, S.D., 1937
The Life of John Sell Cotman, London

KLIMA, Slava (ed.), 1975
Joseph Spence: Letters from The Grand Tour, Montreal

KUSTODIEVA, Tatyana, et al, 1989
The Hermitage, Leningrad: Western European Printing of the 13th to the 18th Centuries, Leningrad

LARSEN, E., 1988
The Paintings of Anthony van Dyck, 2 vols., Freren

Le BLANC, Charles, 1970
Manuel de l'amateur d'estampes, Amsterdam

LEWIS, W.S. (ed.), 1937–83
The Yale Edition of Horace Walpole's Correspondence, 48 vols, New Haven

LOUDON, J.C., 1841
The Gardener's Magazine, p. 271

MACKIE, C., 1901
Norfolk Annals: A Chronological Record of Remarkable Events in the 19th Century, 2 vols., Norwich

MACQUOID, Percy, 1906 (1987 edn)
A History of English Furniture: The Age of Mahogany, London

MACQUOID, P., and EDWARDS, R., 1954
The Dictionary of English Furniture, 3 vols., 2nd edn, London

MARILLIER, H.C., 1926
Christie's, 1766–1925, London

MEYER, Arline, 1984
John Wootton, 1682–1764: Landscapes and Sporting Art in early Georgian England, The Iveagh Bequest, Kenwood

MILLAR, Oliver, 1963
The Tudor, Stuart and Early Georgian Pictures in the Collection of Her Majesty the Queen, 2 vols., London

MILLAR, Oliver, 1994
'Philip, Lord Wharton, and his collection of portraits', *Burlington Magazine*, CXXXVI, No. 1097, August, pp. 517–30

MOORE, Andrew W., 1985
Norfolk and the Grand Tour Eighteenth-Century Travellers Abroad and Their Souvenirs, Norwich

MOORE, Andrew W., 1988
Dutch and Flemish Painting in Norfolk: A History of Taste and Influence, Fashion and Collecting, London

MOORE, Andrew, 1993
'La collection de Sir Robert Walpole (Houghton, 1676–Londres, 1745)', in *L'Age d'or flamand et hollandais, collections de Catherine II, Musée de L'Ermitage, Saint Petersbourg*, Musée des Beaux-Arts de Dijon, pp. 65–71

MOORE, Andrew, and CRAWLEY, Charlotte, 1992
Family and Friends: A Regional Survey of British Portraiture, London

NAGLER, G.K. 1835–52
Neues Allgemeines Künstler-Lexicon..., 22 vols., Munich

NICOLSON, N. (ed.), 1968
Harold Nicolson: Diaries and Letters, 1945–1962, London

PAULSON, Ronald, 1971
Hogarth: His Life, Art and Times, 2 vols., New Haven and London

PEARS, Iain, 1988
The Discovery of Painting: The Growth of Interest in the Arts in England, 1680–1768, New Haven and London

PETERS, Beverley, 1991
'The Development of Wolterton Hall', MA Diss., Centre of East Anglian Studies/University of East Anglia

PIPER, David, 1963
Catalogue of the Seventeenth Century Portraits in the National Portrait Gallery, 1625–1714, Cambridge

PLUMB, J.H., 1956 (1972 edn)
Sir Robert Walpole: I, The Making of a Statesman, London

PLUMB, J.H., 1960 (1972 edn)
Sir Robert Walpole: The King's Minister, London

RAJNAI, M. (ed.), 1982
John Sell Cotman, 1782–1842, London

REITLINGER, Gerald, 1961
The Economics of Taste: The Rise and Fall of the Picture Market, 1760–1960, London

ROBINSON, Sir Thomas, 1731
Historic Manuscripts Commission, XV, Appendix pt vi, Carlisle, p. 84

ROSOMAN, Treve, 1986
'The Chiswick House Inventory of 1770', *Furniture History*, pp. 81–106

RUBINSTEIN, Gregory, 1991
'Richard Earlom (1743–1822) and Boydell's "Houghton Gallery"', *Print Quarterly*, VIII, No. 1 March, pp. 2–27

RUSSELL, F. 1989
'The Hanging and Display of Pictures 1700–1850', in Jackson–Stops, pp. 133–53

SANI, Bernardina, 1988
Rosalba Carriera, Turin

SINGH, Prince Frederick Duleep [1927]
Portraits in Norfolk Houses (ed. E. Farrer), 2 vols. published ?1928, Norwich

SLIVE, Seymour, 1970
Frans Hals, 3 vols, London

SOTHEBY'S, 1992
British Drawings, Sotheby's sale catalogue, 19 November, London

SOUCHAL, François, 1977
French Sculptors of the 17th and 18th Centuries, I, Oxford

STEWART, J.D., 1971
Sir Godfrey Kneller, London

STRONG, R., BINNEY, M., and HARRIS, J., 1974
The Destruction of the Country House, London

STUKELEY, W., 1880
The Family Memoirs of the Rev. William Stukeley, Surtees Society, III, London

SURTEES, V. (ed.), 1995
The Grace of Friendship: Horace Walpole and the Misses Berry, Wilby

SUTTON, Denys, 1966
'A King of Epithets: A Study of James Christie', *Apollo*, November, pp. 364–75

THORNTON, Peter, 1993
'Soane's Kent Tables', *Furniture History*, pp. 59–69

TIPPING, H.A., 1921
'Houghton Hall, Norfolk', *Country Life*, XLIX, 1, 8, 15, 22 January, pp. 14, 40, 64, 98 et seq.

VARDY, John, 1744
Some Designs of Mr Inigo Jones and Mr William Kent, London

VERTUE, George
Notebooks I–VI, The Walpole Society, XVIII, XX, XXII, XXIV, XXVI, XXX, index XXIX, 1930–55 (reprd. 1968, Oxford)

VICTORIA & ALBERT MUSEUM, 1984
Drawings by William Kent from the Print Room Collection, London

VIVIAN, Ralph, 1907
'Houghton Hall: I', *Country Life*, 27 July, pp. 126–34; 'Houghton Hall: II', *Country Life*, 3 August, pp. 162–71

VSEVOLOZHSKAYA, Svetlana, and KOSTENEVICH, Albert, 1984
Italian Painting, The Hermitage, Leningrad

WALISZEWSKI, R., 1894
The Romance of an Empress: Catherine II of Russia, II, London

WALPOLE, Horace, 1747
Aedes Walpolianae..., London

WALPOLE, Horace, 1784
Essay on Modern Gardening

WALPOLE, H., 1888
Anecdotes of Painting in England 1765–71, ed. R. N. Wornum, 3 vols., London

WARD-JACKSON, P., 1958
English Furniture Designs of the Eighteenth Century, London, 1984 ed.

WARE, Isaac, 1731
Designs of Inigo Jones and Others, London

WARE, Isaac, and RIPLEY, Thomas, 1735
The Plans, Elevations and Sections; Chimney-pieces and Ceilings of Houghton in Norfolk..., London

WATERHOUSE, Ellis, 1958
Gainsborough, London

WATSON, F.J.B., 1940
Thomas Patch (1725–1782); Notes on his Life, together with a catalogue of his known works, The Walpole Society, XXVIII, Oxford

WATSON F.J.B, 1965, see above.
COOPER, D (ed.), 1965

WEBB, Margaret I., 1954
Michael Rysbrack: Sculptor, London

WESSELY, J.E., 1886
Richard Earlom: Verzeichniss seiner Radierungen and Schabkunstblätter, Hamburg

WHITE, Edwin, 1868
Lord Orford's voyage round the Fens in 1774, Doncaster

WHITLEY, William T., 1928
Artists and their Friends in England, 1700–1799, 2 vols., London and Boston

WILLIAMSON, Tom, 1995
Polite Landscapes: Gardens and Society in Eighteenth-Century England, London

WILLIS, Peter, 1977
Charles Bridgeman, London

WILSON, Michael I., 1984
William Kent, London

WILTON, A., 1992
The Swagger Portrait: Grand Manner Portraiture in Britain from Van Dyck to Augustus John, 1630–1930, London

WORSLEY, Giles, 1990
'Riding on Status', *Country Life*, 184, 27 September, pp. 108–11

WORSLEY, Giles, 1993
'Houghton Hall, Norfolk', *Country Life*, 187, 4 March, pp. 50–3

YAXLEY, D. (ed.), 1984
Survey of the Houghton Estate by Joseph Hill, 1800, Norfolk Record Society, L, Norwich

YAXLEY, D., 1988
'Houghton', in Davison, 1988

YAXLEY, David, 1994
'The Tower of Houghton St Martin Church', *The Annual Bulletin of the Norfolk Archaeological and Historical Research Group*, 3, pp. 46–50

YAXLEY, David, 1996
'The Houghton Gallery', *East Anglian Studies*, ed. A. Longcroft and R. Joby, University of East Anglia, Norwich (forthcoming)

Exhibitions

Referred to in abbreviated form

Bristol, 1982	*Michael Rysbrack*, Bristol Museum and Art Gallery
Chicago and New York, 1990	*From Poussin to Matisse. The Russian Taste for French Painting, A Loan Exhibition from the USSR*, The Metropolitan Museum of Art, New York and the Art Institute of Chicago
Dulwich, 1991–2	*Palaces of Art, Art Galleries in Britain 1790–1990*, Dulwich Picture Gallery; National Gallery of Scotland
Kingston-upon-Hull, 1985	*A Tercentenary Tribute to William Kent*, Ferens Gallery
London, 1820	British Institution, Annual Winter Exhibition
London, 1838	Old Water Colour Society, Annual Exhibition
London, 1914	*Summer Exhibition 1914*, Royal Academy of Arts
London, 1925	*John Singer Sargent Memorial Exhibition*, New English Art Club
London, 1929	*Exhibition of works of the late John S. Sargent, RA*, Winter Exhibition, Royal Academy of Arts
London, 1929	*Loan Exhibition of Old English Plate and Decorations and Orders, for the Benefit of the Royal Northern Hospital*, Residence of Sir Philip Sassoon, 25, later 45, Park Lane
London, 1930	*Loan Exhibition of Eighteen Century English Conversation Pieces*, 25, later 45, Park Lane
London, 1938	*The 'Old London' Exhibition in Aid of the Royal Northern Hospital*, 25, later 45, Park Lane
London, 1950	*Three Centuries of British Silver, Loan Exhibition in Aid of the Citizens' Advice Bureaux*, Mallett's Galleries
London, 1959	*The Houghton Pictures*, Thomas Agnew & Sons Ltd.
London, 1961	*Architectural Drawings from the Witt Collection*, Courtauld Institute of Art
London, 1971/A	*Hogarth*, Tate Gallery
London, 1971/B	*Sir Godfrey Kneller*, National Portrait Gallery
London, 1978	*Giambologna*, Arts Council
London and tour, 1982	*John Sell Cotman, 1782–1842*, Victoria and Albert Museum; Manchester, Whitworth Art Gallery; Bristol, City Museum and Art Gallery
London, 1984/A	*John Wootton, 1682-1764*, The Iveagh Bequest, Kenwood
London, 1984/B	*Rococo*, Victoria and Albert Museum
London, 1987	*Designs for English Picture Frames*, Arnold Wiggins & Sons Ltd.
London, 1987–8	*Manners and Morals*, Tate Gallery
London, 1990	*Paul de Lamerie, At the Sign of the Golden Ball. An Exhibition of the Work of England's Master Silversmith 1688–1751*, Goldsmiths Hall
London, 1995	*Drawing in Eighteenth-Century Britain*, Courtauld Institute of Art
Norwich, 1985	*Norfolk and The Grand Tour*, Norwich Castle Museum
Norwich, 1992	*Norfolk Portraits*, Norwich Castle Museum
Twickenham, 1966	*The Countess of Suffolk and her Friends*, Marble Hill House, Greater London Council
Washington DC, 1984	*Hogarth*, National Gallery of Art; Berlin, Schloss Charlottenburg; Paris, Grand Palais
Washington, DC, 1985–6	*The Treasure Houses of Britain*, National Gallery of Art
Washington, DC, 1990–1	*Van Dyck*, National Gallery of Art

List of Lenders

British Museum, London 6, 48, 50, 54, 57, 68

The Marquess of Cholmondeley 4, 7–10, 13–4, 16, 19, 21, 23–5, 27–9, 31, 33–6, 40–4, 46, 49, 56, 59, 63, 69, 70, 74, 76–80

Christie's, London 72

Courtauld Institute Galleries, London 32

Fitzwilliam Museum, Cambridge 20, 75

The State Hermitage Museum, St Petersburg 11, 45, 51

Hertford Record Office, Hertfordshire 18

The Hon. Christopher Lennox Boyd 5, 37, 53, 55, 65–7

Metropolitan Museum of Art, New York 61

Museum of London 64

National Gallery of Art, Washington, DC 12, 26, 52

National Portrait Gallery, London 1

Norfolk Museums Service (Norwich Castle Museum) 30

Norfolk Record Office 73

J. Ortiz-Patiño 22, 62

Pierpont Morgan Library, New York 17

Private Collections 2, 3, 15, 38–9, 58

Victoria and Albert Museum, London 47, 60, 71

Contributors

Chloë Archer worked at Sir John Soane's Museum and at the Victoria and Albert Museum before joining Norfolk Museums Service as Assistant Keeper of Art with responsibility for the Decorative Arts.

Geoffrey Beard was Director of the Visual Arts Centre at the University of Lancaster 1972–82. His publications include: *Georgian Craftsmen (1966); Decorative Plasterwork in Great Britain* (1975); and *The Work of Grinling Gibbons* (1990).

The 7th Marquess of Cholmondeley inherited Houghton Hall and estate in 1990 when he embarked upon a programme of refurbishment of the Hall.

John Cornforth has been writing about country houses for *Country Life* since 1961 and during the past twenty-five years has concentrated on the history of English interiors and decoration.

Sebastian Edwards is Assistant Curator with the Historic Royal Palaces, formerly Assistant Curator with English Heritage's London Properties, responsible for Furniture and Decorative Arts and curator for the collection and historic interiors at Chiswick House.

John Harris was the Curator of the British Architectural Library's Drawing Collection and Heinz Gallery, 1960–86, and consultant to Heinz Architectural Center, Carnegie, 1991–4. His publications include *The Artist and the Country House* (1979) and articles in *Country Life*, *Apollo* and other journals.

Andrew Moore has been Keeper of Art for Norfolk Museums Service since 1980, and since 1994 Curator of Norwich Castle Museum. He has organised a number of exhibitions focusing on the historic and private collections of Norfolk, including *Norfolk and the Grand Tour* (1985), *Dutch and Flemish Painting in Norfolk* (1988) and *Norfolk Portraits* (1992).

Gregory Rubinstein was Assistant Curator of Drawings, The Royal Collection, Windsor Castle 1989–90, and is now Director of Old Master Drawings, Sotheby's.

William Speck is Professor of Modern History at the University of Leeds. His published work includes *The Butcher. The Duke of Cumberland and the suppression of the 'Forty-Five'* (1995).

Tom Williamson is Lecturer in Landscape Archaeology in the Centre of East Anglian Studies at the University of East Anglia. Recent publications include *Parks and Gardens* (with Anthea Taigel, 1993), *The Origins of Norfolk* (1993); and *Polite Landscapes. Parks and Gardens in Eighteenth-century England* (1995).

Index

Page numbers in **bold** indicate illustrations

Albani, Francesco
  Baptism of Christ 50
Aliamet, François-Germain 67
Artari, Adalbertus 27, 113
Artari, Giuseppe 26-7, 33
Arundel Castle 54
Atterbury, Francis, Bishop of Rochester 15

Badeslade, Thomas
  map of Houghton 20, 41, 42, **43**
Bagutti, Giovanni 26, 27
Bandinelli, Baccio 114, 116
Barrett, Ranelagh 52, 85, 149
Bartolozzi, Francesco 67
Bassano, Jacopo 121, 138
  Christ laid in the Sepulchre 53
Batoni, Pompeo
  George James, 4th Earl of Cholmondeley **74**
beds 31, 35-7, 37-8, 40, 102, 132
Belchier, John 130
Bell, Henry 20, 22, 24
Bellini, Giovanni
  A Holy Family 50
Bentinck, Henry, Duke of Portland
  sale 49
Bernini, Giovanni 125
Blakiston, Sir Matthew 57
Blount, George 74
Bodham, P. 146
Boeckhorst, Jan 147
Bol, Ferdinand
  Old Woman Reading 49
Borghese Vase 116
Bourdon, Sebastian 136
  Jacob burying Laban's Images 68, **136**
Boydell, John 60, 65-70, 111, 129, 132, 137, 147
  The Houghton Gallery 65-73, 137, 147, **154**, 154-5, 167
  ... *Most Capital Paintings in England* 65-6, 67, 68, 72, 73, 136
  Shakespeare Gallery 66, 67, 68, 72, 73
Boydell, Josiah 68, 69, 72
Bradshaw, William 35
Bragge, Robert 48, 56-7
Breughel, Jan 49
Bridgeman, Charles 42, 43, 46
British Museum 60, 67, 152, 154
Bromley, Henry, 1st Lord Montfort 100
Brouwer, Adriaen 137
Browne, John (engraver) 67
Browne, John (subject of portrait by Gainsborough) 158
Browne, Samuel 25
Brydges, James, 1st Duke of Chandos 53
Buchanan, William 152
Burges, Elizeus 108
Burlington, Richard Boyle, 3rd Earl of 23, 28, 29, 30-1, 38, 92, 111, 125, 135, 148
Burlington House 23, 24, 29, 33
Burrell, Peter 101
Byres, James 99

Cadogan, William, 1st Earl of 52
caffoy 31, 34, 39
Calke Abbey, Derbyshire 37-8
Cambridge
  King's College 22
  Senate House 22
Campbell, Colen 20, 22, 23, 24, 27-8, 29, 32, 42, 112
  design for court front **21**, 22
  design for portico front **21**, 22
  plan of Houghton **42**, 45
  Vitruvius Britannicus 20, **21**, 22, 32, 41, 98, 167
Canons, Middlesex 53
Canot, Pierre-Charles 66
  Dogs and Still Life **129**
  The Goats-Herd **132**
Caroline, Queen 12, 13, 46, 165
Carriera, Rosalba 106, 107, 108-9
  Edward Walpole **108**
  Horace Walpole **109**
  Robert Walpole **107**
'Carton, Peter de'
  Abraham, Sarah and Hagar 52
carving 27
Cass, Christopher 25
Castle Howard, Yorkshire 26
'Catalogue ... 1736' **99**
Catherine II, Empress of Russia 153
  busts **152**, 152-3
  portraits 153
  purchase of Houghton picture collection 52, 56, 60, 61-4, 95, 96, 100, 107, 135, 136, 152-5
  rumour of wreck 155
Cavendish, William, 3rd Duke of Devonshire 54
chairs 35, 91-2, **91**, 92-3, **92**, 126-7, **127**, 146
  armchair 121-2, **121**
  gilded 38-9
  servants' 32
chandeliers 34, 95, 114, 142
Chatsworth 54
Chesterfield, Philip Stanhope, 4th Earl of 114, 115
Chevening, Kent 35
Chiari, Giuseppe 35
Chicheley Hall, Buckinghamshire 34
Chiswick 23, 92, 141
Cholmondeley, Charlotte, Lady 35, 75
Cholmondeley, David, 7th Marquess 81, 156, 157, 160, 171
Cholmondeley, Frederick 158
Cholmondeley, George, Viscount Malpas, 3rd Earl 114, 157, 158
Cholmondeley, George, 4th Earl and 1st Marquess 24, 35, 74-6, **74**, 125, 157
Cholmondeley, George, 2nd Marquess 76, 77
Cholmondeley, George, Earl of Rocksavage, 5th Marquess 79, 80, 81
Cholmondeley, Hugh, 6th Marquess 79, 81
Cholmondeley, James 158
Cholmondeley, Lavinia, Lady 156
Cholmondeley, Mary, Lady *see* Walpole
Cholmondeley, Robert 158
Cholmondeley, Sybil, Lady 6, 78, 79-81, 96, 156, 161
  portraits 80, **81**, **161**
Cholmondeley, William, 3rd Marquess 76, 77
  4th Marquess 79
Cholmondeley Castle (Hall), Cheshire 24, 75, 76, 79, 80, 81
Cholmondeley family
  genealogy 163
Christie, James 7, 60, 61, 101, 152, 153, 154
  letter to Cony 154
Christie's 7
  sales 68, 84, 85, 101, 105, 142, 153, 155, 167
Churchill, Charles 53, 91, **91**
Chute, John 57
Cignani, Carlo 96
Cipriani, Giovanni Baptista 61, 63, 64, 101, 152, 153
Clandon Park, Surrey 26,140
Claude Lorrain 57, 68, 95
  Morning in the harbour **59**
Cleaves, John 27
Clement IX, Pope
  portrait 99, 124, 125-6, **126**
Clerk, Sir John 41-2
Clinton, Henry Fiennes, 9th Earl of Lincoln and 2nd Duke of Newcastle under-Lyme 147
Cocchi, Antonio 100
Cock, Christopher 56, 129
Coke, Thomas, Earl of Leicester 24, 29, 30, 35, 61, 125
Cole, William 61, 63-4, 100, 155
Colebrooke, Sir George 60
Compton Wynyates, Warwickshire 160
Connoisseur 144
Conway, Francis, Marquis of Hertford 62
Cony, Carlos 61, 154
Cortona, Pietro da 51
Cotman, John Sell
  Lee Shore **155**
Courtois, Jacques 49
Craftsman, The 114
Crown Office 142

da Campidoglio, Michelangelo 69
da Cortona, Pietro 148
Dahl, Michael 83, 103
  Catherine Shorter 102, 103, **103**

Danvers, Sir Joseph 54
David, Claude
 Vulcan chained to the Rock 53
de Lamerie, Paul 101, 142, 143
 strawberry dishes **143**
 Walpole Inkstand **101**
 Walpole Salver **142**
de Thoms 99
de Vos, Martin 96, 137
Decker, Sir Matthew 41, 42, 43, 88, 92, 97, 102, 117, 119
Devall, George 25, 28
Didlington Hall 79
Dighton, Robert
 The Specious Orator **153**
dishes, strawberry **143**
Ditchley Park, Oxfordshire 22, 23, 29, 35, 38
Dobson, William
 Abraham van der Doort 63
Duane, Matthew 61
Dughet, Gaspar 104, 120
Dunkarton, Robert 68, 69

Earlom, Richard 65, 66, 67-72, 73, 136, 137, 154
 Agrippina landing ... 67
 Bathsheba bringing Abishag to David 71
 A Concert of Birds **89**
 A Flower Piece 69, **70**, **137**
 The Fruit Market **146**, 147
 Jacob burying Laban's Images 68, **136**
 John Wilkes **151**
 Mary Magdalene washing the Feet of Christ 71
 Meleager and Atalanta 71, **147**
 Prodigal Son 68
Eccardt, John
 Sir Robert Walpole and Catherine Shorter 83, 103
Edward VI, King, portrait 53
Edward VII, King 77
Ellys, John 52, 56-7, 88-9
 Fulke Harold **88**
Erddig, North Wales 31, 37, 130
Esher 30
European Magazine, The 152

Farington, George 61, 68, 96, 147, 148
Farington, Joseph 68, 71, 75, 129, 147
Faustina the Elder 115
 bust **115**
Fleuriau, C.-J.-B. 149
Flitcroft, Henry 30, 38, 115, 165
 ... Stone Hall chimneypiece **114**
Fountaine, Sir Andrew 53, 79, 111
Fourdrinier, Pierre 65, 72, 115
 Cross-sectional elevation of the Staircase ... **111**
 Plan and Elevation of Houghton Hall **66**
Francis I, Duke of Lorraine 132

Gainsborough, Thomas 81, 158
 Mr and Mrs Browne **158**
Gambarini, Count Carlo 100
Gamble, Ellis 142
Garter, Order of the 26, 30, 54, 105, 114, 115, 130, 162
Gay, John
 The Beggar's Opera 84, 104
Gentileschi, Artemisia 160
Gentleman's Magazine 61, 64, 67
George I, King 165
 portrait 50, 94, 96, 97-8
George II, King 12, 13, 46
George III, King 62
George IV, King (as Prince of Wales) 35, 75, 125
George V, King 78
George VI, King 81
gesso 130
Giambologna 111, 123
Gibbons, Grinling 48, 94
 collection 50, 87, 89, 119
 portrait 94, 96
Gibbs, James 20, 22-4, 29, 30, 32, 34, 38, 90, 112
 bust 115
 plan for Houghton **23**
Gibson, Thomas 83
Gideon, Sampson 57
gilding 34, 38-9
Giordano, Luca 106, 119-20
 Birth and *Presentation of the Virgin* 49
 The Cyclops at their Forge **48**, 50, 119-20, **119**
Girardon, François 116
 Laocoön 107, 114
Gladiator 32
Glover, John 25
Gobelins 35, 40
goblet **144**
Goodison, Benjamin 35
Goodwin, Arthur, portrait 54
Goupy, Joseph
 Sir Robert Walpole addressing the Cabinet 18
Grand Tour 100, 107, 109, 116, 137
Gray, Thomas 31
Green, Valentine 65, 66, 69, 71-2, 154
 The Assumption of the Virgin **72**
 Sir Thomas Wharton **71**
Griffier, Jan 48
Griffiths, John 25
Grigor, James 24, 76-7
Guelfi, G.B. 115

Hall, John 67
Hals, Frans 96
 Portrait of a Seated Man **95**
Hamilton, Gustavus, 2nd Viscount Boyne 108
Hardy, Robert 22
Hare, Francis 103
Harley, Sir Edward, 2nd Earl of Oxford 22-3, 48, 90, 102, 111, 121, 140
Harold, Fulke 42, 87, **88**, 101
Hartshorne Collection 144
Hay, Andrew 48, 51
Heins, John Theodore 83
Hervey, John, Baron Hervey of Ickworth 113, 119, 125, 140
Hill, Joseph 76
Hogarth, William 52, 83, 84, 142
 The Cholmondeley Family **157**, 157-8
Holbein, Hans
 Portrait of an Unknown Woman ... 80-1
Hondius, Abraham
 A Crowd watching Bear-baiting **160**
Hoppner, John 75, 157
Houbraken, A. 107
Houghton Hall, Norfolk
 architecture 20-4
  building 25-6
  front designs **21**, **22**
  plans **23**, **42**, **44**, **66**
 costs 16, 24, 156
 craftsmen 25-8
 first floor, plan **86**
 inventories
  1736 10
  1744 10, 99-100
  1745 10, **101**
  1792 10, 40, 159
  1797 10
 dilapidated, *1773* 60
 fire, *1789* 62, 75, 146
 on death of 3rd Earl, *1791* 74
 on death of Walpole, *1745* 56-7
 owned by Cholmondeleys 74-80
 owned by Robert Walpole 9, 20, 24, 30-1, 38, 41, 46
 tenants, *19-20c.* 77-80
 today 156-61
 view from west **98**
 Arcade 32, **87**, 91
 Breakfast Room (Gun Room) 87-9
 Cabinet Room 75, **134**, 135-8
  picture hang plan **138**
 Coffee Room 31
 Common Parlour 94-6, **94**
  plan of hang **96**
 Drawing Room (Yellow) 31, 35, 105-9, **105**
 Dressing Room (Tapestry Dressing Room; Vandyke Dressing Room) 37, **128**, 129-30
 Embroidered Bedroom 37-8, **131**, 132-3
 Family Bedroom 39-40
 Gallery, Picture 38, 100, **145**, 145-50
  east and west elevations 149-50, **150**
  fire 62, 75, 146
  lighting 150
 Great Door **24**
 Green Velvet Bedroom 31, 35-7, **36**, **37**, 48
 Hunting Hall (Dining Room) 29, 31, 90-3, **90**
 Little Bed Chamber 102-4, **102**
 Little Dressing Room (Marble Dressing Room) **102**, 102-4
 Marble Parlour 27, 31, **37**, 38-9, **39**, **139**, 139-44
  west wall design **141**
 old manor house 20, 41
 park and gardens 41-7, **41**, **43**, **44**, **45**, 76, 77, 81
  gardens 41-2, **78**
  gates 75-6
  land sold 81
  utensils 101
  Wash Meres 45
  woods 47
 Saloon **28**, 31, **33**, 34-5, **118**, 119-23
 second floor (attic storey) 39-40

Staircase 27, 31, 32, **40**, 81, 110, 110-12, **111**
Stone Hall 27, **27**, 32-4, **38**, **77**, **113**, 113-17
ceiling 26, **26**
Study (Library) 97-101, **98**
Water Tower 44-5, 47, 81, 111, **112**
White Drawing Room (Carlo Marratti Room; Velvet Drawing Room) 75, **124**, 124-7
Houghton village 42, 46-7, 76
church of St Martin **41**, 47, 76
schools 76
Howard, Henry, Earl of Surrey
portrait 54
Howard, John 29, 48, 51-2, 105
bill 49, 52, 99
Howard, Thomas, 2nd Earl of Arundel 116
sale 116
Hubert, William
bill 34, 99, 142
Hudson, Thomas 83
Huyssing, Hans 83

Idol Worship **17**
inkstand 101, **101**
Innocent X, Pope 135-6

Jenkins, Edward 50
Jerningham, Charles 144
Jervas, Charles 48, 52, 83, 106, 125, 129-30, 158
Dogs and Still Life **129**
portrait of Walpole 84
studio sale 130, 148
Jones, Inigo 115, 127
Designs of ... 30, 39, 115, 141, 169
portrait 99
Queen's House 113
Whitehall 105
Jordaens, Jacob
The Family of Rubens 138
Self-portrait ... 49, 121

Keene, Benjamin 53
Keller brothers 107
Kelmarsh Hall, Northamptonshire 32
Kent, William 20, 22, 23, 24, 26, 28, 29-40, 47, 110-12, 113-4, 115, 116, 119-22, 125, 139, 164
armchair 121-2, **121**
character 30-1
designs for
elevation with picture hang ... Saloon **120**, 120-1
Great Door **24**
Hall settee **112**, **117**
Marble Parlour, west wall **141**
pier table **141**
Stone Hall chimneypiece **114**
Designs of Inigo Jones ... 115
Meleager and Atalanta **40**
Kimbolton Castle, Huntingdon 22
Kit-cat Club 84
Kite, Ralph 27
Knapton, George 108
Kneller, Sir Godfrey 96
portraits by 50, 63, 83, 94, 103
Grinling Gibbons 50, 63, 94, 96
Joseph Carreras 50, 80, 94, **96**
King George I 50, 94, 96, 97-8
Sir Robert Walpole **84**

Langford's auction room 57
Langlois, Jacques 52
Lansdowne House 61
Laocoön 107, 114
Law, John 50
le Brun, Charles 119
Le Maire, Jean
Consultation of the Sibyllic Oracles 129
Le Sueur, Eustache
Moses in the Bulrushes 53-4
Le Sueur, Hubert 111
Borghese Gladiator 53
Legat, Francis
The Continence of Scipio 148-9, **149**
Lely, Sir Peter 51
Lerpinière, Daniel
A Hunting Piece **91**
lighting 34
Locke, John, portrait 50, 63
Lombe, Thomas 100
London
Arlington Street 60, 164
Clarendon House 22
Dover Street 164
Downing Street 99, 104, 108, 136, 149, 164
Exchequer Offices 49, 164
Greenwich Hospital 88, 142
Queen's House 32, 113
Grosvenor Street 99, 104, 164
Henrietta Place 30
Kensington Palace 29, 120
Cupola Room 23, 29, 30, 34
King's Gallery 32
Orford House, Chelsea 54, 56, 99, 103, 138, 165
Pall Mall 165
Piccadilly, Great Gate 24
Rolls House, Chancery Lane 28
St James's Square 165
St Martin-in-the-Fields 27
Treasury, Whitehall 28, 30, 49, 165
Twickenham 165
Orleans House 33
Strawberry Hill 52, 99, 100, 115, 142, 143
Whitehall Palace 111
Lukin, William 142, 143
wine coolers **143**

Mackreth, Robert 75
Macky, John 50-1
mahogany 92, 117
Mann, Sir Horace 60, 100, 117, 123, 155, 159
Horace Walpole's letters to 49, 54, 56, 57, 60-1, 62, 109, 117, 123
Manners, John 60
Mansfield, Isaac 27
Maratti, Carlo 35, 64, 75, 99, 124-6
Pope Clement IX 99, 124, 125-6, **126**
Mason, James 67
Medici Vase 116
Methuen, Sir Paul 57
mezzotint 66-7, 68-9, 71-2, 137
Michel, Jean-Baptiste 65, 66, 72, 96, 137, 154
Boors at cards **137**
A Captain of Banditti 95
The Prodigal Son 72-3
mirrors 130
Mola, Pietio Francesco 50, 99
Montagu, Charles, Earl of Halifax 89
Montagu, John, 2nd Duke of Montagu 54
Moor Park, Hertfordshire 27
Moore, James 112
Morgan, J. Pierpont 99
Morris, William 25
Mortlake tapestries **128**, 129, 130
Seasons 39-40
Murillo, Bartolomé
Ascension 100
The Assumption of the Virgin **72**
Virgin and Child 53
Murphy, John C.
Abraham's Sacrifice **148**
The Cyclops at their Forge **119**
Musin-Pushkin, Aleksei Semonovich 61, 152

Narford Hall 53
New Houghton, Norfolk 42, 46
Nicolson, Harold 80
Nonsuch Palace 25
Norfolk
18th c. 16, 18, 29, 57, 78-9
Crostwick Hall 164
Holkham Hall 24, 29, 30, 35, 57, 61
Sculpture Gallery 116
Raynham Hall 22, 23, 29, 30, 34, 38, 46, 84, 112, 139
Sandringham 77, 81
Stanhoe Manor House 49, 164
Wolterton Hall 30, 46, 164
see also Houghton Hall
Norfolk, Dukes of 54
Norfolk Chronicle 76
Norfolk Gazette 115
Norfolk Militia 57
Norsa, Hannah 164
Northampton
Sessions House 22
Northwick Park, Avon, 38
Nuzzi, Mario 87, 89

O'Hara, James, 2nd Baron Tyrawley 53
Opie, John 157
Orpen, William 81
Oudry, Jean-Baptiste 81
Oxburgh Hall 144

Paine, Ambrose 150
letter **145**, **150**
Palmezzano, Marco 160
Patch, Thomas 75, 159
View of Florence **159**
patronage 24, 52, 83, 84, 85, 101
Pelham, Sir Henry 30, 164
Pembroke, Henry Herbert, 9th Earl of 111, 165
Pembroke, Thomas Herbert, 8th Earl of 44, 47, 53, 111
plate 39
pewter **93**
Platel, Pierre 143

Plumb, Sir John 18, 97, 98
Pond, Arthur 106, 108
Pope, Alexander 29, 30
porcelain plates **144**
Poussin, Gaspar 89
Landscape with a cascade ... 52
Poussin, Nicolas 133
The Continence of Scipio 133, 148-9, **149**
Holy Family ... 53, 64, 132, **133**, 138
Moses striking the Rock **59**, 64, 133,149
the Sacraments 99
Poyntz, Francis 37, 129
Pratt, Roger 22
Prideaux, Edmund 98
Houghton Hall from the west 11, 23, 42, **98**
Pulteney, William 84

Rape of the Sabine Women 123, **123**
Ravenet, Simon-François 66, 67, 73
Reinagle, Philip 61
Reitlinger, Gerald 64
Rembrandt van Rijn 148
Abraham's Sacrifice **58**, 64, 99, **148**
Reni, Guido 72
The Adoration of the Shepherds 100
The Doctors of the Church 64, 99-100
Ricci, Marco (Ritzi) 99
Richards, James 27-8, 29, 34, 112, 117, 121, 141
Richardson, Jonathan 83-4
Sir Robert Walpole 84
Richmond
Park 16, 85
Ranger's Lodge 85, 165
Sudbrook Park 32
Ridding, Thomas 93
pewter plate **93**
Ripley, Thomas 20, 22, 23, 24, 25, 31, 47, 111, 112, 164, 165, 169
Roberts, Thomas 34, 39, 119, 121, 126
Robinson, Sir Thomas 34, 39, 42-3, 46, 57, 92, 111, 139, 145, 146
Rocksavage, Countess of *see* Cholmondeley, Sybil
Roesslin, G. 153
Rolfe, Jonas 98
Rolle, Margaret, later Countess of Orford 26, 57
Romanelli, Giovanni Francesco
Hercules and Omphale 51
Rosa, Salvator 68, **95**
Democritus and Protagoras 95
Portrait of a Man **95**
The Prodigal Son **62**, 68, 72-3, 95, 100
Rosa da Tivoli (Philip Roos) 133, 160
The Goats-Herd **132**
Rosalba
Apollo and *Diana* 72
Rosebery, 6th Earl of 84
Rottenhammer, Johann 49
Royal Academy 71
Royal Institute of British Architects (RIBA) 22
Rubens, Peter Paul 51, 52, 138
Hélène Fourment **63**, 135, 136
Mary Magdalene washing the Feet of Christ 64, 71
Meleager and Atalanta 71, 135, 145-6, **147**, 147-8
Moonlight Landscape ... 52, **55**
Susanna and the Elders 90
Ruslen, John 101
Rysbrack, John Michael 27, 32, 33, 38, 114, 115
Bust of Sir Robert Walpole **115**
Peace and Plenty figures 38
Roman Sacrifice **140**

Sacchi, Andrea
Venus bathing ... 52, 96
Sacheverell, Dr 14
Sackville West, Vita 80
Sailliar, Louis 72
Helena Forman **73**
salver 142, **142**
Sang, Jacob **144**
Sargent, John Singer 80, 161
Lady Rocksavage **81**
Lord and Lady Cholmondeley **81**
Sybil, Countess Rocksavage **161**
Sassoon, Aline, Lady 79, 80, 161
Sassoon, Edward 79
Sassoon, Philip 79, 80, 156, 157, 158, 161
Sassoon, Sybil *see* Cholmondeley
servants 32, 81, 88
settees 112, **112**, 117, **117**, 122, **122**
Sherbourne Lodge, Gloucestershire 112
shooting 77, 78-9
Shorter, Catherine (1st wife of Sir Robert Walpole) 9, 16, 102, **103**
portraits 26, **83**, 101, 102, **103**, 114
Shubin, Fedot Ivanovitch 153
Bust of Catherine II **152**
Shuvalov, Count Andrew 152
Skerrett, Maria (2nd wife of Sir Robert Walpole) 9, 16, 19, 85, 104, 164, 165
portrait 102, **104**
Slaughter, Stephen 85
Sir Robert Walpole **85**
Sleter, Francesco 28
Smith, Joseph 108
Smyth, Sir John 161
Snyders, Frans 50, 51
A Concert of Birds 50, 87, **89**
family portrait 120, **121**
market scenes 99, 120, 145-6, 147
The Fruit Market 99, **146**, 147
Sotheby's 84, 88, 99
South Sea Bubble 15-16, 162
Spence, Joseph 109
Stanhope, James 84
Stanno 49 *see also* Norfolk, Stanhoe Manor House
Stature of The Great Man, The 13
stipple 72
Stones passed by Sir Robert Walpole **19**
stools 122, **122**
Stowe, Buckinghamshire 46
Strafford, Countess of 77, 79
Strawberry Hill sale 99, 142, 143
stucco 25-8, 30, 33
Stukeley, William 56
Suares, Teresina 108
Susini, Antonio 123
Swan, Abraham 27, 38, 140
Swizer, Stephen 20
Sympson, Joseph 142

tables
chamber 92, **92**
pier 122-3, **123**, 127, **127**, **141**
side, mirrored **130**
Tacca, Ferdinando 123
Talman, John 29, 120
tapestries 35, 37, 39-40, **128**, 132-3
The Goats-Herd **132**
Tassaert, Philip 101, 153
Teniers's Kitchen 68
Teniers, David 65, 96, 137
Boors at cards **137**
A Cook's Shop 137
Thornhill, Sir James 88, 142
Thurlow, Samuel 25
Tijou, Jean 75
timber 25
mahogany 92, 117
Towneley, Richard 26
Townshend, Charles, 2nd Viscount 12, 13, 15, 30, 46, 87-8
Treasury inkstands 101, **101**
Trent Park 79
Trent Place, Middlesex 75
Tuckfield, Margaret 57
Turner, Hill and Pitter 37, 126
Turner, Thomas 91

van der Werff, Adrian
Bathsheba bringing Abishag to David 53, 71
Van Dyck, Sir Anthony
Head of a Horse 87
portraits by 51, 69, 105, 106-7, 120
Arthur Goodwin 54
Charles I 72, 105
Helena Forman **73**
Henry Danvers 54
The Holy Family **51**, 52, 64, 89, 119
Inigo Jones 99
Philip, Lord Wharton **106**, 106-7
Sir Thomas Chaloner **54**, 96
Sir Thomas Wharton 69, **71**
van Gunst, Pieter 72
van Huls sale 49
van Huysum, Jan 52, 137-8
A Flower Piece 64, 69, 70, **137**, 138
Fruit Piece 138
Vase of Flowers **63**, 64
van Huysum, Michiel 138
Van Loo, Jean-Baptiste 83, **104**
Maria Skerrett **104**
van Steenwyck, Hendrick
A Noble Palace 50
Vanbrugh, John 26, 165
Vardy, John 127
vases, antique bronze 116, **116**
Vassalli, Francesco 26
Vecchio, Palma 99, 100
Velázquez, Diego 135-6
Death of Joseph 136
Pope Innocent X **136**
velvet 31, 35-7, 125, 126, 135

Vertue, George
engraving by 103, 116
Notebooks 48, 49, 50, 51, 52, 83, 85, 88-9, 96, 104, 105, 108, 115, 125, 126, 147, 169
Vittoria, Alessandro 114

Wade, George 148
Waldegrave, James, 1st Earl of Waldegrave 53, 133, 149
Walpole, Catherine, Lady (1st wife of Sir Robert) *see* Shorter
Walpole, Catherine (daughter of Sir Robert) 103
Walpole, Sir Edward 60, 87, 103, 105, 108, 116, 164, 165
portrait **108**
Walpole, George, 3rd Earl of Orford 81
character 57
sells pictures 35, 57, 60-1, 64, 81, 100, 153, 154, 157
death and wills 74-5
Walpole, Horace, 4th Earl of Orford 10, 24, 31, 44, 47, 50, 51, 52, 73, 103, 108-9, 146, 148, 159, 164
after father's death 48, 56, 57-61, 67, 151-2
death 74
Grand Tour 100, 109, 137
inherits estates 74-5
letters to Horace Mann 49, 54, 56, 57, 60-1, 62, 100, 109, 117, 123, 151
portrait 52, **109**
Aedes Walpolianae 48, 49, 52, 53, 56, 64, 65, 66, 82, 86, 87, 89, 95, 96, 99, **100**, 100-1, 135, 137, 146, 150
dedication 25
Anecdotes of Painting in England 96, 169
Essay on Modern Gardening 42
'Sermon on Painting' 100
see also Strawberry Hill
Walpole, Horatio, 1st Baron Walpole of Wolterton 22, 23, 24, 30, 33, 53, 85, 116, 144, 164, 165
Walpole, Maria, Lady (2nd wife of Sir Robert) *see* Skerrett
Walpole, Maria (daughter of Sir Robert) 106, 108
Walpole, Mary (later Viscountess Malpas, then Countess of Cholmondely) 74, 103, 106, 158
Walpole, Robert (1650-1700) 9
Walpole, Sir Robert, 1st Earl of Orford
bust **115**, 141
as collector 9, 32, 48-55, 56, 57, 107
chronology 162
correspondence 50, 98-9
death 19, 24, 47, 56, 151
finances 9, 16, 24, 56, 151
Houghton owner 9, 20, 24, 30-1, 38, 41, 46
marriages 9-10, 16, 19, 103, 104
Order of the Garter 26, 30, 54, 105, 114, 115, 130, 162
as patron 9, 24, 52, 83, 84, 85, 101
personality 9-10, 12
political career 9, 12-19, 85, 142, 164
portraits **12, 18**, 49, 83-5, **84, 85**, 103, 114
residences 164
scholarship 9, 97, 116
stones passed by **19**
Walpole, 2nd Earl of Orford 26, 34, 47, 52, 54, 85, 97, 103, 107, 164
death 57
on father's death 56, 57
paintings sale 56
portraits **107**, 114
Walpole family
genealogy 163
motto 144
Waltham Black Act 18
Ware, Isaac 20, 28
Designs of Inigo Jones and Others 30, 39, 115, 141, 169
The Plans, Elevations, and Sections ... 20, 24, 43-4, 72, 111-12, 115, 145, 155, 169
plan of Houghton Park 43-4, **44, 66**
Watson, James 72
Watteau, Jean Antoine 52
The Artist's Dream 52
Sulking Woman 52
Wedgwood, Josiah 62
Wehrlin, Voldemar 152
Wellington, Arthur Wellesley, 1st Duke of 76
West, Benjamin 61, 63, 64, 67, 101, 152, 153
West, Charles 72
Wharton, Anne, Lady 96
Wharton, Philip, 4th Duke of 105, 106-7, **106**
Whitehall Evening Post 155
Wilkes, John 60, 67, 152, 154
portrait **150**
Willaume, David 143
Wilton House, Wiltshire 22, 23, 53, 111, 122
Wimpole, Cambridgeshire 46
Windham, Sir Charles, 2nd Earl of Egremont 116
wine 141
coolers 143, **143**
Wise, Henry 46
Woburn Abbey, Bedfordshire 115
Wootton, John 53, 63, 83, 85, 87, 104
Classical Landscape 103, **104**
Hounds and a Magpie **50**, 85
Hunting Piece 90, **91**
Sir Robert Walpole **12**, 49, **84**
... and Catherine Shorter 83
World War I 79
World War II 80
Wouvermans, Philip
A Stud of Horses 49
Wyck, Jan 87

Zinke, Christian Friedrich 103
Zoffany, Johann 93

Photographic Credits

All works of art are reproduced by kind permission of their owners.
Specific acknowledgements are as follows:

Ashmolean Museum, University of Oxford: Fig. 10.
The Bridgeman Art Library, London: cat. 24.
British Architectural Library, RIBA, London: Figs. 6-9; cat. 30.
British Museum, London: Figs. 2-4; cats. 6, 48, 50, 54, 57, 68.
The Marquess of Cholmondeley: cats. 76-8.
Christie's, London: Figs. 43, 45-6; cats. 10, 21-2 (A.C. Cooper), 33, 46, 72, 79.
Country Life Picture Library: Frontispiece; Figs. 23, 49, 50, 53, 54.
The Courtauld Institute of Art: cats. 2-3.
Courtauld Institute Galleries: cat. 32 (Conway Librarian, Witt Collection 3217).
M.R. Dudley: cats. 5, 37, 55, 65-7.
Fitzwilliam Museum, University of Cambridge: Fig. 38; cat. 75.
R.M. Goodchild: Figs. 42, 44; cat. 19.
The Gulbenkian Museum, Lisbon: Fig. 36.
Angelo Hornak: Fig. 17.
Neil Jinkerson: Figs. 11, 13-16, 18-20, 51, 55-62; cats. 25, 31, 35, 36, 63.
The Metropolitan Museum of Art, New York: cat. 61.
Museum of London: cat. 64.
National Buildings Record: Fig. 12.
Board of Trustees, National Gallery of Art, Washington, DC: cats. 12, 26, 52.
National Portrait Gallery, London: Fig. 64; cat. 1.
Norfolk Museums Service – Derek A. Edwards: Fig. 21; GGS Photography: Fig. 48; cat. 69, endcovers (hardback edition).
Pierpont Morgan Library: cat. 17 (PML 7586).
The J. Ortiz-Patiño Collection: cats. 22, 62.
Peter Rogers: cat. 15.
Martin Smith: Figs. 24, 37, 39-41; cats. 4, 7-9, 13-4, 23, 27-9, 34, 43-4, 49, 56, 59, 70, 74, 76-8, 80.
Sotheby's, London: cats. 38-9, 58.
The State Hermitage Museum, St Petersburg: Figs. 26-35; cats. 11, 45, 51.
C. Simon Sykes: Figs. 1, 52, 64; cat. 40.
Board of Trustees of the Victoria and Albert Museum, London: cats. 47, 60, 71.
The Lewis Walpole Library: Fig. 47.
Wellcome Institute Library, London: Fig. 5.
Tom Williamson: Figs. 22, 25.

F. Zinke effig. p. 1735

G. Vertue del. & sculp. 1748.